For Berta, and for Rebecca, Nigel, Martha, and Hannah,

with my dearest love

TREAD THE MAZY ROUND

George Wrangham

ISBN-13: 978-1511499965
ISBN-10: 1511499966

"[Through these my tales] tread the mazy round...
The groves of Eden, vanish'd now so long,
Live in description, and look green in song:
These, were my breast inspir'd with equal flame,
Like them a beauty, should be like in fame."

Alexander Pope

TABLE OF CONTENTS

CHAPTER 1

ALL THOSE AEROPLANES

I t was early afternoon on a pleasant day in June. Two young teen-age girls, cousins, rose from the table where they had just fin-ished midday dinner, the principal meal of the day. It was spartan fare, cabbage soup and boiled potatoes, with a slab of bread and a tall mug of milk from the farm next door. But at least there were a few strawberries, the very first of the season, just a small handful for each girl. After eating they left the room and went upstairs to the small bedroom they shared, where they changed from stan-dard daytime clothes into heavy work clothes, corduroy and stiff canvas substitute. This was wartime, and there was not much avail-able in the way of food or clothing: one took what one could and made the best of it. Downstairs again, they called out goodbye to the hardworking wife of the farm laborer now away somewhere at war, no one knew where -- what news there was was always highly censored. She was the mother of one of them, Marjorie Abney, and the aunt of the other, Sheila Wheeler. Sheila had been born and brought up in Coventry where her father had held a steady job as a shop foreman in the BSA Works, until that terrible day of the massive air raid that killed him, his wife, all their children but one, and many, many others besides. Sheila alone had been at school and had escaped the bombs. So her aunt Lucy Abney had taken her into her family and her farm cottage in the village of Huby in County Durham. The girls were much the same age and got along well, except when there was work to be done, which Sheila faced with a passive and blank face, but which Marjorie found every opportunity to shirk: she found pleasure in so many other things that work had a low priority for her.

School was open only in the mornings so that the students, and the teachers for that matter, could make their contribution to war work in the afternoons. School sports were laid aside for the duration, only to be seen on Sunday afternoons. Marjorie and Sheila had been assigned to farm work; there was not much else available anyway in this country village, and as luck would have it they had been listed to work together helping the Brackenthwaite family up at Huby Hall to grow the prosaic vegetables of wartime instead of the gay flowers of peace. Most of these vegetables would continue to be the property of the family, but a good proportion was taken away to feed factory hands, dock workers and coal miners, a great number of whom lived and worked in the industrial heart of County Durham. And not a few vegetables found their way into the stew pots of such as Mrs. Abney.

In the extensive walled garden up behind Huby Hall old Albert Sherrington the gardener set the girls to the task of digging over the long bed where the last of the spring carrots had just been pulled. Sherrington was too old to serve in the war, but he had a sharp way about him and he worked those girls just as hard as he could. His son Geordie had been gardener, chauffeur and jack-of-all-trades at Huby Hall, but now he had gone away for the duration, enlisted in the RAF. Sheila Wheeler accepted old Sherrington's acerbic comments with staring stoicism: poor girl, she had yet to recover, if she ever would, from the death of her entire family and the extinction of her world. Marjorie on the other hand always resented Sherrington's authority, sticking her tongue out at him behind his back and imitating his limping walk. She had wanted to work in a hospital or in a daycare centre for children of families where both parents went off to work all day, but she had been assigned to her present lot, and in wartime one had no choice. That was that, and get on with it – which she did, albeit with sullen reluctance.

Marjorie waved cheerfully to me, Eddy Brackenthwaite, as she made her way past Huby Hall and up to the walled garden beyond. I had just turned four years old and had been chatting offhandedly with Joyce Carndale the scullery maid as she hung up the laundry on the washing line. Catching sight of Marjorie, however, I forsook the staid company of Joyce for the fun and good cheer that I had come to expect from Marjorie. This was the first time I fell in love, I remembered with a smile fifteen years later, and she and I used to walk around the garden together, I stretching up for her hand since I was only a small child and she was in her teens. The robin redbreast that perched upon the handle of her spade or on a nearby clod of earth was a special friend to both of us.

Looking around warily to make sure that Sherrington was nowhere in sight, Marjorie invited me to skip out of the walled garden with her down to the lane that ran behind the home farm, separating it from the field of Landwick Hill where an open grove of oak trees stood in the centre of a rolling pasture. Next to the lane stood a stretch of thick, lush grass, and beyond that ran a low drystone wall with a couple of lines of barbed wire stretched atop to provide a barrier of sorts to any farm animals that might be put out to graze on Landwick Hill. Today there was only one animal there, Alfred the bull, a heavy and placid beast. Marjorie, a country girl born and bred, knew well enough not to play any provocative games with a bull and certainly never, ever to go into the field with him, but Alfred always seemed to all intents and purposes to be the very personification of peace and gentleness.

Marjorie knew very well what Alfred wanted from her, and she and I would give it to him, long bunches of lush green grass pulled from the roadside and the ditch, far superior to the downtrodden, well-grazed sod that covered Landwick Hill. So we both picked great handfuls and carefully leaned across the low stone wall to offer them to Alfred, who had come lumbering up to us for this treat. With his long blue tongue he pulled sharply at the grass as Marjorie called out to me to let it go. What grand fun that was, giving a treat to this enormous quiet animal! Marjorie and I were both beaming with delight.

And then we paused, stood back and looked at each other quizzically. At the same instant we had both become conscious of a vibration, a gentle but deep and insistent sensation somewhere in the region of the breastbone. The feeling increased in intensity, and sound began to accompany the vibration: a deep, very heavy note such as one encounters from time to time as the ultimate lowest note of a great organ in an old cathedral. The teenage girl and the little boy forgot the bull and looked at each other with a curious feeling tinged with anxiety. Whatever was going on? It had to be real rather than imaginary since we both felt it in the same way at exactly the same time.

First Marjorie's head and then mine swung round slowly to gaze to the north, away across Landwick Hill. That was where the sound was coming from, far to the north, and the vibrating resonance too. And then at the same time we both began to see something unusual and distinct: first no more than tiny dots above the horizon set against the open sky, and then dot after dot, ever increasing in rows and clusters. As they approached – they were still far from overhead – the dots became identifiable: they were aeroplanes, aeroplanes beyond number, aeroplanes probably countless to Marjorie, certainly so to me. They were large planes too, each one far, far larger than the army lorries or tanks that ground their way periodically through the village of Huby on their way to or from the artillery training grounds up on the open moors above the villages clustered along Teesdale.

Now the noise was no longer a simple bass note from a cathedral organ, oh my goodness no, it had grown beyond belief into a tempestuous roar, such a chaos of tumult that it became utterly impossible for Marjorie and me to communicate, shout as we might right into each other's ears! For the two of us on the ground the entire universe had turned into noise, pure incalculable, undiluted noise, ornamented by flight after flight of great aeroplanes, many of them doubles such as neither of us had never seen before or imagined: a big plane pulling another along on a thick wire rope, the second plane having no engine at all. The pair of us on the ground stared up in disbelief at a phenomenon that just had to be believed because there simply wasn't any choice but to accept it. The aeroplanes wore the familiar wartime camouflage colors of dark subdued greens and browns, but they were also decorated with great broad bands of black and white, something we had never, ever seen before. They almost looked like giant wasps.

After what seemed an age, the last of the great aeroplanes passed overhead and the whole fleet began to slip away, down to the southern horizon, and as they did so the overwhelming roar began to moderate, to diminish, to drop away. Finally only ever-shrinking black dots remained visible in the sky, and the sound of all those massed propeller engines faded down to no more than the deep bass note of a cathedral organ. Last of all, the breast-bones of the teenage girl and the little boy lost their resonant vibration – and the scene was over.

This was the third time, only the third time, that this great and terrible War had touched the little community of Huby. First, to my great excitement as a little boy, our house, or rather my uncle's, Huby Hall, where we were living for the duration, far from the blitz in London, had been designated 'Enemy Headquarters' in a modest joint training maneuver involving the British and American armed forces. The British defended: the Americans attacked. And we, the family in residence, were, to our great excitement, permitted to look down out of the attic windows and watch the fighting below, just so long as we stayed put and never, ever came downstairs until the All Clear sounded: we might be hurt! I can remember the terrific thrill of the American assault when GIs, all firing blanks to left and right, charged across the tennis lawn and vaulted the flower beds to leap in at the library windows. I just could not believe they were allowed to tread in the flowerbeds at all and, heaven help us, to climb in at the windows, great grown men, jumping in and shouting, mud all over the carpets. Well, when all was over and done with and the fury of battle abated, we, the family, were permitted to come downstairs once more. I remember making my way out into the garden (through the veranda door, not over the window sills), across the tennis lawn and into the orchard, where the GIs were now squatting down, eating a meal out of their mess tins. Old berries and leaves, I thought? Americans actually like those? Well, we have plenty more, and to spare. So I stumbled around, picking up old grass and dead leaves and obligingly pushing them into all the mess tins I could see – doing my bit for Uncle Adolf. Smiling and doubtless missing their own children three thousand miles away or more, the GIs pulled from their rations my humble contributions, and I was not shot out of hand.

And the second time the War had made itself felt? Our nanny from the village, Marjorie's older cousin Winifred, one day was taking the children out on an afternoon walk: my older brother Harry wobbled along on his first bicycle, my younger brother Francis sat in his pram, and I steered an unsteady course on my tricycle along the lane between the farm fields. "Quick!" suddenly called out Winifred. "Turn round! We aren't going this way any more. Come along now, boys, do as I say -- no time to be lost!" She looked anxious, frightened even, so we swerved around and started back the way we had come, but not fast enough. Along the farm lane behind us a small, shambling procession of men was approaching, a dozen perhaps, with a soldier in front and another behind. These must each have been each carrying a gun, but I never saw that. The men, farm laborers in old and dirty clothes, looked tired, worn and thin, but as they approached us and passed right by they waved cheerfully and called out endearments, breaking into great smiles. We could not understand a single word, and Winifred's fearfulness had been infectious. So we said nothing to them and never waved in return. Looking back years later, my brothers and I have concluded that these bleak farm laborers must have been prisoners of war, Italians in all likelihood, set to work in the fields like POWs everywhere. They must have been homesick for their own bambinos and so cast warm and friendly glances on the three little children they encountered on the dreary march back from the fields to the barracks. The incident was over.

Now it was the final moment of the third and final time the War put in an appearance at Huby. The last wave of aeroplanes was sinking out of sight, but Marjorie and I still looked open-mouthed at each other. "Lawd's sakes, never would I 'ave believed it, not in all me born days!" came the hoarse gasping voice of Albert Sherrington close behind us, as the aeroplanes faded from the southern sky and took their final departure. We spun round with a start, and there Sherrington stood, staring, his mouth and eyes wide open in his weather-beaten face. "No, nor wouldn't I ever 'ave believed it," he went on, "not if you'd told me over and over, ever so many times. Not now, nor never would I 'ave believed I would live long enough to see such a sight. Why, I truly believe, the whole bloody RAF was up there, yes they was, with my beloved Geordie-boy and all, right there in the middle of 'em. Which of them aeroplanes are you in, Geordie, I kept on asking all the time they was a-flying by, which aeroplane? Then I could have blown him a special kiss and sent the aeroplane a special prayer, yes I would 'ave done that and all, and sent a blessing right from the parson and the church, yes, I really would 'ave done that, right and all!"

In his emotion he paused to catch his breath, and then continued. "Well, I comes out 'ere to the back lane, mind you, Miss Marjorie, when I doesn't see you a-workin' in them carrot beds alongside of Miss Sheila, she the young lass what's come up from Coventry after all them Jerry bombs what fell on the city and killed all her family, God save 'em all … well, what was I a-saying? Ah yes, I sees her, diggin' away right as rain she were, payin' no attention to them aeroplanes what would make your 'eart stop dead, they would, never lookin' up she didn't, and never a word to me as to what you had gone and done with yourself, not a word, mind you! So I comes out here to the lane, see, knowing you likes to go off sky-larkin' with young Master Eddy here, and what does I see? There's the two of you, a-feeding that there bull of Farmer Heatherman's across the way, all as if he were as friendly and loving as your own little pussycat. Good Lord, Miss Marjorie, doesn't you 'ave the common sense the good Lord gave you to know as how he could have killed you, both you and little Master Eddy here, right as rain and just as easy as apple pie, if ever he had caught a hold of you and pulled you back into his field? Why, I gets all of a tremble just a-thinkin' of it, I does." And he shook his head in disbelief.

"But look 'ere, let's get back to all this, these 'ere aeroplanes and all. Why, I can't be angered at you now, not to anyone now, not now when the whole blessed RAF has just gone and flown right over our heads! You knows very well what that means, doesn't you? All of them lads, me own Geordie right there in the middle of 'em, are flying right out of the training grounds up here in the North and in Scotland, to go down there to fight them bloody Jerries in France or wherever! That's what they're all a-doin', make no mistake abaht it! And me Geordie's right there with 'em, with his Mum passed on and all, and he being all as I've got left in this world, yes he is. Oh Lordie me!"

8

Here Albert Sherrington broke down, took a ragged handkerchief from his pocket, blew his nose long and hard, and presently took up his story again.

"So just for today let's forget about you two sky-larkin' around, shall we, and now please to drop to your knees, both of you – yes, you too, young fellow me lad – and we'll ask the good Lord to save our boys and send 'em safe back 'ome. That's all I asks for, dear God, really it is. I'll leave it to the good Lord to think what to do with them blasted Jerries, that's not my business at all. Just send me back my Geordie! Send 'im 'ome safe to me!" And here his voice broke down into sobs.

With that Albert Sherrington, Marjorie Abney and I sank down onto our knees together, in the long grass by the side of the back lane at Huby Hall, while Alfred the bull gazed at us with his large and uncomprehending eyes. Sherrington could not speak, so Marjorie did.

"Dear Lord," she started, "please help our men, our boys, especially Geordie, in their battle. Think of them, and keep them alive, specially Geordie 'cause he's all his Dad's got left… For now and forever and ever, world without end" – she did not know quite why she said those closing words, but they felt right and she knew they were important whenever you said your prayers – "Amen." Sherrington echoed the Amen, and I tried to too.

We rose from our knees, and then we did something very unusual among those dour and undemonstrative villagers living in the North, far up the Pennine dales: we hugged, all three of us, in a tight and tearful embrace. We truly believed that the entire RAF had flown over us that afternoon on its way to do battle for Good against Evil.

And we were not very far wrong in that, for many years later, when I had grown up, when my family had moved away from County Durham to the south of England and I had long ago lost touch with my dear Marjorie Abney, I, no longer little Eddy but

Edward Brackenthwaite, was able to set a date to that miraculous event. It had certainly to have been just a day or so before June 6, 1944, a date that will live forever in the history of all free men, in triumph and in sadness.

And Flt. Lieut. George Sherrington, D.S.O.? No, he didn't come home.

CHAPTER 2
UNCLE DIGBY

The village of Bradfield Tye lies in Suffolk, not many miles
from Sudbury in the valley of the River Stour, well known
for Constable's rural scenes. My family lived there for most of my
childhood, and indeed the atmosphere of the place, not the acci-
dentals such as cars and the like, but the essentials, the steady pace
and the sturdy reliability of rural life, had remained very much
the same since the days of the great artist. At least that was how
it seemed to a boy growing from the age of five to twenty in that
village. In my memory it is one long sunny day in our home at
Bradfield Tye, with a few flies and an occasional bluebottle hum-
ming casually around in the library from which French windows
open onto the capacious garden. It was here that I really learned
to know my Uncle Digby.

Our home there, Ewesholme, is a long white house descending
in slow steps down the incline from the village towards the River
Stour that flows, oh so gently, past the tall trees and across the
foot of the meadow, where it forms the border between the two
parishes of Bradfield Tye and Bradfield Hinton. The oldest part of
Ewesholme, now the downhill end of an extended house, was built
as long ago as the late seventeenth century. Fifty feet or so of lawn

in front, an irrepressible bank of St. John's wort, a tall and straggling box hedge and a steep brick wall, hold Ewesholme back from
the road that leads from Bradfield Tye across to Bradfield Hinton.
The uphill end of the house is much grander than the old farm-
house below, with tall rooms on the ground floor remodeled in
Edwardian times so that their ceilings intrude above the bottoms
of the windows of the modest bedrooms above; such a thing can
scarcely be imagined but nevertheless it is so, the product of the
artistry of a local architectural craftsman over a century ago. Attic
bedrooms up a contrary and backwards-turning narrow wooden
staircase, and a deep-delving warren of dark and cobwebby cellars
below ground, complete the picture: there you have Ewesholme.

We came to live there in 1945, at the end of the War, when my
father, Gerald Brackenthwaite, thought it safe to bring his family back from County Durham to somewhere not too distant from
London, where he lived and worked in the world of finance, something infinitely far removed from the cognition of a young boy.
My father had performed yeoman service in London in the ranks
of the government for all the war years, working right through the
Blitz and earning his CBE. At the outset of the War in 1939 the
family had consisted only of my father, my mother and my older
brother, then just a year old. My father's older brother, Digby, had
been a lawyer of some consequence in the city of Durham before
the War, and lived in a handsome limestone house, a former rec-
tory built in the reign of Queen Anne in the village of Huby in the
Teesdale countryside. The doors of this house, Huby Hall, Uncle
Digby generously threw open to any and all members of the extended family who wished to take refuge from the bombing in the
cities, while he himself departed as colonel of his county regiment
to serve King and Country in defence of the Indian Empire. My
own memories of Huby Hall in Teesdale, where I was born, and
where my younger brother and sister also saw the light of day, are
necessarily fragmentary since we left Huby for Bradfield Tye when

I was just five years old. In my mind's eye as a child Uncle Digby always stood strongly athwart the front door at Huby, a mythic figure when he came home on leave from the army, who had provided a heaven-sent refuge for us all, and the father of Cedric and Brenda, who came home in their holidays from boarding school together with assorted cousins and friends from the bombed ports and cities, all towering above my siblings and me as great grown-ups visiting the children's world. When I was alone and could pluck up the courage to do so, I would on occasion speak in my mind to Uncle Digby, even though he was ever so far away in India and there was of course no telephone. But my make-believe best friend, CowCurtain, who lived in the sandy rabbit warrens beneath the tall oak trees on Landwick Hill in the farmland stretching up to the moors behind Huby Hall, could also talk to Uncle Digby, and it was through him that I used to ask my uncle what India was really like, elephants, jewels, dark-eyed ladies in saris and all that, seen through a child's listening to the stories of Rudyard Kipling. I had to imagine Uncle Digby's answers, for it was only through CowCurtain and imagination that I could receive them.

In 1945 Uncle Digby came home from the East and established his residence once more at Huby, moving after a while to Portsbridge St. Leger on the borders of Cambridgeshire when his career took him to the law courts of London, where soon enough he was awarded a knighthood for his legal distinction and in recognition of his elevation to a High Court judgeship. For us at Ewesholme he remained a lofty and remote figure, a relative of the greatest moment, one to whose personal grandeur one could scarcely dare to aspire. But he was also my godfather, my very own godfather, and that was a great treasure to me.

We lived a very quiet and domestic life at Ewesholme, with my mother Teresa and her companion-nanny Jenny Macaulish taking care of the household all week long. Mrs. Bunyan from the village was our daily lady, sweeping the front stairs and scrubbing the back steps, her kind and weather-beaten face creasing into the broadest and most welcoming of grins as she broke off from her wearingly slow rendition of last Sunday's hymns in order to caution us "Mind you don't never get the cane at school!" A succession of gardeners, Crowell, a frightening figure for youngsters since he looked to us exactly like Stalin *sans* the moustache, Moss, a tall and rotund soft-spoken countryman, and the irrepressible Trimbleton, a natural elf if ever there was one, completed our household: Trimbleton polished the shoes, emptied the grates of the three miscellaneous central-heating boilers in the coal room, and took out the household rubbish, chuckling happily with us all the while. All in all, it was a quiet, almost secret life that we lived, except at weekends when the all-encompassing figure of my Papa would appear from London: then, from Friday evening to Sunday afternoon, the whole pace and atmosphere changed, for like his brother he had a commanding presence and we all stood in awe of him, delighting in his smile, amazed at his knowledge of just about everything, and fearful indeed of his disapproval. Occasionally family visitors came to call or to stay for a few days or a weekend to escape from London, my two widowed grandmothers, aunts and great aunts, uncles and cousins – and Uncle Digby, his wife Aunt Grace and their young twin children.

Uncle Digby did not have the height of my 6'3" father, but he had a manner all his own, and we children soon appreciated that even Papa looked up to him and deferred to him. Uncle Digby was sturdily built, with a large and handsome domed forehead. He spoke with authority: one would not want to be caught contradicting him or even failing to catch his meaning. His frequent laughter was strong, deep, sonorous and completely infectious: when he laughed the whole house laughed, and I can see him still, standing before the fireplace in the library, his feet planted well apart, hands thrust deep in his pockets pulling sideways the dark green thornproof tweed breeches that he seemed always to wear whenever he visited our family, with a matching suit jacket and waistcoat with a silver watch chain.

I knew, I really knew, how privileged I was to be his godson, to have a unique relationship with this great man that I did not have to share with anyone else. (I regret to say that in my own family containing three young boys with scarcely six years between the oldest and the youngest some measure of rivalry was inevitable, and any point in which one brother excelled was surely treasured by that fortunate individual.) Each time Uncle Digby visited, perhaps two or three times in the year, he would take me by the hand and propose a walk around the garden so that he could reacquaint himself with the life of his godson. These gardens covered an acre or so, providing all the fruit and vegetables we needed so that, all unconscious of the outer world, we never knew what it was to shop for such things. The gardens contained three sizeable lawns as well, stretching away beyond the great copper beech, the locust trees ('acacias') reputedly the offspring of those brought home from the Carolinas by Mark Catesby generations ago, beyond the spreading mulberry tree with its never-to-be-excelled, unbelievably delicious fruit, beyond the flower gardens and the broad vegetable beds, past the raspberry and currant cages and the wide-spreading orchard, right out to the paddock and farm outbuildings beyond the farthest hedge.

One time on just such a walk – I believe I was six years old at the time – Uncle Digby suddenly broke off from the remarks he was making, the questions he was posing.

'Listen, Edward! That's a Yellowhammer over there, singing his heart out," he exclaimed.

I was taken aback by the suddenness and inconsequence of this. I just didn't know what to do, what to say or what to think.

"Don't you hear it, Edward? I'm telling you, there he is again! 'A little-bit-of-bread-and-<u>no</u>-cheese!' That's what he's singing. Now let's go and look for him, shall we?"

Well, I had already had some incipient interest in birds, brought on no doubt by a couple of volumes from the extensive collection of bird books that Uncle Digby, a lifelong birder, had maintained at Huby and which had somehow crept into the many boxes and suitcases of our possessions when we removed south from there to Ewesholme. But I had never really looked hard at birds in the field or concentrated upon them, let alone being aware of anthropomorphic renditions of their vocalization. I was stumped.

"Come along, my boy, come along, I say! We're going to find that Yellowhammer and you can see for yourself what a beautiful bird he is, singing all the time 'A-little-bit-of-bread-and-<u>no</u>-cheese!'"

So Uncle Digby and I stalked stealthily around the top of the lawn, peering past the Ribes bushes, the straggling yews in that corner of the garden, the branching hazelnut tree, and the tall dark Ilexes. And then, wonder of wonders, oh my goodness, then the unbelievable actually happened! I am not referring to our catching sight of one little bird, no, not that at all, but to the fact that Uncle Digby actually dared to defy all the rules of the household, the strictest instructions of my much-to-be-feared Papa, and there we were, actually walking, one foot set carefully down after the other, through the flowerbeds! Imagine that, we were really making our own pathway, each of us stealthily treading between the treasured flowers. I would have been in for such a scolding if I had dared to do that alone, likely being sent to my room by Papa to contemplate my sins in solitude, or having to confront the sad and deeply disappointed look on my dear Mama's face if I had breached her instructions, her rules so few and so easy to obey. But with Uncle Digby before me I could do no wrong. "In his master's steps he trod, Where the snow lay dinted..." Those well-known words did not occur to me the time -- I was too small then -- but they have crossed my mind repeatedly ever since.

And then, almost as an anticlimax, there at the tip-top of a tall straggling rose bush in the hedgerow perched the little Yellowhammer himself, a yellow-brown finch with a brilliant yellow head, singing away to establish his territory and to attract a mate. "A-little-bit-of-bread-and-<u>no</u>-cheese!" he repeated over and over again. The delight spread all across Uncle Digby's face was palpable indeed, a joy to behold. That image has indeed stayed with me ever since, and when I close my eyes I can see with the greatest clarity my revered uncle/godfather standing in his dark green tweeds beneath the Ilex, casting his glances back and forth in triumph up to the Yellowhammer in the bush and down to his nephew-godson beside him, with the very broadest of open-mouthed smiles lighting up his entire countenance.

It is no wonder that at that precise moment Uncle Digby made of me a lifelong birder, and that now, some sixty-eight years later, I still talk to him in my mind, while CowCurtain still lives and passes his time quietly beneath the oak trees at Huby -- and now I live an ocean away, grateful all the time to the man who gave me the gift of birding.

Uncle Digby lived well into his eighties, a man venerable and duly venerated, deeply loved by his family and sincerely mourned by all who knew him. Speaking strictly for myself, I have to admit that at the moment when I heard that he had left us I did not altogether feel that a light had been extinguished in my life, since it had been many years since I had last seen him and really talked with him. Indeed the two final occasions when I was truly with him were first, when he with wonderful tolerance allowed my infant son to poke his finger into one of Uncle Digby's beloved Alpine plants, a smooth and solid mound of vibrant jade green, nourished in a limestone trough in the garden of his home in Portsbridge St. Leger, and secondly, when I visited him and Aunt Grace in their retirement in their country cottage on the Northumberland coast where he spent the last years of his life a few miles from Lindisfarne.

I treasure a photograph I took of them both there, walking home over the sands after an exhaustive attempt to establish the identity of a far-off shore bird – a Knot, we concluded.

The vagaries of my life wafted me away after that, and I had not been able to attend his funeral, save in spirit. I have come to rest in America, in the state of Delaware. There it is that a group of my friends, fellow members of a local birding club, venture out on our annual New Year's Day excursion. This is not a trivial ramble for those who have celebrated New Year's Eve late and long, for we assemble before six o'clock in the darkness of a January morning at an appointed spot some twenty-five miles south along the highway. Our aim is to sweep down to the southern tip of Delaware, staying by the Atlantic shore, and then to make our way north and homeward, stopping at each well-known estuary or stretch of wetland as long as the hours of daylight might last. Our first stop on our way south is always on the Cape Mahon road, really no cape at all and not so much a road as a deserted gravel drive right along the shoreline of Delaware Bay. There at the appointed hour the sun could be relied upon to rise, slowly, with almost imperceptible motion but with unutterable romantic charm, clear out of the salt waters of the Bay. So we scanned the miles of open and deserted marshland for Short-eared Owls, Bitterns and Black-crowned Night Herons. We found them all, what a delight, and heard a Great Horned Owl hooting from the woods a mile away across the marshes. I have taken to the habit of naming each year after the first bird seen that day, with deference to the Chinese. So 2013 was the Year of the Swamp Sparrow, 2014 the Year of the Black Duck, and 2015 the Year of the Northern Harrier.

Then, in the fiery glow of a winter sunrise, we took up our drive southward for the Indian River Inlet, just a couple of miles short of the point where Delaware yields the seashore to Maryland. Here a long, slow river meandering through the wetlands and riverine woodland debouches into the Atlantic Ocean, and here, where fresh water meets salt, where tides flow in and ebb back again endlessly over the hours and the years, here of all spots along the calm and sandy coastline that extends from southern Maine all the way to the coast of the Gulf of Mexico and beyond, here, at the mouth of a tidal river, here something notable might indeed be found. Expectation and the rapture of chancing upon that something special and unexpected glinted in everyone's eyes as we climbed out of our cars bundled up in our warmest clothes against the freezing dawn, shouldering our 'scopes and wreathed in binoculars. We headed out of the parking lot toward the three hundred foot wide channel hemmed in by rough stone jetties where the fast-flowing Indian River greets the ocean. Tripods were erected in place, telescopes mounted, binoculars focused with care, -- and the birders' calls began to ring out.

"Red-breasted Mergansers, ten or more, in the main channel, some of them diving."

"Double-crested Cormorants, a dozen at least, swimming on the far side, some drying their wings on the groins."

"And that's not all! Look at the tall buoy light out there by the ocean. There's a couple of Great Cormorants there. See their white fronts?"

"And Long-tailed Ducks scattered everywhere, some on the water, some flying by. Say, did you know that they are fastest flying ducks? Eighty miles an hour or more, they've been clocked. But don't you dare call them Old Squaws any longer: you can be indicted for racism, sexism and ageism on those two syllables alone!"

"Lookee out there, way beyond the inlet. There's a raft of Common Eiders there... Keep your eyes open for a King Eider: They say one was seen right here not three weeks ago."

"And the Scoters, take them in! They're all there: American, Surf and White-winged. This is a great chance for anyone new to them to sort out the species and photograph them in your mind's eye."

"Couple of Turnstones out there on the rocks. And look, half a dozen Purple Sandpipers just below them at the water line. Why did anyone ever call them purple? They always look dark grey to me."

"Anyone seen a Black-headed Gull yet? Look for it in this flock of Bonaparte's, feeding off the surface of the water. There's occasionally one or two to be found right in there with them, if anywhere, and we had one at this spot just a couple of years ago on this trip. And keep an eye open for Icelands among the Ring-billeds, no black wing-tips..."

Gradually the conversation died down, the watchers calm and entranced, alert with hope for the best and the greatest, and filled with appreciation and gratitude for all the familiar species, some of them observed by many of us only once or twice each winter, somewhere or other along the many miles between New England and Cape Hatteras.

But what has all this to do with Uncle Digby? Nothing at all -- yet.

Then the word slipped around, passed from mouth to mouth, that a Razorbill had been sighted precisely here, not two weeks ago, far out, floating at sea, looking at first glance like a dark marine duck, black above and white below, but with the short upturned tail and the stout, solid black bill that would soon identify it as an auk rather than anything else. But how in the name of all that is good and gracious could one possible discern those fleeting field marks on a bird floating up and down, now totally hidden in the dip between waves and now for an instant riding on a crest, a hundred yards or more out to sea? So, being by no means an expert birder, I came close to giving up hope of what would be my first American sighting of a bird common enough around the seabound crags of Scotland and the northwestern reaches of England and Ireland, as well as of Labrador, Newfoundland and Nova Scotia. Of course the Razorbill had been an old and familiar friend to Uncle Digby. He had on one occasion taken me out in a small boat to the lonely and windswept Farne Islands off the coast of Northumberland, where we found Razorbills among many other birds,, and to the crags of Bamburgh Castle, where in the breeding season the screams of Carracks and adult Kittiwakes at their nests make human conversation quite out of the question.

Razorbills can be found occasionally in the western North Atlantic at the latitude of the State of Delaware, but in winter it is generally their habit to keep themselves far out to sea, nowhere near the stormy cliffs with which one always associated them in one's mind – and there are no cliffs at all on the sandy coast of Delaware, from one end of the State to the other. So we looked at each other, promised mutually to keep a good eye out, and returned to our more rewarding perusal of Mergansers, Long-tailed Ducks, Great and Double-crested Cormorants, Red-breasted Mergansers, Common Eider and the three species of Scoter, as well as the Purple Sandpipers and the Ruddy Turnstones that had flown in to keep each other company on the rocks.

"Quick, quick, look there!" the cry went up. "It's the Razorbill, it really is! Well, it's quite a long way off" (Read: quarter of a mile or more, binoculars no use, try a telescope, good luck among all those dancing waves and with your tiny field of view anyway). So one groans and faces the fact that in all that great spread of land-mark-less ocean one has a less than a minimal expectation of seeing the blessed bird – and blessed it is and would surely be, if only it would comfortably show itself to us, its true devotees ashore. We strain our eyes and stare out to sea, all of us.

"There it is! – No, that's a Lesser Black-backed Gull, wings too long, wingbeats too slow, not jet black on the back, no great solid bill, how could I ever be so dumb as to make that mistake?"

"This one may be it -- no it's a dark female Long-tailed Duck."

"How can you tell the Razorbill from a Scoter? White stomach? Yes, I'll look for that."

"No, I haven't seen it, where is it anyway? In fact, has anyone seen it at all?"

Then gradually the excitement began to fade into disappointment, with most of us thinking that the chance had gone by ... perhaps it wasn't really a chance after all, ... and anyway who on earth was it who ever claimed he had actually seen the bird in the first place, and what in heaven's name does <u>he</u> know about anything?

And we returned to our careful identification of all the birds we had seen on the rocks and in the river and the sea over the past half hour. It was almost time to go: a great flock of literally tens of thousands of Snow Geese had been seen in the neighborhood of Slaughter Beach some miles to the north of us, enough to whiten the sky like snowflakes or, on turning in the wind, to darken it like the smoke of a distant forest fire. That was a sight never to be missed: we all wanted desperately to own a part of it. So we betook ourselves to the task of hefting our telescopes and tripods onto our shoulders and turning back to the cars above the shore.

Suddenly, from someone: "There it is! Oh my God, it's right in front of us, right now, the Razorbill!"

I whirled around, heaving my telescope off my shoulder and swinging my binoculars up to my face. And there indeed it was, sitting in the channel at the river mouth right in front of me, not even twenty feet away, bright as a button and clear as daylight, a true adult Razorbill, in full plumage no less, glistening with droplets sliding off its back after the bird's ascent from a long, deep dive. I swear, he and I almost looked each other in the eye! A couple of other people saw him too, but no one was half as close as I -- and then he was gone, gone, upending and vanishing into another long, deep dive that took him right out to the centre of the inlet and washed him away upstream on the swift-flowing tide, so that after that he could only be seen with any clarity through binoculars or perhaps through a telescope if anyone had the time to catch his image in the lens.

And then – and here at last is the point of all this – at that very moment I heard a familiar full-bodied laugh right behind me, close at my hand, a laugh I knew and recognized instantly, and of course it was Uncle Digby! He and I gave not a thought to the other members of the group standing around, congratulating or commiserating each other on the view or the non-view of the Razorbill. For an instant he and I just had each other, face to face. It was indeed Uncle Digby, it really was him, just for a flash of time. I had no chance to speak to him, no chance to call out his name, no chance even to show any recognition at all. But there he was, truly standing there, stalwart in his old familiar country tweeds, hands in pockets, his face flushed with joy and excitement, his glance congratulating me and congratulating himself on this delightful close sighting of a bird he knew so well from the cliffs of far-off Northumberland. And then in an instant he was gone, vanished.

Well, in sober fact had he ever really been there? Had he indeed come back from the other side in order to celebrate with me, the godson-nephew he did not really know all that closely, certainly far less intimately than his four dear children, the unlooked-for arrival of a special bird? Or was I simply imagining the whole thing, having for so long associated Uncle Digby with the delights of birding that my mind created at the appropriate moment the image of the favorite uncle? How can I tell which of these it was, or indeed whether it might have been something else entirely? But there was indeed a certain true, albeit evanescent, reality to his absolute presence alongside me. This was indeed infinitely less overwhelming than the many spiritual visions that have been vouchsafed over the ages to saints of deep religious faith. If it is not too much to say this, I can perhaps assert that my experience had something more in common with what Winston Churchill narrates, of the visit of his long-dead father to his painting studio some years after he had retired from the monumental contributions he had made to Britain's survival, endurance and victory in the Second World War – but unlike Churchill, I had, alas, no extended one-to-one conversation at all with my uncle when he appeared, only the certain conviction of his ineffable presence and then of his immediate absence.

So, may I ever meet Uncle Digby Brackenthwaite again, this side of the grave? I dearly hope so -- and indeed I look forward most warmly to seeing him again on the other side if that gift may be afforded me, then to thank him for the very special and vaulting delights of birding that he bestowed upon me in this life.

CHAPTER 3
THE WALTZ OF NOAH STUBBLEFIELD

After the war my family, the Brackenthwaites, left my uncle's house at Huby in County Durham and moved south to Suffolk, where once again I struck up a special friendship with the gardner, whose name was Noah Stubblefield.

"'Be ye strong and of a good courage,'" intoned Noah one day. "'Fear not, neither be dismayed.' Those are the words in the Good Book, and many's the time they've come to my rescue when I was all adrift and I didna know what to do, where I was a-going. And lookee here, Master Eddy, it's all turned out very well for me. Here I am, seventy-eight year old if I'm a day, strong as an 'orse I be, a-doin' what I loves best, helping all God's good plants to grow."

I looked up at Noah very doubtfully, my eyes swimming with unshed tears. "It's all very well for you,' I managed to say. "You're doing everything you want, but here am I, about to be carted off again to that beastly boarding school. I got through it all last term, which was my first, you know. I just thought and thought of being home, in my own room with all my books and toys and things, and with the garden outside and you in the garden for me to talk to for hours and hours. That's what I did, you know, just thought as hard as I could about you and old Groby and Mummy and Daddy and my brothers and everything, and I felt if only I could go on thinking about it, it would all come true and I would be home again and that awful school would be gone forever. But now I've got to go back, tomorrow, oh tomorrow …" My voice trailed off, quiet sobs taking the place of coherent words.

"Well, Master Eddy," answered Noah Stubblefield, "there's good and there's bad to be found in everything, y'know. Here, just you take a look at me. Don't you think I wouldn't be happier if I was to be a-planting all these 'ere flowers for me own self and my little family, and the fine, big vegetables and beautiful flowers that I grows in this 'ere your family's garden, and not any of them, nary a one of them, I tells you, belongin' to me? I'm not complainin', mind you, not complainin' one little bit. I likes nothin' better than to get a bit o' fresh air, you know, and this 'ere garden has that all right, so big and airy it is. It's a marvel to me, really it is, this piece of land, stretching from down there by the old house away over across to the meadow and back by the lane and the little plots, the way it gives you and all the family all the fruit and vegetables you could ever eat all year long – not bananas or oranges or any of them foreign fruits, mind you – but all the greens, root veg, apples and pears, strawberries, currants and rasps, oh I could go on a long time about that, couldn't I ever, and ever so many flowers, gorgeous really, one season after the other – with no hard feelin' at all for me and my 'umble lot. The good Lord has given me this row to plough, and that's what I'll do, thank you very much, for as long as the strength of me right arm holds out."

"That's what I really like about you, Noah," I said with all the honest forthrightness of my ten-year old self. "There's no fooling you, and you're just about my best friend in the whole wide world, you and old Groby – better anyway than just about every one of the boys back at school. They're only your friend if you're good at soccer or can help them with their prep, or have extra sweets from home. Sometimes I just hate school, I really do, and I don't know if I can go on with it – but I would be in awful trouble with my father if I absolutely refused to go back – he would drag me back there by my hair, I swear! But this is where I really belong, in this house and garden, I know it, and I can really talk with you, and what's why I'm going to miss you just dreadfully." And here I broke down and sobbed to myself, trying to conceal my weakness from my friend the Stubblefield.

"Nah then, nah then," said Noah. "That won't do at all, y'know, Master Eddy, not at all it won't, no, not one little bit. Just pay you heed to what I say, young sir, straight from the mouth of the Lord it is: 'Be ye strong and of a good courage, fear not, neither be you dismayed.' Why, I really believe it was you He was a-thinking of when He spoke them very words, yes it were. So when you feels downhearted just say them words over, think of God and remember me a-standing 'ere when I should be digging the beds over, talking to you and getting myself the sack for nattering on and on when I should be a-doing all the work what I was paid to do."

Here Noah Stubblefield shouldered his garden fork, turned round and trudged heavily up the garden path, past the old mulberry tree and the two broad flower beds, past the crabapples that stood guardian at the pathway crossing, and across the tangled rough grass into the orchard, and thence up to the top of the garden to the long, long vegetable beds. I trailed behind, not really consoled by Noah's words of wisdom.

"Tell you what, Eddy me lad," said Noah, turning on his heel just before digging in the fork to turn the first heavy sod at the start of a row of French beans that had produced their crop and were now dying back. "I 'ave found me a keepsake for you, so mind you takes this, and thinks on me and this 'ere garden every time you touches it in your pocket." And he picked up off the top of the garden gatepost where he had laid it a day or two beforehand

27

a fine smooth piece of white quartz, translucent where its surface was free of earth and even with a hint of transparency. "There, me boy, that'll bring you luck, that and the photos you took of our good old friend Groby. Why, just you look at those cracks and lines in the stone – lookee close, I do believe it looks like my own poor old face with its lines and all. Don't you see, let me show you, it's me and all, though I don't quite looks like that, not with all them deep cracks, but never mind that. So I'll be a-watching you, my friend, you can be sure of it, when you're far away at that there school of yours."

My lip trembled again as I took the special little stone and held it hard as I thrust my hand deep into my pocket.

"And now, Master Ed, do please be so good as to run along and leave me be. I do have this here piece of work in front of me, the sun's past the half day already and we can't spend all day a-nattering, now can we? Your father would give me the sack and all, and he'd be right and proper to do that, wouldn't he? So run along now, have a word or two with old Groby, and I'll be sure to see you before I goes home tonight, 'cos I might miss you in the morning, you being packed up and ready for boarding school and all. No more tears now, and that's an order -- far as ever I could give you one. Just remember to say your prayers at night, that's right, and always be of good courage, and then there's nothing can't never hurt you."

And as I moved reluctantly away down the garden path I heard Noah Stubblefield break into his favorite verse, the one he always saved for digging rows of vegetables, beds of flowers, or circles for potash around the many apple, pear and plum trees in the orchard. "The earth with its store of wonders untold..." slowly creaked out the antique voice, and I remembered the triumph of a couple of days ago when Noah had disinterred the red glass reflector from the back of a long-gone bicycle: "See, young Eddy, what was I a-telling you? Rubies they is, purest ruby jewels, and don't you never tell me nothing otherwise. Just you look at them all a-glinting and sparkling fresh as ever from a crown or tea-arrow or whatever you calls it, right from the brow of a fairy princess, maybe from Cinderella herself, or Queen Victoria, or Kelly Patrer far away in Egypt. No nonsense, mind, I'm a-telling you the truth, and this only looks like a bike reflector to then as can't see straight, ain't that right? Course it is." And I smiled gently to myself as I made my way to the greenhouse where I could lie down on the floor and talk for awhile with Groby, my other special friend. He was sure to be there.

Old Groby was the love of my heart. Indeed, very much of the love of which my young self was capable was directed toward my endlessly patient confidante Groby. Why, I could tell him things I never would have dared to tell even to Noah Stubblefield, and Groby would never, never betray a secret, however special, dangerous or exciting it might be.

A few weeks earlier the Brackenthwaite family had left our home in the Suffolk countryside for our annual summer holiday in the Scottish highlands, a wonderful time of breezy fresh air redolent with the scent of pine trees, bracken and heather, a time of clambering over great rocks as high as houses – nothing like that back in gentle, comfortable Suffolk – and icy cold dips in the northern waters off the coast of Nairn or Findhorn, together with picnics after a long steep walk high in the Cairngorms, with my father puffing furiously away at his pipe to drive off the gnats and midges. While we Brackenthwaites were away, we entrusted Groby to the care of Noah Stubblefield since there was no way at all that Groby could look after himself: he would probably just wander away in the high grass along the hedgerows and never be seen again.

So Noah had constructed a small grassy plot behind his cottage by the medieval village church, protected by fieldstone walls, and it was there that Groby could spend his daylight hours in the sunshine while I was away. And Groby was comfortable with that, being looked after and cared for by Noah, who always had a kind word for him and who brought him special treats to eat, like crisp bright green hearts of lettuce and the delicate white inmost stalks of celery. But, oh dear, Groby had tried to climb the wall one day, and had tumbled over, scratching the nape of his neck on the wire. Groby did not complain, not in the least, but poor Noah was quite beside himself.

"Oh, whatever will Master Eddy think of me now, taking no good care of poor old Groby? How ever could I have let such a thing 'appen? Oh, if only it won't lead to disaster. That would be the death of me, really it would. Master Eddy would never forgive me, no more he wouldn't, and he'd be right about that, right as rain he would be. And then I simply couldn't face him. I would never see that boy no more. Oh dear, oh dearie me, whatever shall I do?"

Well, Groby seemed to be not put out at all, and Noah applied home remedies as well as first aid cream from the village post office shop, and all seemed well – but the sore never truly healed, continued to ooze just a little blood and liquid each day, only a very little, but there it was, a wound that didn't heal.

When we Brackenthwaites came home from the Highlands all seemed well. Noah was consumed by apologies, but since Groby appeared to be to all intents and purposes just the same individual he had always been in my memory or Noah's or the family's, no one thought very much about the little sore on the back of his neck.

With the imminent approach of autumn the time was certainly coming when everything would have to be made ready for Groby's hibernation since tortoises in the wild sleep through the winter months. I chose a stout box of the right comfortable size, filled it with dry dead leaves from the great copper beech in the garden, and gave Noah all the instructions I could possibly imagine. The box, and Groby, would then spend the winter in the frost-free but chilly greenhouse. The plan looked perfect. So I made my way back from the vegetable garden where Noah was still singing, or rather trying to sing, last Sunday's hymns, this one about the hart panting for cooling streams when hunted in the chase. Whatever had that to do with church, I wondered vaguely. But I let that pass, sat down by Groby and told him all about how I hated, how I dreaded, how I shivered all over at the prospect of going back to that boarding school. "I got through one term, couldn't that be enough?" I asked Groby, blinking back my tears. But Groby said nothing, just reached up for the fistful of tender clover leaves that I had brought for him. Then I picked Groby up, held him tight and kissed him on the hard curve of his back.

"Goodbye, best friend," I murmured. "The first thing I'll do when they let me out of that jail for Christmas will be to run right back here. I'll run right up the garden path, and then I'll tiptoe in so as not to wake you up, and I'll whisper to you all my secrets, just like I do every day."

I couldn't let Groby see my tears or hear the gulping in my throat, so I carefully set him down and slipped away out of the greenhouse. Back in the house with the family, it was time for tea.

At last mid-December came, and with it the Christmas holidays from boarding school. The autumn term had turned out much better for me than I had dared hope: I had been elected head of my classroom with the responsibility of seeing that all was straight in the room, chalk by the blackboard, ink in all the inkwells, and desks neatly in rows, my own being in the front right-hand corner by the door for the honor of my position; I had also won for myself a place as substitute full back on the Under-Twelves Cricket team, a position much coveted by my fellows; and I had to my surprise discovered in myself a notable aptitude for Latin translation, earning me the respect and compliments of my form master, and even on one occasion having my work 'Sent Up For Good,' which meant being presented by Dr. Cratton the Headmaster with the promise of a prize book if I could repeat such excellence. All this delighted my father and warmed the heart of my mother. With success and recognition in the ascendant I felt less and less often the need to squeeze the white quartz pebble that Noah Stubblefield had given me, though I still did so from time to time for Noah's sake and for Groby's. And after the first week or two back in September I never had to repeat to myself the incantation "Be strong and of a good courage, fear not, neither be dismayed," though I remembered with warmth and gratitude how cleverly and affectionately Noah had found the way to strengthen my resolve.

Home again! And after loving family greetings all around, I dashed out of the house and up the garden path, first to pay my respects to the hibernating Groby in the greenhouse, and then to have a good long conversation with Noah Stubblefield, whose cracked and lilting voice I could just hear wafting down from the vegetable garden. "I feel myself so different," I said to myself, "I'm not a little boy anymore, scared of going away, scared of boarding school and everything. Why, I have a place for myself there, and it's a jolly good one too. I'm proud of it. So I can't be little Eddy anymore. My name is Edward, Edward Brackenthwaite, and Edward I'll be from now on, thank you very much, and that's flat. No more little Eddy, goodbye to him."

I carefully opened the greenhouse door, creaking on its rusty hinges, noticing from the torn and scuffed leaves around the door that no one had been in there for a good long time, in fact since the autumn leaves had fallen. At once there was a peculiar smell in the greenhouse, one that caught in my throat and which grew stronger and nastier as I cautiously approached Groby's box. I slowly lifted the lid. All was quiet. "Well, he's asleep, that's good," I thought, and I slowly parted the leaves covering the tortoise.

Something was wrong, I knew, and tried to convince myself that the source of the ever-stronger smell could only be some feces that Groby had passed in his sleep. But it wasn't that kind of smell, oh no, not that kind of smell at all.

I gently parted the dry leaves that covered Groby and then noticed that there was black dirt and what looked like long-dried blood on the leaves closest to Groby's head and front legs. This was absolutely wrong -- something dreadful had happened. So I carefully and ever so gently picked Groby up, but his hind legs hung loose, not tucked comfortably up as one would expect of a sleeping tortoise. I turned him around in order to take a close look at his dear, wise, wrinkled old face, and then gazed in. Horror, utter God-rending horror confronted me just six inches before my face, and the whole world swam around. There was no skin and precious little flesh left on Groby's entire head and neck. His eyes were gone, and the bones lay exposed, his skull and sharp jaws painfully clear, with every groove, every curve, every detail of his bones shining dull and yellowish-grey. A ghastly smile was fixed upon his horny jaw. Behind his shoulders, in the dark recess of his body beneath the back of his shell countless maggots twisted and turned, disturbed that Groby had been picked up and that daylight now played upon them. And Groby stank, oh my, how he stank.....

I dropped Groby back into his box in horror and stumbled to the rear of the greenhouse where an old wooden kitchen chair had been left for years. My chest was heaving, my wide eyes were staring at nothing, and I was panting deeply. I could not cry, it was all too deep for tears, sweet, simple everyday tears. In fact I was close to passing out: I realized that I was losing consciousness since the vision of my beloved Groby's corpse was taking the place of every single other thing in the entire universe, filling infinite space with that dreadful image of the grinning jaws and the wriggling maggots.

"Oh no,' I gasped, "I can't, I can't! I must get out – that smell, it's going to make me faint..." I managed to take sufficient hold of myself, made a dash for the door, flung it open and rushed out, across to the tall grass beside the hazelnut tree, and there I sank down on the ground, and, out of sight of everyone, cried and cried my heart out. When there was no more crying to be done, when I had no more ability to cry at all, I just lay there on my back, screened by the tall grass from the eyes of anyone passing nearby, and there I lay motionless for what seemed to me to be hours and hours. Then I arose, brushed myself off, and moved over to make sure that the greenhouse door was securely closed again. Everyone knew not to disturb Groby's sleep, but an open door would invite investigation, and that would be sacrilege indeed.

"And now I must break the news to Noah Stubblefield," I thought to myself. "Poor old Noah, he will take this very hard. He loved dear Groby, especially when he could take care of him by himself when we were all away in Scotland. Well, it's my duty to tell him, and to stand by him. Then together we'll bury poor Groby."

I walked slowly and mournfully up the path to the vegetable beds where Noah Stubblefield was plucking iced-over Brussels sprouts off their tall and rigid stalks.

"Well, Eddy, old son!" he called out gleefully in his familiar cracked voice. "How are you? A sight for sore eyes you be, and make no mistake about it. I've been a-looking forward to this day for ever so long, marking it on the calendar ever since you went away in September – just you ask me old lady if I ain't."

Then he noticed my slow steps and downcast face.

"Why, what's wrong, me lad, eh? Ain't you glad to be 'ome and even to see old Stubblefield again, eh? What's all this grief and grieving all about now? Come on, tell me, you've got to do that, you trusts me, doesn't you, same as ever?"

"Oh Noah, I don't know how to tell you! Something dreadful has happened, something absolutely dreadful! Poor Groby won't be waking up in the spring, he won't ever be waking up again. He's gone – and, and, and you and I must bury him together."

Noah Stubblefield staggered, his jaw dropping and his eyes staring wildly. He threw one arm around the branch of a nearby apple tree in order to prevent himself falling down onto the ground, which would have been painful to a man of his age.

"What? What's that?" he asked incoherently. "Why, I made him as nice a bed as ever I could, and I laid him on it nice and soft and easy after he had gone to sleep in the dry grass at the back of his hutch. He's dead and gone, you say? However did that happen? Oh my poor old Groby!" and he pulled from his pocket an old handkerchief, wiped his eyes and then blew his nose ferociously

"Well," I said, "you know how a whole lot of tortoises in England just don't make it through the winter. They come from Greece and Africa, see, and they just can't manage the cold up here. He must have just slipped away while he was asleep. I don't suppose he felt it at all, just stopped dreaming."

Noah could say nothing more. He just stood there, looking far off into the distance, thinking perhaps that Groby had had a gentle death and praying that he in his turn might have one too. Then a frightening thought suddenly took hold of him.

"It weren't that there cut on his neck, were it? The one he got while staying at my place, the one that never 'ealed? Did it get really poisonous and kill him in his sleep? Did it now? Come on, lad, you're not talking to me. I believes you knows something you're holding back from me. What is it? Out with it. Oh my Lord, oh my Lord!"

"Oh, Noah," I cried, "I don't know if it was the sore or something else, but somehow maggots got into him and he's been eaten up, and now all his bones are showing and the smell is dreadful! Anyway, if it was that hateful sore – and we really don't know that

--, that's absolutely not your fault, and you're <u>not</u> to go blaming yourself. You never meant for him to cut himself on that wretched wire, and we all did everything we could for his sore. We asked the chemist about it and all, and Mummy even had Dr. Putnam, our family doctor, take a look at him. So you must never, ever blame yourself, do you hear? Promise me now."

After a long silence the two of us looked at each other and slowly left the rows of Brussels sprouts, stopped in at the potting shed for a pair of spades, and then proceeded to the greenhouse, where I insisted on stepping in alone and retrieving the now closed box. I could not bear the thought of what might become of dear Noah if he should encounter that dreadful odor or see the wreck of his beloved friend. I now left the door wide open to clear the air, and the two of us paced slowly over to the orchard, choosing the tall and stately Blenheim as being the best tree to give shelter to poor old Groby's earthly remains. We took turns digging, and settled Goby's box at the foot of the hole. I was just about to shovel in the first of the earth that would cover the coffin box, when Noah called out "Stop, I have 'ere a little cross for him, just two sticks twisted together, mind you, but that'll be a comfort to him anyway, all alone in the orchard." And I murmured "Father, Son and Holy Ghost," not knowing what else to say.

At the end of the burial Noah was devastated, lost in his dry sobs, and it was for me, Edward Brackenthorpe, not little Eddy anymore, to comfort this man, so much older and more experienced than myself in the ways of the world.

"Remember what you told me before I went away to school last September?" I said. "'Be strong and of a good courage, fear not, neither be dismayed.' All that came straight from the Bible, you told me so yourself, and I completely believed you, and you were right. Well, you gave that to me when I needed it – or rather, you told it to little Eddy when he needed it. Well, I'm not little Eddy now, I've grown up and I'm Edward Brackenthwaite – and now I have something to tell *you.* They're really true, you know, all those lines from the Bible. Say them to yourself and it really helps. It helped me lots at the beginning of last term, and it'll surely help you now. Come on, Noah my friend, let's us both say the helpful words together."

What could then be heard in the orchard was the cracked voice of an old man close to his second childhood and the confident alto of a young boy eager to approach his adulthood, as together they recited the verse that held them together: "Be ye strong and of a good courage, fear not, neither be dismayed." And then we recited it again, and a third time.

What neither of us noticed or understood at the moment was that the effect of the agony of one of us when confronted by boarding school, and the overpowering grief of both of us at the death of a dearly loved friend, had in fact brought about a sea change in how we stood, one to another. Noah Stubblefield had been the comforter and little Eddy the one needing comfort, and now it was Edward Brackenthwaite who was offering the comfort and old Noah who stood in sore need of it. We had changed places: we had waltzed around each other.

CHAPTER 4

"PILE ON! EVERYBODY
PILE ON!"

"Oh-oh-oh-oh! Every-body pile on! Every-body pile on! Oh-oh-oh-oh!" These were the singsong cries of some thirty or forty young boys, aged from nine or ten to twelve or even thirteen as they huddled together as close as they could against the old brick walls in a corner of the school playground. This happened on all the coldest days of the winter as long as no sleet, freezing rain or heavy wet snow was falling, and the winter of 1950 was surely cold. At Hallworthy House, a boys' boarding school far out on the windswept fens beyond Ely, the half hour between boys' breakfast and chapel was always spent on the playground if the weather was at least halfway tolerable. Acute cold for the boys was felt by the masters to be perfectly acceptable, as indeed it was to the masters themselves as they supervised the boys and broke up fights before they fairly got underway, for the adults were warmly clad in winter trousers and tweed jackets with thick scarves around their necks, often in the colors of their own boarding schools or colleges. But the boys, oh the young boys, they had to wear the regulation school uniform which did indeed include a grey flannel jacket and schoolboy cap but also required them to wear grey flannel shorts all year round, with knee socks and everyday school shoes.

So in winter the boys grew pitiably cold, never having really warmed up after the regulation morning cold bath, for which they had lined up in the dormitory passages, naked except for bedroom slippers and a skimpy towel around their shoulders, until the moment should come when one boy was allowed to leap out of the cold bath, to be succeeded in the same water by the next in line until the last had come and gone, by which time the leaden bathroom floor stood a quarter inch deep in cold water and even the wooden duckboards were sodden.

After that and an unvarying breakfast of tea, toast and indeterminate red jam, only a few boys wanted to run mindlessly around the brick-walled gravel playground in order to try to keep warm. Most took refuge in a traditional Pile-on, chanting lugubriously "Oh-oh-<u>oh</u>-oh! <u>Pile</u> on! Every-body <u>pile</u> on! Oh-oh-<u>oh</u>-oh! <u>Pile</u> on! <u>Pile</u> on!" They had no idea that their chant was distinctly reminiscent of that of the Volga boatmen, which poses an interesting question. Did some Old Hallworthian compose the tune for the schoolboys' chant in a direct echo of the strain of the Volga boatmen, or was it a case of wholly independent creation? There is no way to tell, but there it is. Trying to beat the elements by crowding ever closer together, the half-frozen boys in fact shared something with the Emperor Penguins of the black Antarctic winter night since they too crowd together in great droves – except of course that penguins recite no long sad chant. The masters at Hallworthy House had for a long time tried to discourage Pile-ons, maintaining that some small boy might fall down in the midst of the crowd and be trampled under, but the boys refused to be discouraged and eventually had their way: Pile-ons became part of School Tradition, and Hallworthy House was very fond of its traditions, always on the lookout for something new and distinctive to keep its rival academies at bay. On any raw wintry day in London a gentleman on his way to the office had only to call out at the entrance to the Underground "<u>Pile</u> on! Every-body <u>pile</u> on!" and a face in the crowd might indeed warm up, glance around and smile in recognition at the memory of his schooldays, 'the best days of your life.'

But for all the "Oh-oh-<u>oh</u>-oh!" the Pile-on never really worked. Certainly it gave companionship and the boys' bodies pressed so close together shared their warmth, but the icy cold hung about their bare knees and penetrated their everyday shoes. Chilblains were endemic, just part of the system, nothing to go running off to Nurse about unless one wanted to be labeled a sissy, a cry-baby or worse. Of course when the red, shiny and swollen toes with their scuffed skin actually began to bleed, well, that was something else, and the complainant would be patched up with a few Elastoplasts and sent back to the daily routine of school life. One boy, Edward Brackenthwaite, could not help groaning and gasping out loud at the sharp and unremitting pain. He was only ten years old, and he was close to tears. For that shameful performance he was labeled Bye-Baby-Bunting for weeks afterwards, and he never forgot it, vowing never to send *his* son, should he ever have one, to Hallworthy House or anywhere like it, a vow that he kept all his adult life.

After the half hour in the playground the boys were allowed back into the school building, where they lined up and processed in pairs into the chapel for another half hour of ritual, this time religious exercises. The rest of the morning was taken up by several classes, in Latin, Greek, divinity, English, French, history, geography, mathematics or science.

Then the boys lined up once again and processed down the long corridors to the dining hall for lunch. Meals were spartan indeed, and they were always accompanied by baskets of bread, always the same baskets with just a hint of green mould in the interstices of the open weave. It was a peculiar quirk of Matron, who also happened to be the dietician and commandant of the kitchen, that she sincerely believed that fresh bread was indigestible to the young and should be consumed only by the adults in the school community. So all the beautiful great crusty loaves delivered fragrant and steaming hot from the bakery were cut up into slices one day and the hard, dry pieces presented to the boys on the next, having spent the intervening twenty-four hours loosely stacked in those familiar woven baskets. But by a dreadful mischance one day a basket of fresh soft bread with crackling crust made its way into the pile of baskets of day-old bread and was served at Brackenthwaite's table. As soon as he realized what a joy had presented itself to his senses – oh, the creamy delight of fresh-baked soft white bread! -- he seized upon slice after slice, piling them up on his plate and taking a hasty bite out of each in turn so that no one else would want it. Otherwise, even his best friends might go so far as to commandeer a slice or two of *his* bread for themselves, such a rare and delectable treat it was. In his overflowing enthusiasm and, yes, in his reprehensible greed, Brackenthwaite had overreached himself: he could not possibly eat all he had taken, despite valiant efforts to stuff himself. The bell rang! Time was up -- lunch was over. He could not possibly take any food out of the dining hall, almost a capital offence at Hallworthy, so he piled up into the basket again the slices he could not eat, and prayed that the callow serving girls would not notice the semicircular bites.

But one man did notice, oh yes, he did notice indeed. This was Isaac Spendleton, a tall, sardonic, lanky man with heavy straight black hair, who happened to be young Brackenthwaite's math teacher. Now math was Brackenthwaite's worst subject: he simply could not persuade the numbers to arrange themselves in the right order, and once arranged to stay so. At that time no one knew much at all about learning differences – indeed the phrase had not yet been coined – so failure to learn meant one of two things, either laziness on the part of the student or inefficient teaching on the part of the master. Dr. Ludovic Cratton, the Headmaster, had his eye on Mr. Spendleton, rumors and more than rumors having reached him of Mr. Spendleton's aggressive, even bullying, manner in the classroom and on the playing fields where he, like virtually all the masters, taught the boys soccer, rugby and cricket. Indeed Dr. Cratton would be just as happy if Mr. Spendleton chose to leave the school as to stay, and Mr. Spendleton knew it. Employment was hard to find in the years after the war, so he determined to watch his step. Inefficiency in teaching would certainly bring about his departure, so he applied his fiercest efforts to turning each and every one of the boys in his classes into top-flight mathematicians. And now along came young Brackenthwaite, the incorrigible Edward Brackenthwaite, who was well on his way to spoiling Mr. Spendleton's outstanding record. Well, that boy should pay, and Mr. Spendleton was always on the lookout for a way. And here it was, heaven-sent, he told himself, as he carefully observed the boy's greed and vile wickedness. As the masters were making their stately way out of hall before the procession of boys, he leant across and slipped a word into Dr. Cratton's ear, knowing full well that the Headmaster, a most abstemious man, abhorred greed and waste as he abhorred little else, judging greed to be one of the most horrendous of the deadly sins, and waste, if unchecked, to be a sure and certain way to bring a school to its knees.

"Dr. Cratton, Sir, I do think you should know this," began Mr. Spendleton. "I distinctly saw one wretched boy, Brackenthwaite I believe it was, Sir, seize slice after slice of bread right before the end of luncheon and then take a bite, one single bite, out of each, and finally pile them up for himself on his plate. Now why would he be doing such a thing, I wondered? So, if you will allow me, Sir, I will just slip back there to the serving room and see what it was all about. We can't have every little boy taking good bread and spoiling it for others when he cannot possibly eat it himself, can we now?"

"Very well. Go and find out, and then come and see me afterwards, will you?" said Dr. Cratton, reluctant to pass more words with a master whom he wished to shed.

The serving room was all astir, no one being able to remember such a thing ever having happened before. Here was a pile of half-eaten slices, broken crusts spilled this way and that across the long trestle table in the dining hall, and the bread basket empty! The kitchen maids could not explain it, but Matron soon discovered the cause: some careless serving girl, doubtless some dimwitted creature from the village, had carelessly given the boys a basket of today's fresh and crusty bread instead of the hardened slices of yesterday. All this Matron explained with indignation and apologies to Mr. Spendleton, who spun round on his heel and took his departure, eager to impart the horrific news to the Headmaster, who in turn would doubtless be grateful to him for his vigilance and his evident care for the dietary correctness of the provender offered to the schoolboys. But Dr. Cratton had already been called away to other capito-magisterial duties, as Mr. Spendleton secretly named them to himself, and had left word with his secretary that Mr. Spendleton might be coming by and if so he was to make his report in writing, briefly.

Alas, it was math class right after lunch for Brackenthwaite, and there stood Mr. Spendleton glowering down upon him, bitter that he had not been able to ingratiate himself further with Dr. Cratton and eager to vent his spleen upon the young boy. The lad had no means of self-defence and he knew himself to be in the wrong, expecting condign punishment to be visited upon him at any moment.

"So you have condescended to grace our little circle with your presence," sneered Mr. Spendleton. "How very nice of you, how very nice. Ah yes, I thought you might have had an appointment you could not pass up with a slice of bread! Ha, ha, ha! Well, let me tell you, young sir, that if I had had anything to do with the matter I would have called you up before the whole school, the entire body, masters, boys and servants, ordered you to pull down your trousers and then thrashed you within an inch of your life! My goodness, yes, I would certainly have done that, and no regrets! When I think of all the poor starving children in India, China, any of those sorts of places, and you guzzling away at your pleasure – and what's even worse, spoiling good, honest, heaven-sent bread, the staff of life itself, by taking bites with your miserable little jaws out of that first-rate sustaining food, why, my blood just boils! It boils, you loathsome little wretch, do you understand that?"

Well, young Brackentrhwaite understood that all too well, and could not help himself, try as he might, from breaking down in audible gulps and sobs at Mr. Spendleton's tirade. The only consolation that came to him was the recollection that it was absolutely forbidden for any master to inflict corporal punishment upon any boy, whatever the provocation. Mr. Spendleton knew that too, of course, and this alone restrained him: he had to keep his job. But Brackenthwaite feared for his life.

So math class passed, and it cannot be said that Brackenthwaite learned one single thing, further infuriating Mr. Spendleton, who counted upon victory in the classroom as the key to saving his position in the school.

And now it was time for sports, outdoor exercise to be followed later on by two more hours of classes. In winter at that latitude the afternoons drew in early and it grew dark by half past four, so it was time to shepherd the boys out to the playing fields. A thick wet snowfall had succeeded to the icy blast of the early morning and the playing fields looked more like an Arctic vista than anything else, goal posts standing forlornly here and there in the clear and unmarked whiteness. So, no football, and no practice either since the balls would not bounce to the satisfaction of the games masters. What to do? The answer: Run. Why not set the boys to running around the periphery of the broad playing fields?

And no childish snowballing nonsense either, nor, heaven help us, snowmen and snow forts. A good long run would keep the boys warm, several times around the playing fields, that would set the blood coursing through their veins, and it would help them run with less fatigue when they could be playing soccer again – and the whole thing would also be a blessing in disguise to the masters, or at least to most of them, who had no more desire than the boys to stand about or run around the fields under these conditions. Why, it would only take one or two of the masters to supervise the whole school, and the rest could slip away to the staff room, to sit by the fire with a hot cuppa tea, ostensibly to prepare tomorrow's classes or to mark the test papers from yesterday's. There were always one or two hearty members of the teaching staff who took especial pleasure in the great outdoors as it presented itself to them on the playing fields, and of course one of these was the Head of the Athletic Department, Harry Glempsey, a strong, heavy-set fellow with a clipped mustache, sandy hair and sleepy, light blue eyes, but little intellect. These masters had no compunction in pushing the boys to the limit of their endurance, maintaining with blind sincerity that the whole thing was good for their young minds and bodies. Toughen them up, it would, teach them to be men, real men, not dull little scholars always perched on benches at their school desks.

So running in deep snow it was to be for one and all, even though more heavy snow was falling all the time. The boys were told to change into their soccer clothes, shirt, shorts, knee socks and football boots, and to fall in by class outside the school building where they were ordered to start running, and to keep running until one of the masters should dismiss them. It was bad luck for all the boys and especially bad luck for Brackenthwaite that it was the cold-hearted Isaac Spendleton who had volunteered to supervise this activity along with Harry Glempsey. This Mr. Spendleton had done not from a love of it all, far from it: like everyone else, he would much have preferred that cuppa by the fire. But he knew that, for some reason he could not fathom, he had fallen out of grace with the Headmaster, so he had set himself to ingratiate himself with the other members of the staff. Then, if ever the need should occur, he would have at least a few of his colleagues to stand up for him in the presence of the Headmaster.

For the first hundred yards or so the running was rather fun for the boys, leaning back to catch the falling snowflakes in their mouths, swishing through the deepening snow under foot, and kicking it up at the back of the boy in front. But then they began to grow tired, particularly the youngest of them, no more than nine years old. Finally some of the nine- and ten-year old boys, with Brackenthwaite at their head, turned to Mr. Spendleton and to Mr. Glempsey, formerly Colour Sergeant of the King's Own Gloucestershire Rifles. Together they begged for time out for a rest and to warm their gloveless hands, their bare heads and knees, and their feet too, for the snow had by now found its way into their football boots. But Mr. Spendleton was immovable, stony-faced, obdurate, and Mr. Glempsey said nothing at all although in his heart he thought Mr. Spendleton was a cruel man.

"You were told to run, and run you will," barked Mr. Spendleton. "Be off with you, and don't you dare come sniveling up to me again!"

"I say, old man," murmured Mr. Glempsey with some hesitation. "Don't you think we're perhaps a little 'ard on 'em? They're only kids, after all. Can't have them calling in sick on account of us, can we now?"

Mr. Spendleton shrugged him off with an angry glance: "Don't you know I'm in charge here? I was the first to volunteer for this duty."

So the boys set off once more, not having heard Mr. Glempsey's asides to Mr. Spendleton and hoping that their strength would hold out until the whistle should blow and they could come in out of the cold. But the waiting time was too long, and by ones and twos the boys began to falter, even to stumble and fall down for a moment before dragging themselves on and on and on.

"Look here, Hulbert," said Tom Mallory, the Head Prefect of Hallworthy House, a tall, clean-cut youth with striking good looks, to his friend Bob Hulbert, a short, lean lad with wiry red hair, Captain of Hallworthy House's First Eleven Soccer Team, as they ran smoothly together. "That bloody Spindles has gone too far this time. Those little'uns just can't take it much longer, and I don't want to be any part of this. Remember Old Crat making each of us promise individually that as leaders of the School we must take our responsibilities seriously, and as good citizens and Christians and all that rot we have a real duty to help those who are in trouble? Well, what do you think? Isn't it the time for that now?"

"By golly, you're right, you're absolutely right!" answered Hulbert with enthusiasm. "But what shall we do? Go up to old Spindles and ask him to let them off? He would be mad as hell at us for that, and find a way to take it out on us later somehow or other – and we wouldn't be helping the little'uns either. So what to do? But, I say, here's an idea! Let's just peel off as we pass the side door and go and see if Old Crat's in his study. He would know what to do and he would respect us for speaking up for the little'uns. He always has a soft spot for them, and I get the feeling he's not too fond of old Spindles."

"Great idea, Hulbert! And let's pick up a little'un or two so Old Crat can see what's what, how icy and shivering they are."

And that's what they did, sweeping almost off his feet the first young boy they came across – it happened to be Brackenthwaite. They bundled him in at the side door by the pantry and rushed along the corridors, hoping to encounter no master who would stop them and ask what the blazes this was all about. They slipped through all right, and breathlessly passed the outer green baize door to Dr. Cratton's study, and then knocked cautiously on the oak inner door.

"Come in," he invited them, not looking up from the pile of papers and correspondence to which he was attending. "Who are you, and what can I do for you?" he asked, still not looking up from his desk, where he sat with his back to them.

"Goodness gracious, what on earth is this all about?" he asked, his eyes opening wide as he finally turned to face the three boys. "You are soaking wet, all of you, and dripping right onto my carpet. At any rate we must put a stop to that right away. Here, Hulbert, these are yesterday's newspapers. For goodness sakes, throw them down on the bare floor beyond the carpet, and all three of you stand there, and then if you please, explain yourselves. I am all ears. Two great Sixth Formers and one very much younger boy. Hm, let's see. Now, am I right? I believe you are young Edward Brackenthwaite, son of my old school friend Gerald. He's in business now, isn't he? Yes? Well, that's established, and now let's go on from there. Who is going to tell me? Mallory, Head Prefect of Hallworthy House, I think this is up to you."

"Well, Sir, it all began with this snow. It's really heavy now and –"

"Snow, did you say, Mallory? Snow? Upon my soul, I didn't know about that. Let's take a look at it, shall we?" So saying, he edged himself past the corner of his great desk and ambled over to the window. "Great Scott, my boy, you're right! And I never noticed it, never noticed it at all. Why, bless my soul! All of you lads must be having the time of your lives out there, snowballing and making snowmen and attacking each other's snow forts! Who has the biggest and best fort? My money's on the Sixth Form. Ha, ha! Oh, how I envy you! School days were the best days of my life.

But now we are wandering from the point, aren't we? What are two of the leaders of the School, greatly respected youths, two of the Mighty Ones in fact, if I may be permitted the phrase, doing in my study with this jejune youngster today? I have asked you to explain yourselves, you know, and you haven't even begun to do that. Please proceed. I am waiting, very patiently, I may say, and I am all ears – I rather believe I told you that, didn't I? Well, never mind, get on with it, my lads, why are you hesitating?"

"Well Sir, things aren't going on well out there, if I may make so bold as to say so," started Mallory. "Yes, all of us are out there, that is, all the whole School, Sir, from the First Form to the Sixth, but no one is allowed to make a snowball and no one is allowed to make a snowman."

"*Not allowed?*" interjected Dr. Cratton. "*Not allowed?* Whatever do you mean? Why, God Almighty gave us winters and snow so that we could play in them, didn't He? 'All work and no play, makes Jack a dull boy.' So what on God's good earth is all this nonsense about no snowball fights and no snowmen? I can see I had better get out there myself and teach you ignorant youngsters how to have a good time in the winter! Whatever is the world coming to, I'd like to know?"

"Let me try to explain, Sir, if I may," interjected Hulbert. "You know I'm fearfully keen on soccer and all that, and everyone who plays has to have stamina, has to be able to run up and down the field for the entire length of the game. Well, Mr. Spendleton and Mr. Glempsey decided that rather than have all of us just lark around with snow forts and snowball fights, we ought to be training since we can't actually play football in six inches of snow. So everyone had to get on their soccer togs and run laps all around the whole playing fields, which is quite a long way, Sir, for the little'uns. It must be as much as a quarter of a mile, I think. After half an hour or more, with the snow coming down something fierce, well, the little'uns have had enough and some of them are starting to cry what with the cold and all, and them with no hats or gloves or anything. So a few of them plucked up their courage and asked Old Spindles – pardon me, Sir, I meant Mr. Spendleton – if they could just come indoors and rest for a spell, but he would have none of it. And Glempers, -- er, Mr. Glempsey that is, -- he just let Mr. Spendleton have his way, and there weren't any other masters anywhere to be seen." He paused for breath, and to think what to say next.

"So you both came to see me, isn't that it?" asked Dr. Cratton, taking off and polishing his *pince-nez* as he spoke. "Just why did you do that, please, what was in your minds? Why didn't you step up and have a word with Mr. Spendleton and Mr. Glempsey? And what has young Edward to do with all this?"

Mallory took up the narrative. "If I may say so, Sir, with great respect, Hulbert here and I got to talking as we ran round the fields, about how you took aside all the School leaders, captains of the boarding houses and what not, just a week or two back, and told us that with our privileges come responsibilities, and the greatest of those responsibilities was to help any boy, particularly the little'uns, -- sorry, Sir, I mean the First and Second Formers – if they are in any trouble. It was a Christian duty, I can hear your words now, Sir, if I may say so, and I got to thinking about your talks in Chapel and all that. They mean so much to us, you see, they really do. So that's why we're here. We've come to ask you to stop this running before some young fellow really collapses for good and all. And, and, and, please do hurry, Sir, please hurry right now! I know I shouldn't talk to you like that, Sir, but I'm really scared! Oh, and I didn't think Mr. Spendleton would take kindly to it if I were to ask him right in front of all the other boys to change his mind and call the whole thing off. I heard for myself how he had torn a strip off some little'uns who asked him, ever so politely, and young Edward here, he was one of those."

"Very good, very good," said Dr. Cratton, with a black look on his face. "You three gentlemen please wait right here on this very spot, and I'll be back in a trice. I have to see to this, find out what is happening, and' – with a slightly threatening glance at the three boys – "I have to discover whether there might not perhaps be another side to this yarn that you have spun to me. But first you'll have to tell me why you have brought young Edward along with you. For myself, I cannot for the life of me imagine why you did that." And he was gone.

"Well, why did you come with us?" asked Hulbert, looking across at Brackenthwaite. "I for one don't remember asking you." Mallory said nothing, his face a study in anxiety and distress.

"I don't know at all, I don't know at all," gasped Brackenthwaite, close to tears and overawed by the questioning presence of two of the Mighty Ones. "You just took me and I couldn't help it. I was, I was" -- he swallowed hard – "kidnapped, you might almost say. But I am awfully glad you did, awfully glad, really, 'cos now I can tell Old Crat" – thus did this innocent youth refer to the Reverend Ludovic Cratton, D.D., Canon Emeritus of Ely Cathedral and Headmaster of Hallworthy House -- "what it's really like being a younger boy, almost a new boy really, running and running in all that terrible storm." His face brightened. "Wouldn't you like me to do that? Please? I really want him to know."

"Yes, yes," mused Mallory. "Of course that *is* exactly why we asked you to accompany us, and you were kind enough to come along. Yes, yes, that's exactly how it was. And you can tell Dr. Cratton anything, anything at all that he asks you – but it might be a good idea to let Hulbert and me do the talking first, that is, unless Dr. Cratton asks you directly."

Meanwhile Dr. Cratton had rushed as fast as his short legs and advancing years permitted him to the great doors that led out from the changing rooms to the playing fields, the spot where he would be closest to Mr. Spendleton and Mr. Glempsey without having actually to equip himself with clothing suitable in a snow storm. For a moment he thought with some regret of the splendid felt and reindeer leather boots he had acquired almost half a century ago in Lapland while following the path Linnaeus had trodden in those latitudes in the middle of the eighteenth century, but it would have taken far too long to don them, and if those older boys were speaking only half the truth there was indeed no time to be lost.

It took the Headmaster no more than a minute to see that this 'running' had gone on far, far too long, and that if prompt action were not taken forthwith, there might be some real disaster in the making – a boy in collapse, a boy taken to the hospital, parents distressed, newspapers on the scent, the School in the 'papers, Old Boys full of questions, fund-raising dwindling, oh dear, oh dear, and all because of that infernal ass Spendleton. I should never have let him enter the premises, thought Dr. Cratton, the worst mistake I ever made in my life. And why hadn't Glempsey had more sense? Obeying orders like the dumb soldier he once was, I suppose.

"Mr. Spendleton," he called out in the loudest tone he could command, "and Mr. Glempsey, I believe the lads have had quite enough exercise for today. So please dismiss them forthwith, and send them in to tea."

With that, and knowing that he would be obeyed at once, he turned sharply on his heel and ambled as fast as he could back down the corridor to his study, where the three boys stood waiting, a little anxiously.

"Edward," he said, "would you mind please just stepping out into the hallway for a few minutes? I believe I ought to talk to these gentlemen first."

Frightened now that he might be in trouble with the Headmaster, Brackenthwaite left the room and paced up and down the narrow hallway, his anxiety increasing with every passing minute. He knew he had done nothing wrong, that it had not been his idea that they should turn sneak and run off to the headmaster as tattle-tales, that he had in plain fact actually been kidnapped – he liked the word and told himself to remember it – but the truth was that as only a Second Former his word would count for very little. That nasty little nursery rhyme kept thrumming through his head:

"Tell-tale tit,
Tell-tale tit,
Your tongue shall be slit,
Your tongue shall be slit,
And every puppy-dog in town
Will have a little bit!"

He had worked himself up almost into tears by the time the two Mighty Ones stepped out of the Headmaster's study, and with long faces beckoned him to enter.

Meanwhile, what had happened in the study? It had taken Dr. Cratton several minutes to collect himself, to calm down, as he went over and over in his mind the callous brutality – he could find no other words – of that godless wretch Spendleton and that thick-headed Glempsey. Well, Glempsey had not been so very wicked, just weak in the face of malignity. But Spendleton! Anyway, time for that later. What to do with these boys? They had after all only done their duty as they saw it, in response to his, Ludovic Cratton's, inculcation to them and all the young gentlemen in his charge, always to live by their Christian consciences. Yes, they should have plucked up their courage to face the two masters directly, before seeking him out if that should indeed prove to be necessary. But that was a matter of judgment, and one must always err on the side of forgiveness for those whose sincere judgment proves to be a little awry. So that is what the Headmaster explained to the Head Prefect and the Captain of the Soccer Team, and he was on the point of dismissing them when he remembered young Edward Brackenthwaite.

"Ah, one moment more of your valuable time, please, if you would be so kind" he called out as Mallory was in the very act of opening the study door. "May I please ask you just a few more questions? What, pray, was the reason why Edward Brackenthwaite accompanied you in your visit to my place of refuge? Surely a lad of his tender age would not be privy to your councils, an active companion to this distinguished pair of Mighty Ones that saw fit to come calling on me? Share with me, I pray you, gentlemen, share with me."

The boys shuffled uncomfortably, and the Headmaster saw that. "Well, Sir," began Mallory, the better speaker of the two. "It was like this. Just as Hulbert and I were heading for the changing room door to come and see you, Brackenthwaite came up to us looking perfectly miserable, and when he saw that we were going indoors, really, truly and truth going indoors, he pushed his way in past us, to stay indoors for just few minutes, mind you, so he could get a little warm. And then when he saw that we were coming to see you, Sir, he begged and begged to come along too and was going to put up a real fight about it, and, and, and we just hadn't the heart to tell him not to – he looked so miserable, and he was really furious at Spindles and Glempers, particularly Spindles, blubbering that Spindles always had it in for him and now this was his one and only chance to speak out for his side of the case."

By this time Hulbert was staring open-mouthed at his friend, for that was not at all the way it had in fact happened. He was on the point of speaking out when he realized that telling the Headmaster that the Head Prefect was adjusting the truth was going to land him with a whole lot of problems as well as being disloyal to the closest friend he had made over their five years together in the school.

The Headmaster caught his expression and looked him straight in the eye, saying "Bob Hulbert, you have something to say. Out with it, Sir, out with it!"

"Er, no, nothing Sir, nothing at all. I was just remembering how awfully angry Brackenthwaite was." Dr. Cratton left it at that, and the interview was over.

Outside the study, the two boys paced along the hallway and Hulbert turned on Mallory. "What the devil did you have in mind? Those were stark lies, and now weak little Brackenthwaite is going to tell Old Crat what actually happened. He used the word kidnap, and by God he was right. Oh Lord, what do we do now?"

"Do? We do nothing at all, Hulbert, nothing at all. Brackenthwaite will think twice about turning in the Head Prefect and the Captain of Soccer, and anyway I don't suppose for one moment that Old Crat would believe his word over ours. It's not a hanging offence anyway. And, listen to me here, Hulbert my good friend, I believe I have saved you and me from a whole packet of trouble. Old Crat would not at all like the idea of us, two of the Mighty Ones as he is so fond of calling us, frog-marching a helpless little'un into the Headmaster's *sanctus sanctorum* solely in order to bear witness to the truth of our story – particularly as its truth was self-evident to Old Crat the moment he poked his bald head out of the changing room door and saw the whole school slowly, slowly, faltering and tramping through the deep snow round and round those bloody playing fields."

"Jesus, Mallory, you've got it right! I have to admit it, you thought quicker than I did. And I'm sorry I got angry with you. So, yes, mum's the word." And the two of them made their way back to the changing room and the studies where all the boys were warming up and chattering excitedly about the clash of wills between Headmaster and a member of the teaching staff. "Old Spindles is on his way out, make no mistake about it, and good riddance!" was the popular judgment.

Meanwhile it was Brackenthwaite's turn to take his place in the Holy of Holies. He stood nervous and twitching as Dr. Cratton looked him over, scrutinized him from head to toe for a full two minutes with no smile on his lined face. Brackenthwaite's trepidation turned slowly to despair, and despair turned to terror. What was Old Crat going to do? And why was he so angry? What had

I done, he asked himself? Oh Lord, if this gets back to Dad, and Dad just worships Old Crat, next hols will be no fun at all. I'll be in disgrace the whole damn time.

"So you were so angry at Mr. Spendleton that you came to me rather than face him like a man? Isn't that it? Isn't that called being a sneak, and being a sneak is just about the lowest thing a schoolboy could be. Why, in my time, the other boys wouldn't stand for it, no sir, they wouldn't stand for it, not for an instant. Why, they would beat the boy themselves, and the masters would let them. However" – and here his expression returned to its characteristic benignity – "times have changed, and for the better, I do believe. So let us set that aside, loath though I am to do so.

But I have another bone to pick with you, young man, indeed I do. This same Mr. Spendleton has informed me that thanks to his scrupulous watchfulness he observed you at luncheon today exhibiting such a foul and repellent display of hideous greed as I have seldom come across in all my born days. What do you have to say to that, sir? Am I right, and is not greed one of the seven deadly and almost unforgivable sins?" Here he glowered again, and left Brackenthwaite for what seemed like an eternity to choke and come up with an answer.

"If you please, Sir," he mumbled. "I was awfully hungry, and that fresh bread was just yummy, and we don't ever have real, honest-to-goodness fresh bread here, Sir, not ever, and I just couldn't stop myself, and I know I was wrong, I think I knew it at the time, but it all just happened, don't you see, Sir, I just didn't think, I just went on and on, it was such awfully good bread, Sir, it really was, and, and, and ..." His voice caught in his throat and trailed away to silence.

Dr. Cratton studied him for a few moments. "Well, my lad, I can see that you have perceived the error of your ways, and I feel sure you will never commit so heinous a crime again. Enlightenment must precede repentance, and repentance must precede confession, and confession must precede absolution. I believe I have accurately described the course of events in your case. So I have changed my mind, something I very rarely do. I may tell you I had decided, firmly decided, to deal with you seriously, and you know what that phrase means at Hallworthy House. It means a beating, and it is a severe beating that you well deserve. But that punishment, though richly merited, will not fall upon you. Instead, this is what I will do. I hereby now charge you, upon your honor for I take you to be a thoroughly honorable boy although also a manifest sinner, I charge you, Edward Brackenthwaite, to think this all over very deeply, for some hours if need be, to go to bed this evening in good time, early would be best, and to spend your time praying for further enlightenment and for divine forgiveness. And one more thing: I will spare my dear friend your father from all knowledge of this utterly lamentable business. Finally I ask you, I invite you, I urge you, to come back to see me, either as your Headmaster or as the Canon and Priest that I am, if ever you want to at a time when you have collected your thoughts, to discuss these matters with me in greater depth. So go now, go, and remember – early to bed, as early as you can, and think deeply."

Brackenthwaite stumbled from the room, muttering his gratitude and feeling relief flooding right over him.

"I say, Brackers, old man," called out one of his friends when he got back to the classroom. "Buck up! What's the matter with you? You look downright glum. And where have you been all this time anyway? There's a super film tonight, all about Robin Hood -- and Errol Flynn's in it! Won't that be absolutely super!"

Brackenthwaite had forgotten it was Saturday, and there was always a film for the boys on Saturday evening. His spirits soared: a film, a really super film, just what he really needed after all he had been through – the way Spindles had cursed him out in front of the whole math class, the terrible cold, above all the fearful moments in Old Crat's study. A film! And such a film! His heart leapt at the prospect – and then it came crashing down again, slamming into the floor. He could not see the film. He just couldn't see it. Not only would he miss it and all the fun of being part of it and shouting at it with all his friends, but tomorrow everyone would be talking about the film, rehearsing their favorite scenes, and he would have to sit out all that fun, all that friendship. And why? Because Old Crat had sentenced him to bed! To bed, for really nothing he had done that everyone else wouldn't have done too if they had had the chance.

Being sent to bed early on a Saturday evening and thereby missing the school film was a well-known and standard punishment at Hallworthy House, not nearly as severe as a beating but all the same considerably worse, being public, than having to write out, in one's spare time, half of one of Vergil's *Georgics*, all the hundreds of lines of it. Had Old Crat really given him this sentence? Or had he just told him to be quiet and think, think, think about what he had done? There was no way to tell, and Brackenthwaite simply didn't dare go back to the Headmaster for a more detailed explanation. Why, if he went back his punishment might grow by leaps and bounds! Better suck it up, make the best of it, slip off to bed early, and keep out of all his friends' way for the next day or two until the predictable excitement and constant references to Robin Hood had had time to die down. So, when the time came for everyone else to assemble in the school hall in a sparkling mood of excitement, Brackenthwaite took his lonely path along the corridors and across the corner of the snow-bound playing fields to his boarding house, where, alone and in silence, he changed into his pyjamas, brushed his teeth, and climbed into bed.

At first he lay very quiet, with the pale light from the stairwell barely illuminating the dormitory room, flat on his back, trying his hardest to do everything that Dr. Cratton had instructed him to do. After all, thought Brackenthwaite, Old Crat really was a priest, so he should know about such things. Since this was now getting close to an atmosphere of prayer, Brackenthwaite folded his hands together on his chest as he lay on his back, in the stance taken by the effigy on the tomb of a medieval knight in armor back in his parish church at home. But it wasn't much use. Brackenthwaite had thought about everything there was to think about on that subject, several times now, and his mind kept wandering back to that brute Spindles and the cold fear that he felt that Spindles would lose his temper over him once again in math class – why, oh why wouldn't those wretched numbers behave as they should? Why ever did they flicker and move around when his attention touched upon something else even for an instant?

And then he did think of something else, and it wasn't good. Mr. Glempsey was his housemaster, and once the boys were all back from the film he would be making his rounds of the dormitories, chatting with the boys and seeing that all was well as they prepared for bed. What would he make of Brackenthwaite being in bed already? He might think it had something to do with Brackenthwaite on the playing fields that afternoon, or to the way all the boys were talking now about Mallory, Hulbert and, yes, young Brackenthwaite going off to see Dr. Cratton about the running in the snow. So the boy lay wide awake with his fears, his confusions and his sorrows, anxious now about Mr. Glempsey, but growing at the same time more and more bored as each quarter hour passed.

It was altogether more than flesh could bear: he simply could not go on lying there thinking of all that had gone wrong that day, trying but completely failing to force himself to go to sleep. What made it worse was that right there on the shelf next to his bed lay the book he was reading, Sir Percy FitzPatrick's *Jock of the Bushveld*, a wonderful account of the life of a mongrel dog among the hunters and trekkers of South Africa in the first years of the twentieth century. He looked up longingly at the book, remembering so many of the scenes, such as when Jock's master and his friends got lost in the bush. They thought they were walking in a straight line through unknown territory, but then they came across tracks from the boots of men who had gone before them. After a while there were twice as many tracks, and they noticed that the same boot with a split heel was among them, twice. It was Jock's master's boot! They had been walking in wide circles, and now they were truly lost -- but not far from a dry stream bed, which led them back to the camp. Brackenthwaite loved that particular story, and he wished he dared just take a peek at it once more. So he plucked up his courage and did exactly that, after listening to the silence and drawing the book under the bedclothes to the safety of his flashlight, for reading in bed was a very serious offence in one sent there in disgrace.

Presently he heard the voices of the other boys coming in, so he bade adieu to Jock, the hunters, the tang of the strips of *biltong*, and the lowing of the oxen being hustled to the *vorspan*. He turned off his flashlight but still kept it and his precious book tight to his chest, poked his head out onto the pillow, and pretended to be waking from deep sleep. The boys trooped in and at once began telling him how much he had missed, how glorious it had been to watch Errol Flynn sailing through the air on the branch of a vine, knocking the sheriff of the Earl of Nottingham clear off his horse and galloping away on it himself. Yippee!

"All of you just have to stop that at once," called out Kendall, the boy who was captain of the dormitory. "You know someone sent to bed has been sent to Coventry and we're not allowed to talk to him at all. So just shut up, will you?" Brackenthwaite groaned and turned over in his bed, his face to the wall to conceal the tears that were collecting on his cheek. The other boys soon lost all interest in him as they prepared for bed, brushing their teeth and whooping it up so loudly that Mr. Glempsey had to come upstairs himself to quieten them down. He glanced over at Brackenthwaite but made no move in his direction.

"Just keep it quiet," he said. "Talking's fine, but no shouting and jumping around. Lights out in fifteen minutes." And he left the room, to keep an eye on how things were progressing in the seven other dormitory rooms..

After lights out Mr. Glempsey moved softly through the corridors, glancing in at each room to see that all was well. He passed by Brackenthwaite's room and then paused and silently stepped back. What was that glow on the other side of the room? It was coming from someone's bed. Brackenthwaite's, by God! Mr. Glempsey strode into the room and whipped back the bedclothes, and there lay the criminal, curled up and reading his book by the light of his flashlight.

"Aha, so what have we here?" roared Mr. Glempsey with a note of triumph in his voice. "I haven't heard why you were sent to bed early in disgrace, but sent to bed you were, and now you've really it got it coming to you. Who sent you, boy? And what for?"

"Oh Sir, please don't be angry," mumbled Brackenthwaite, horrified now that he had got himself into the deepest trouble. "You see, Sir, this is such a super book, and I just had to go on reading for a little bit. Please don't be angry, Sir. I promise I won't do it again."

"Well, dammit, answer my question, won't you? Who sent you, and for what?"

"Please Sir, it was Dr. Cratton, and I think it was because I went to see him with Mallory and Hulbert, but I don't really know. I'm not sure. I can't quite remember." And indeed he had clear forgotten all about that yummy bread.

"Dr. Cratton, eh? And now you're reading in bed after lights out, offence number one, and reading in bed when you've been sent there in disgrace, offence number two. This calls for serious action, my boy. Go right down to my study and fetch my stick. Mrs. Glempsey will show you where I keep it for such times as this."

"Oh Sir, please ..." the poor boy whimpered.

"Shut up, you nasty little creature, and get out of here this instant! And come right back with my stick."

Brackenthwaite crept out of bed, pulled his dressing gown around him, and in his slippered feet slowly descended the staircase to the housemaster's private wing of the boarding house. In a daze he asked Mrs. Glempsey for the stick, which she handed to him with a soft and pitying look but nary a word. He climbed the staircase again, and solemnly handed the stick to the expectant Mr. Glempsey.

"You miserable little worm," said Mr. Glempsey. "I have thought about this. It was the Headmaster who sent you here in disgrace, so I think it would be right for him to decide what is to be done with you. Take my stick back to the study, thank your lucky stars that I am not beating you tonight because I have a strong right arm, go to bed, and then report to Dr. Cratton first thing in the morning. Got it, you nasty boy?"

"Yes, Sir, please Sir, I do understand," stuttered poor Brackenthwaite. And he carried the cane back downstairs, mumbled something incoherent to the surprised Mrs. Glempsey, and took himself off for a long, tortured and almost sleepless night.

Even before all the boys lined up for breakfast Brackenthwaite opened the outer baize door and knocked at the inner door of Dr. Cratton's office.

"Why, Edward my lad, please come in! Delighted to see you, delighted indeed. To what do I owe the pleasure of this visit?"

"Oh Sir, please Sir, it's just dreadful," began Brackenthwaite, his heart pounding furiously. "You're going to be so angry with me, and I can't stand it. Well, I did something very naughty and wrong, and it was all my fault, and I'm so sorry, Sir, I really am." Here once more his tears got the better of him, and he had to stop.

"Very wrong, Edward, very wrong? And here I was, thinking we had put all of that firmly behind us. But the Devil is very strong:

the spirit may be willing but the flesh is weak. Remember those words, I charge you: the spirit is willing, but the flesh is weak. Well, dear lad, out with it. What on earth has happened this time?"

"Well, Sir, I went off to bed early as you had sent me, and I missed that film about Robin Hood and all, and I tried, I really did, I tried just as hard as ever I could, to think over all you had said to me yesterday, I really did, I promise, Sir. But it just didn't make me go to sleep. I really tried, I kept my eyes shut and all, and I prayed just like you tell us to in Chapel, but I just couldn't sleep. So, oh Lord, I took down the book I am reading, *Jock of the Bushveld* by Sir Percy Fitzpatrick, a really super book, Sir, and I started to read it with my flashlight under the covers, 'cos when you're sent to bed early you're not allowed to read. And then old Glempers – sorry, Sir, I meant Mr. Glempsey – caught me and sent me down to his study for his stick. He was going to beat me, Sir, he really was. Well, when I got back with the stick he said that you had sent me to bed early and it would only be fair for you to punish me. Oh Sir, I am so sorry! I really didn't mean anything by it! I just couldn't stop myself." And he added sheepishly "Do you really think it was the Devil?"

"My goodness gracious, my boy, here's a great how-d'ye-do! Yes indeed, if ever I saw one. Confusion worse confounded, eh? Don't ye think so, what? But you have no idea what I am talking about. Yes, my friend Edward, I do distinctly recollect talking with you yesterday, about Christian responsibility and the correct course of action when one is confronted by a moral dilemma. Quite an interesting discussion it was, if I remember correctly. At its conclusion you had seen the error of your ways, the regrettable slips in your judgment, your dreadful lapse into unconscionable greed." And here he scowled at poor Brackenthwaite, who had no idea where this conversation might be going, but at least he was not being beaten yet. "So we parted on good terms of Christian fellowship, with me as your Priest and Headmaster advising you to give the whole matter serious thought and to determine how best to mend your ways. But I have no recollection whatever, I repeat, no recollection whatever, that I ordered you to miss perhaps the very best film of this entire winter term, and to make your way off to bed in disgrace. No indeed, I never, ever told you to do that! So how can I punish you for disobedience when you disobeyed nothing and no one? It simply cannot be done! It seems to me, my young friend, that you have already punished yourself to excess, and I believe the good Lord may have been behind all that in order to stir in you a true and contrite heart. Be that as it may, Edward, go in peace, go in peace."

As the boy turned to go, astonished and not quite taking in the heavenly good fortune that had descended upon him, Dr. Cratton called out to him.

"Oh, one thing more, my lad. Mr. Spendleton has asked for a leave of absence. It seems he caught a nasty cold out on the playing fields yesterday and it may turn to pneumonia. Mr. Wilson will take his place in your math class at least until after Half Term." And he waved the astonished boy away, asking forgiveness from God for his white lie: he had indeed suspended Mr. Spendleton from Hallworthy House for a week or two until he could sort things out.

Brackenthwaite glided in joy down the corridor, feeling the reprieve of a condemned man at the foot of the gallows, and completely giddy at the thought of Half Term, a long weekend away from school. He was met by a flood of little'uns like himself.

"Have you heard the news?" they called out. " You haven't? Well, the snow's so deep that we can't go out to the playground this morning. Hurrah! Hurrah!"

And now Brackenthwaite floated on air, he positively floated. "No playground," he thought, "No playground... No Pile-on, no Pile-on. Thank God, thank you, lovely God! " Calloo callay, oh frabous day!" he sang to himself,

"Nobody knows, tiddley pom,
How cold my toes, tiddley pom,
How cold my toes are growing!"

Half Term was coming -- a long weekend at home far, far away
from school! Why, it was almost on the horizon, but in all the
trouble he had been through he had clear forgotten it until the
familiar words of a song passed down through generations of
Hallworthians wafted up to him from the Fourth Form homeroom
down the corridor:

"Two more weeks, and where'll I be?
Not in this acad-e-mee!

No more Latin, no more French,
No more sitting on a hard old bench.

No more spiders in my tea,
Making googly eyes at me.

No more froggies in my bath,
Trying hard to make me laugh."

And then there reached his ears that other familiar old song:

"Latin is a language dead as dead can be,
First it killed the Romans, now it's killing me!"

Why, he thought, my blasted chilblains might even get better.
Perhaps they might just stop that awful sore itching all the time
and go away altogether one day, but I suppose that's too much to
ask. Let's just stick with no more playground, no more Pile-On;
that's enough to ask.

He just couldn't help himself calling out loud down the hallway

"Pile-On! Nobody pile on!
Oh-oh-oh-oh! Nobody pile on!"

The Fourth Formers, all of them several years older than him, crowded out of their homeroom at his voice and followed him in the loud rhythmic Pile-On chant along the hallways, picking up ever more boys behind them. To his surprise and delight Brackenthwaite was even allowed by these older boys to keep his well-deserved place at the head of the procession. This isn't so bad, he felt with pride -- in some ways school can be almost all right ... and, praise the Lord, at Half Term there'll be yummy fresh crusty bread at home.

And he wandered away down the passage, singing quietly to himself,

"<u>Pile</u> on! Nobody pile on!
<u>Pile</u> on! Nobody pile on!"

CHAPTER 5
THE FALL OF
DR. SYLVANUS CROFTES

"Oh Sir, please let me help you! Look, I can get your books anyway," I exclaimed as a Fourth Former at St. Adalbert's Academy when I saw the revered Dr. Croftes stumble and collapse to his knees on the two stone steps leading from the pavement up to the apron of the School Library above.

"Well, my boy, that's certainly very kind of you. I do seem to have made a mess of it, don't I? But look here, I think I can manage it now, if you would be so very kind as to extend your arm to me so that I may grasp it." And grasp it he did, making me wince at the strength of that grip. Dr. Croftes tried hard to pull himself to an erect position, or almost erect since he had lived with a game leg since the War. Once, twice and a third time he tried, at last succeeding in raising himself to as close as he could manage to a full upright stance, that posture having escaped him, lo these many years. The scattered books and papers were collected and handed back to Sylvanus Croftes, alas in no kind of order, and he, breathing somewhat heavily after his stumble, now pulled himself together, wrapped his academic gown around him, and with a polite

"Thank you, my dear boy," moved off at a hesitant limp toward the School Library that was his haven and his home from home. It had been a nasty tumble, tearing his clothes and blooding his knee, he thought, but worse than that was that it was unfitting his dignity and unbecoming in one who considered himself, as did others of the faculty, to be the foremost intellect and scholar of the school, a school which he was wont to describe as a community of scholars after the medieval kind.

I followed him slowly up the steps and into the School Library. I had no preps to do at that time, Latin construe and science lab reports being behind me and math waiting till I could secure the assistance of my friend Hazleham who was ever so much brighter than I in everything mathematical, and I was free from the football field, thank goodness, so, with a delightful three-quarters of an hour to spare before tea with my friends in my room in my boarding house, I made my way, as I so often did, to the School Library. The multitude of books there intrigued me, held me in a kind of spell. With no particular volume or even section of the library in mind, I wandered around the shelves and the galleries, pausing here and there to pull a book out for an instant, my attention caught by the wording of its title (*Nostromo* – what does that mean, 'our' something? *The Descent of Man* – where did he go down?). Suddenly I stopped in my tracks, taken aback: Dr. Croftes stood there before me, right in front of me though several paces distant, scrutinizing me carefully.

'Yes, I have been keeping an eye on you," he said. "You were gallant indeed to offer your arm to me out there and to assist me when I fell down. It's a wretched thing, a game leg, and you may believe me that it is not helped by my sciatica and everything else I have to take as the accoutrements of my advancing years. It's worst of all when I have to draw attention to myself – but that's enough of all that, too much in fact. So what are you after, young gentleman, this fine winter day? You have been wandering all over the place in the library, I know that. What are you looking for? Can I help you? I would like to do that, you know. It's what I am here for, and it would be a way of extending to you my sincere gratitude."

"Oh Sir, it's really nothing. I just had some free time, and I really like libraries and books, you know, so I just kind of thought I would look around for a bit. Is that all right, sir?"

"'Is that all right?' 'Is that all right?' It's perfectly splendid! It's just what I like to do myself. But look here, if you're not too busy, I have a job to do and you can help me with it. Would you like to do something for me?"

And that is how it came about that Sylvanus Croftes and Edward Brackenthwaite entered into a partnership that lasted through the years until I graduated from St. Adalbert's, a partnership that in its gentle way came to have a strong meaning to me, the quiet boy in the library. The central reading room of the School Library had been built as a memorial to Old Adalbertians who had fallen in the Wars of Empire in defence of Queen and Country, its high dome supported by ten pairs of broad white columns. Between each pair was suspended a framed picture, perhaps four feet by three. These frames and a copious collection of colored prints of notable paintings through the ages had been donated to the library several years ago, and one of the duties that devolved upon the librarian was to select those pictures that would be mounted on display, and to alter and renew the display every few weeks. It was this task that Dr. Croftes wished to share with me, an honor indeed for an undistinguished boy in the Fourth Form. There was of course something in it for the amiable librarian as well: he would no longer have to limp along the corridors outside the library, bending down to a degree that often brought a jab of pain to his leg, in order to pull forth from their deep shelves the capacious portfolios that housed the collection of prints. As his assistant I would now do all that for him. And what was more, Dr. Croftes was no longer comfortable with the task of setting an old wooden stepladder in place and mounting perhaps as many as four or five steps in order to lean across and first remove and later replace the picture frames heavy with plate glass. Good heavens, he shuddered to think, how unbelievably close I came to slipping last time I had to do that, and what a dreadful catastrophe that would have been, an almighty tumble that would have closed out my days as St. Adalbert's Librarian, even perhaps my days as one of the living. Such close calls had become all too frequent these last few months. For the first several times in his partnership with me Dr. Croftes made all the selections, gently asking the novice student of the history of art for his opinion of the new set, be the theme landscapes, interiors, figures in armor, something ecclesiastical or something royal, something from the Italian Renaissance or something from the South of France as interpreted by the Impressionists. But life moved along in its gentle way, and soon enough it was my responsibility and delight to perform the entire task, being challenged by Dr. Croftes to come up with a theme that he, the older man, the master, the highly respected librarian, would find it an artistic and intellectual effort to discern. This game of course was manna to the young scholar: I delighted in setting Dr. Croftes a challenge, and in doing that I necessarily learned a good deal of the history of art, which was of course the unspoken intent of the old schoolmaster – and it was one of my deep sorrows that when it should come time for me to leave St. Adalbert's and to move on to university, to All Saints College, the sister foundation of St. Adalbert's, I would necessarily have to take my leave of my dear Sylvanus Croftes.

But to my joy I found that I did not really have to leave him behind at all. The university, one of the most ancient and respected in the land, that housed All Saints' College stood not more than forty miles from the small market town that was graced by the presence of St. Adalbert's Academy, and it was a frequent practice for scholars from All Saints and other colleges to pay a visit to St.

Adalbert's, especially to its far-famed Chapel and Select Library. The School sent her sons to the College, and the College in turn made sure that all her most promising students, whatever their background and whatever secondary school they had attended, in the fields of history, English literature, architecture and the fine arts, made a pilgrimage, or several pilgrimages, to St. Adalbert's, and especially to the Chapel and Select Library. This library, housed behind the school's Tudor Court in the tall brick gate-house tower whose deep-toned bell had accompanied hundreds of boys through their hours of slumber each night of the school year, formed a distinct entity, not part of the general School Library at all, but a *sanctum sanctorum* dedicated to bibliophilia. Few boys in the school had ever penetrated there, but I had, oh yes I had, often, escorted carefully by Dr. Croftes, and it was to this library and to my mentor in scholarship that I would return whenever time and the busy life of a college student would permit. On one of my visits from All Saints, on Old Adalbertians Day, I found Sylvanus Croftes in the highest state of excitement.

"Come in, dear boy, come in!" he exclaimed, stumbling over the doorsill in his enthusiasm, and seizing firm hold of the lapel of my tweed jacket in order to maintain his equilibrium. "You simply will not be able to believe what a Red Letter Day this is for St. Adalbert's and especially for our dear Select Library. Would you believe it, the most extraordinary volume has just been given to us, it really has – and it arrived not an hour ago, and you have been chosen by the Almighty to be here this very day and in time to share in the unpacking. What a day, what a day!"

"Why, Sylvanus, whatever is it?" I asked. I was careful to use Dr. Croftes' Christian name although for months, even years, I found it extremely hard to do so, almost an act of sacrilege. When Sylvanus Croftes had insisted that now that Edward Brackenthwaite was no longer a student at St. Adalbert's the two of them should use each other's Christian name, I found that to be one of the most difficult tasks I had ever undertaken in my life. I did manage the transition, however, for all my self-consciousness.

Well, it took me many minutes to calm Sylvanus down sufficiently so that he might share with his pupil the news that had so enraptured him. Here is what it was, the immediate arrival of what in many ways constituted the greatest acquisition that the Select Library had ever seen come its way: an original volume from 1611, a first edition of the Authorized Version of the Bible as Appointed to be Read in Churches, the King James Bible, undamaged, in its original binding, complete with only a very few sheets slightly loosened but not torn from their place, and, *mirabile dictu,* actually signed by His Majesty King James I himself and bestowed as a personal gift upon his dearly beloved friend 'Steenie,' George Villiers, Duke of Buckingham, from his "dear old Dad." Nothing like this exists anywhere else in the world, and the blessed tome had come to St. Adalbert's as the bequest of an ancient Old Adalbertian, the last of his line as a gentleman of county family, a man with no close relatives, his only heir being a rapscallion novelist of racy and fast-paced bestsellers who had taken up residence in the West Indies. To the old gentleman close to his deathbed his youthful memories of St. Adalbert's meant far more to him than the occasional "Hiya, old buddy, old boy!" with which he was accosted by his *soi-disant* heir, and so he had added a codicil to his will bequeathing to St. Adalbert's this unique and splendid volume. The Provost of St. Adalbert's had at first been anxious at the prospect of entrusting Dr. Croftes to open the package alone, since his hands now trembled and the book must surely be fragile, but he had been relieved to hear that Brackenthwaite was due to visit that afternoon and would doubtless assist: now there stood a sterling and reliable Old Adalbertian if ever there was one.

I met Sylvanus at the Front Lodge of the school, the office where packages were received. "Come with me to the Select Library, dear boy, and there let us together dispose of the wrappings," urged

Sylvanus. And so, carefully cradling in my arms the priceless package, I stepped warily out, across the cobbles of the Tudor Court and up the winding staircase of the Clock Tower to the chambers occupied by the Select Library. There were three rooms in all, tall rooms with narrow circular staircases leading to iron galleries, each room a home for several hundred leather-bound volumes. One single broad table, an elegant piece from the middle decades of the eighteenth century, stood in the centre of the middle room, surrounded on all sides by display cases, their treasures carefully screened from intrusive and deleterious rays of sunshine by rolled panels of green baize.

"There now, Edward! Lay the dear package down, my good friend, and let me have at him!" chuckled Sylvanus, flourishing wildly a long brass paper knife and a pair of scissors that lay conveniently at hand. With no more ado and with a few swift strokes he laid bare the outer wrappings, brown paper and layer upon layer of corrugated cardboard, until the soft white tissue paper, the undergarments of the precious package, lay before him. A slit here, a swift cut there with a circular flick of the wrist, and the great treasure lay before them, a handsome dark leather volume indeed, in perfect mint condition, bearing with dignity the impress of the ages and with the Royal Arms stamped in gold upon the cover.

"Oh, I must look, I must look!" purred Sylvanus, "and so must you, m'dear." He leaned forward for the closest inspection that he could manage with his bent back and his enfeebled legs, opening wide the ancient book, cradling in his extended hand the top corner of each right-hand page and delicately peeling them back with as much enthusiasm as scholarly care. He raised himself gently to reach as far forward as he could, but his foot contrived to crook itself beneath the corner of his chair, and oh no, he fell, he fell with a crack against the table and then down onto the floor. It all seemed to me to happen in slow motion, as I stretched out my arms to save both my aged friend and the priceless book. The chair fell backward --- Sylvanus crashed forward -- I held for dear life onto anything my hands encountered – and the room was rent by a second, louder crack from the elegant Queen Anne chair that Sylvanus had been sitting in. When all movement stopped, after indeed no more than a moment although it seemed an age, Sylvanus found himself lying prone on his back on the carpet, his face a mask of ghastly horror, the great book splayed open across his chest, and I leaning over, covering and enveloping all, holding all still, silent, motionless in the cloud of encircling dust, until the two of us could set ourselves to rising slowly and carefully from the floor.

And arise of course we did. The worst sufferer, by far, oh by far, was poor Sylvanus Croftes, agonized by the arrows of pain in his leg and in his back but far more, infinitely more, by the horror of what destruction he might have wrought upon a priceless volume in his own Select Library, in his own School, his very own St. Adalbert's. As for me, I was painfully bruised to be sure, and bleeding from wounds inflicted by what had proved to be a seriously sharp paper knife and the jagged leg of the broken chair, but I was naturally more alarmed for my elderly friend than for myself.

"Oh, Sylvanus, do let's take a look at you first. The book can wait. It can't get any better or worse for waiting, and I just have to get you sitting up." So, gingerly, I raised poor Dr. Sylvanus Croftes to a sitting position, and fetched him a glass of water.

"Yes, thank you, dear boy," he groaned. "But if the Book is hurt, oh my Holy Lord, oh my Holy Lord, then I'll just have to crawl away and die, that would be the only thing left for me honorably to do."

But, *Dei gratia*, the Bible was by some miracle ("a clear case of divine intervention," murmured Dr. Croftes) practically unhurt, undamaged, unmarked, so close to his chest had he clasped it in his fall. All that had happened was that several of the already loose leaves had detached themselves and now floated free, their torn and frayed edges alone witness to the mutilation they had so narrowly escaped. And that that was all, that was all. "We can tell everyone that the Bible came to us that way, that they were like that when we unwrapped the package," I said solemnly. Sylvanus looked at me for a long time, but said nothing.

This was Old Adalbertians Day at the academy and Dr. Croftes had volunteered his services, as he had so often done before, as escort and guide to such returning alumni as might be interested in a tour behind the scenes of the architecture of the Chapel. The Chapel was indeed a truly remarkable building, constructed beyond the Perpendicular style at the close of the Middle Ages, in fact one of the very last works of note designed from start to finish in the final efflorescence of the Gothic style just as the Renaissance broke forth upon the shores of Britain. Indeed, on the very day of its dedication to St. Adalbert, scholars and aesthetes outside the school rued the moment when the Board of Electors (for so the trustees of St. Adalbert's Academy were named) had looked back with affection to the Gothic style of ecclesiastical architecture with which they and their predecessors had for centuries been familiar, rather than forward with courage to the new and daring excitements of the neo-Classical fervor of design that was flooding steadily northwards from Italy – but aesthetes in later centuries were delighted at the steadfast faith of the old master masons, for what they had succeeded in creating in St. Adalbert's Chapel at the last gasp of the Middle Ages was something truly extraordinary, something quite unlike anything else in Christendom. The ground plan of the Chapel was indeed somewhat cramped – it could barely contain the whole School when the boys assembled every morning for prayers and twice on Sundays for full-blown services. But though narrow it was remarkably tall nevertheless, likened by some to Sainte Chapelle in Paris and by others, perhaps less travelled, to Lancing Chapel. And its glory lay in its vault, a great sweep of fans, one counter-balancing the other, not in matched pairs as at Bath Abbey, at Dorchester, at King's College Chapel in Cambridge, or indeed at any other fan-vaulted house of worship, for here at St. Adalbert's the fans, each one spreading so very delicately right across the roof, alternately touched the crest of the opposite wall, so that the line down the centre of the roof was not by any means a straight line as in all other fan vaults, but a sinuous curve, a wave ebbing and flowing this way and that as it carried the eye of the viewer from the western wall to the point right over the altar where the stone face of the east wall was divided by a great ogee arch to close in the gaze of the worshipper with a broad expanse of stained glass. Such an extravaganza, such a playful, almost wanton, treatment of sacred Gothic, was virtually unknown in medieval Europe, only to be found in such places as the vault of the banqueting hall at Hradcany Castle in Prague, where the pattern of the interlacing ribs of the vault takes such precedence over their utility that some ribs of stone even start and stop in mid-leap, as it were, or confound themselves in knotted caprice a few feet above the topmost line of the supporting walls; or again, in the whimsical Apprentice's Column at Rosslyn where a fully-leaved garland of stone spirals up an otherwise straitlaced Scottish pillar; or, once more, in the low, dark crypt of the Mariendom in Freising, where fantasy runs riot in the carved forms of men and animals that cover the Bestiensaule from top to toe.

As a renowned architectural historian and lecturer in the arts of the Middle Ages, it was only natural that Dr. Croftes had become the foremost expert on the local treasures of ecclesiastical art and on the history of our famous Chapel. Over the years he had occasionally taken his topmost scholars among the boys on a tour of the Chapel, behind the scenes, up the narrow circular staircases, along the walkways that edged the open rooftop, screened as they were by tall crockets in the machicolation, and even into the narrow space, not much more than five feet high at its peak, that rose between the stone vault of the Chapel and the lead-covered wooden roof that sheltered the stone vault from the elements. It had become a tradition, warmly recognized and even revered, that on such notable occasions as Old Adalbertians Day, Founder's Day and the Feast Day of St. Adalbert, Dr. Croftes would lead a select few, ten, possibly as many as a dozen, in and out, up and down, around and about, through all the architectural complexities of the Chapel. And so, still fluttering in his heart from the very narrowly averted disaster of the ruin of King James's own King James Bible only an hour or two before, Sylvanus Croftes fortified himself, resolved deeply, took a strong breath, drew himself up to his full height, and prepared to sally forth up those narrow stairs and along those dim corridors of masonry. He had particularly asked me to accompany him, to bring his electric torch and to stay close to him just in case an uneven stone might cause him to waver in his steps.

The tour began out of doors with a lecture on the history of the Chapel, the style of the architecture and the distinguished place that St. Adalbert's Acadamy had earned for itself through the centuries as a seat of learning and a refuge of scholarship. Dr. Croftes held forth on the glories of the Chapel, most especially on the unique character of its fan vault, the very ultimate in that most exalted style of ecclesiastical architecture. He alone of the group did not seem to notice in the least that a bleak February mist had given way to an increasingly cold and penetrating rain, gentle at first but persistent, chilling the hands of the gloveless and the heads of the hatless, so that they cast nervous glances at one another and the most fainthearted even dared to allow themselves to contemplate slipping away to hot tea and crumpets in the Common Room. But all things come to an end in due time, and Dr. Croftes wound up his lecture and ushered the group into the darkened Chapel. He pointed out to them much more than they had remembered from their schooldays, passing over the cramped and narrow desks and benches at which they had been compelled to sit through so very many prolonged sermons, referring, but only in general terms, to the glories of the stained glass in the east window since the icy rainstorm had now dimmed its jeweled colors to shades of flattened grey, deepest blue and dark-blood crimson.

Unlocking a small arched door in the northwest corner of the Chapel, a door whose existence had been passed over by all but a very few of those who had ever entered the Chapel, Dr. Croftes led the way, his electric torch feebly illuminating their steps, up a tightly wound, narrow circular staircase that twisted ever upwards. At the rear end of the group I obediently took my place, assuming the role of assistant guide and escort, if not architectural historian. There were a few small electric lights here and there along the wall, bulbs that burned dimly but did offer some assistance to the visitors who followed in Dr. Croftes' footsteps. After what seemed an interminable series of wheels and turns, so many that it was hard for anyone in the group to maintain his sense of direction, the stairs suddenly terminated at another low stone-arched door.

"Ah, my friends, come in, come in!" welcomed Dr. Croftes, gesturing widely as he beamed upon his flock. "None of you have been up here before, I take it, that is, except my good friend Edward Brackenthwaite who has been kind enough to assist me in this endeavor. Now let me explain a point or two before any of us take one single step, I repeat one single step, from where we now stand. This small area where we are now standing is a level platform of stone, a sill to the narrow circular staircase that will lead us in due course back down once more to ground level and safety. This slab is just that and that alone: a slab, a level platform of stone, of barely sufficient width to take us all. But don't step a foot farther! Not a foot farther, I beg you, with good reason. Look around you, I pray, stand still and look around you."

They did just that, held in obedience to the master, noting that while they stood with the utmost care solely upon the little apron of stone that reached forward only a foot or two from the narrow stone stairway door, Dr. Croftes had with surprising agility edged his way along one of the sturdy curved transverse ribs of the fan vault below, one of the stanchions that supported the stone ceiling as it leaned across from one side of the Chapel to the other. Feeling still the subarctic cold that had assaulted them outside before their long climb to the vault, one or two of the visitors noticed that some small leaks in the roof above had allowed a few lines of rainwater to trickle in, at least while they were still water. But now they were freezing fast into a skin of ice.

"Please note, my friends," intoned Dr. Croftes, "how there are still a few feet between the stone vault that everyone sees from below and the great oaken beams on high that take the weight of the transverse and lesser wooden beams above them that in turn support the crosswise lathes upon which the leaden roof itself is laid. You all thought, didn't you, that the stone vault within was indeed but one and the same with the leaden roof without? No indeed, no indeed, never so, never, my friends! A vault of the purest limestone such as ours at dear St. Adalbert's, could never in the course of the centuries beat back the ravages of winter storms, the assault of the summer sun, without being of such a thickness as no ribs and columns could support. Why, a thin stone vault such as the walls could manage to carry would scarcely last two or three hundred years! But a good solid roof of tried and true English oak, such as Nelson relied upon at Trafalgar, will last till kingdom come, if sensibly sheathed in sturdy sheets of lead. But lead does creep, as surely you know, and that is why we have to renew the topmost leaden roof every half century or so. But let us return to the stone vault itself."

Here he swung his flashlight back and forth across the width of the Chapel and from one end to the other, where the thin yellow beams of light lost themselves in the shadows and the cobwebs. "The weight of a layer of solid stone is tremendous, for solid stone all must be. And how can it be sustained by the delicate fans of the vaulting? This, my good and dear friends, is where I let you into a secret. Only the very ribs of each fan are thick and sturdy stone. Along them one can walk with confidence."

And Dr. Croftes displayed such confidence, extending his arms to balance himself as he made his way, steadily and surely, right across the vault of the Chapel on one curving transverse rib and back across on the next, graciously acknowledging the polite applause of the visitors as he returned to their midst.

"But dear me, I would never try that in mid-fan. There the panels are no more than half an inch thick, the slightest of them so very delicate, appearing to be full of strength to support the vault, even the roof itself, but in fact hanging on for dear life to the slightly more substantial stone of their neighbors, who in turn rely upon the great stone blocks of the ribs, such as I crossed upon, to keep them in their appointed places. Let me show you once again how the central ribs gladly, nay cheerfully, had sustained the weight of a mason of the Middle Ages. But let him surely beware that he never try the thinnest little panels!"

And with that Dr. Croftes proceeded to make his way once again across the entire vault on one curving transverse rib, along the top of the wall and then to start back by the next one. By this time I was gulping in anxiety, almost in terror, I being one of the few that had noticed the little patches of ice. Alas, alas, one of those small frozen circles, no more than two or three inches across, lay precisely where Dr. Croftes set his shoe on the final step of his peregrination.

His foot shot clear out from under him. His body arched back. With his eyes bursting from his head and his gaze fixed upon his young friend, all he could do was gasp out "Oh dear, oh dear, oh dear!' as he crashed backwards full upon the very thinnest reaches of the stone paneling. A resounding crack rent the air, a single crack and then a concatenation of accompanying crackles, as the cartwheeling figure of Dr. Sylvanus Croftes, Architectural

Historian of the School Chapel and Curator Emeritus of the Select Library at St. Adalbert's Academy, spun end over end in its fall and disappeared clear out of sight. A dreadful thud from below and the clatter of stonework hitting the floor told the horrified visitors what had happened.

Some days later the Chapel was reconsecrated. At the Memorial Service for the dearest scholar among all the sons of St. Adalbert the Provost gave the Eulogy and I, Edward Brackenthwaite, was privileged to read the Lessons.

CHAPTER 6
HILDA INGOLSTADT

Taking a commercial flight across the Atlantic in 1955 was an undertaking, a commitment to three flights, from New York to Gander, from Gander to Reykjavik, and from Reykjavik to London, all of them noisy and liable to the sort of bumps in the air that leave the coffee suspended in midair as the plane drops two feet. Gerald Brackenthwaite was not looking forward to this, having pled in vain with his employer, the London-American Trading Corporation, that he might return in greater comfort by sea. But he was in truth Overseas Director of the company, and his presence was essential at the Annual General Meeting scheduled for next week at the Head Office in London. So there it was, no option. He settled himself into his seat for the first flight, took out his copy of *Fortune* magazine, turned the pages idly and looked out of the window at the runway at Idlewild. It was raining, he was tired from a fortnight's travel and from endless meetings in four far-apart cities in the States, and he wished only to catch up on his sleep and to return as quickly as possible to his home and family in Hastings. Ah yes, and he was looking forward to a long, quiet evening one day soon with his close friend Andrew Foyle who always had up his sleeve some interesting story of his father's police work in the Second World War.

Then he noticed the passenger who was taking her seat next to him, passing across him to the window, a young and very pleasant-looking woman, perhaps eighteen years old and clearly excited about her trip. Gerald Brackenthwaite's whole expression lighted up as he took her in. Her enthusiasm and her way of constantly looking around her to make sure all was well, and her prompt adjusting and refastening of her seat belt long before take-off, gave him the hint that this might be, and indeed probably was, her first flight.

"Done this often?" he asked with a friendly smile. "We won't be taking off for quite some time yet, twenty minutes at least, the air hostess told me."

She looked up at him hesitantly, both pleased to enter a conversation and careful at the same time of coming too close to a stranger. But this was safe neutral ground, she thought, in public, inside an aeroplane.

"No," she replied. "This is first time I have ever been in an aeroplane. All is so exciting to me!" And she smiled, a quiet, warm smile.

"Then you must have come over by sea, and that's so much better than this noisy, cramped way of traveling," he said. "And where do you come from, if I may ask? That isn't an American voice I hear. What was it brought you Stateside?"

"Oh, I am student," she said. "I come from Germany, where I learn English in the school. I hope to be international secretary when I speak proper English. Is not so good right now."

"Please don't say that. It is excellent indeed. I am afraid I have no German" – and here a shadow crossed his face, because it was not much more than ten years since the end of the War and all things German sat badly with him – "but I do speak French, and I can manage Latin and classical Greek, not that that's much use in the world today." And he too smiled.

"Sir, you are educated. I can tell from accent. So it is pleasure for me to converse and to learn idioms. Idiom is so very hard! Perhaps you can teach me some while we have to sit here during all these hours." She blushed slightly as she said this, feeling she had been too forward, but it was important to her to learn all she could. Her month in America, first staying with a female middle-aged distant cousin in New York and then working as a mother's helper in the pleasant family seaside resort of Atlantic City in New Jersey, had indeed improved her English, but she knew she needed all the practice she could find, particularly in business English – and this gentleman looked like a businessman.

Soon enough the plane's engines roared into life, the propellers spun round faster than the eye could possibly follow, and the plane trundled forward and took up its place at the head of the line on the take-off runway. Then with ever-increasing speed and deafening noise it hurtled down the runway and rose smoothly into the sky. Conversation was of course impossible, and anyway the young German girl was gazing wide-eyed at the land retreating fast beneath the plane and at the spectacular view of Manhattan opening below.

"Well, let's get to know each other. My name's Gerald Brackenthwaite, and I live in Hastings in England, and yes, I am a businessman. And you tell me you are a student, at university perhaps. Where do you live in Germany? And do you have a family, brothers and sisters?"

"Sir, I am named Hilda Ingolstadt, and I live near Siegen. My parents are both alive, *Gott sei dank*, but not young now, and I have one brother Hans who is very clever technician and works for Telefunken in Berlin. Him we do not see often but rejoice so gladly when he comes home for the vacation days. Then comes me, and then my brother Karl, but he is restless, troubled, not happy – but why do I say this? Last comes little Doerte, my sister, the baby of the family, ten years old. You have family too, Mr. Brackenthwaite, I think. Please, who are they? If you can tell me..."

So the two of them chatted casually for half an hour or so, until dinner was served, and after that they both read for a while, he turning the pages of *Fortune* magazine, she working her way through *The Great Gatsby*. And then they leaned their seats back as far as possible and tried to catch a little sleep before the descent to Gander.

One thing of importance began to happen between them, however, something that was first broached in the most general terms on their next flight, the leg from Newfoundland to Iceland, and was then formally agreed upon on the final flight from Reykjavik to Heathrow. They had neither of them slept very much on those flights. Hilda Ingolstadt now had in her handbag a piece of paper with the name and school address of myself, Edward Brackenthwaite, and she had promised to write to me. I was a couple of years younger than she, which made me sixteen, and I was studying German at St. Adalbert's Academy in England. My father had wanted so very much to find a native German-speaker with whom I could correspond and perhaps even speak to on the telephone if that could be arranged. The teaching of German in English schools, he had discovered, followed exactly the pattern in which the ancient tongues had always been taught, with emphasis on correct grammar and syntax, and lists of irregular verbs to be learnt by heart. He knew that was an absurd, indeed an insulting way to treat a living foreign language, but he had no influence at all on the curriculum. So he had become desperate, looking for ways in which I would really learn, from inside as it were, that modern languages are indeed alive and spoken, not to be reduced to such lists of belabored trivia as Latin gender rhymes.

A few weeks later I received my first letter from Hilda Ingolstadt, a precise, carefully handwritten piece in which she formally introduced herself, described her home and family, and invited me to enter into a correspondence, being sure to let me know that this initiation into a correspondence was not something she had picked up injudiciously from some newspaper or young peoples' journal but that by way of contrast the initiative had come from my own father, whom she had met and become acquainted with on their trip together across the Atlantic. Well, I already knew all that very well, since my father had clued me in as soon as he had come back from Heathrow to our home in Hastings. What is more, Hilda had requested and received her parents' permission to write to a boy none of them had ever met. Hilda, a scrupulous and careful German, had written her letter in English for me in case I might be lost otherwise. She debated long and hard within herself about that: to presume that I could read German would be a compliment to me, but I might not understand the letter at all, yet to write it out in English as well might make it look like a school-book lesson. In the end she wrote it simply in English, explained her dilemma and begged my forgiveness if she had not understood the situation correctly. I was touched by this, and felt flattered that a girl was writing to me: I knew no girls at all in England save my sisters and a couple of their friends from school, all very much younger than myself.

It was not long before Hilda and I were writing to each other almost every month, a journal entry, as it were, of our activities and thoughts over the last few weeks. We agreed early on that each write only in his or her own language, and in that way become acquainted with the other's vocabulary and with idioms that might well not appear in classroom texts or the handbooks of correspondence courses. These letters, somewhat contrived and stilted at first, soon grew into close and personal accounts of our friends and acquaintances, our family members, even of our parents and siblings. It was true, however, that all the time as I grew increasingly personal, Hilda on the other hand maintained a carefully controlled and friendly atmosphere. That must be, thought I, because she is a girl writing to a boy, or because she is a German writing to an Englishman in the late 1950's, only a dozen years after our peoples had been killing each other just as fiercely as ever they could. Anyway, there it was, a slight reserve that I could not penetrate. Never mind, I thought, it does no harm and I am growing very fond of her anyway, eagerly looking forward to her next letter.

And then to my amazement one day there came a letter from Hilda enclosing a missive from her mother, an invitation to me to come visit the family for a week in my spring holidays from boarding school. I could hardly believe it, and was utterly delighted, at once conjuring up in my mind what it might be like to see Germany --- I had never been anywhere abroad – and puzzling how it had ever occurred to Hilda and her mother to invite me. What of the father too, what of him? Hilda had told me that he was a retired and very distinguished railway engineer who had been the top man in his profession fifteen years before, also a serious *paterfamilias* who was in every way the ruling spirit of his hearth and home. Why had no word come from him? My mother could shed no light on this, and I turned to my father. He was more of a traveler and more wise in the ways of the world than she, and he had a good idea of what might lie behind this. The lady of the house in Germany, in a traditional family in Siegerland, would take care of such matters as hospitality, unless they involved business or professional associates of the master of the house, or suitors for his daughter's hand. No way was I a suitor! Of course I was also no professional acquaintance, so the unspoken message was that I must take care not to allow myself to consider myself anything more than a passing 'penpal' or acquaintance of his daughter. I was distinctly ambivalent about this dismissal: I had never truly considered myself as a boyfriend to Hilda, but she was indeed the only girl friend I had ever had, and I did not like to be put down in my place. On the other hand, it was flattering to some degree that it might ever be imagined that I could possibly be seen in that role, as Hilda's beau. Oh well, I thought, let it go. It will be splendid to go over there, actually to see this special friend whom I only know from a photograph or two. We will have endless things to talk about!

I wondered why my father had shown no surprise at the invitation, in contrast to my mother who was delighted at the honor accorded to her son. In due course it transpired that Mr. Brackenthwaite had himself started the ball rolling by enquiring from Herr and Frau Ingolstadt whether they might agree to Hilda's visiting Edward and his family. My father had been very much taken by Hilda during their three plane rides together, and he looked forward to meeting her again. He understood completely the message behind Hilda's mother's note: that it was not appropriate for a well brought-up young girl in Germany to leave the parental home in order to stay in the household of a young man whom her family had never met, a foreign family with whom they had only had the slightest acquaintance of the father, none of the mother, and only indirectly through Hilda of the son. In the traditional atmosphere of old Germany, the Germany of the Kaiser, this approach would all have been entirely comprehensible, correct and acceptable in every way.

So one day at the beginning of April I packed my bags, and my father drove me from Hastings to Dover from where I took the cross-channel ferry to Ostend. And there I was, in a foreign country, and no one there knew me! That was an exciting feeling for a sheltered boarding-school lad of seventeen. I found the train to Cologne, or Koeln as I must now learn to call it, and gazed out of the window for the entire length of the journey, telling myself how silly it was to think of that object in the field over there not as 'a tree' but first as 'une arbre' or later as 'ein Baum.'

And then Koeln – and Hilda! She looked just like her photographs, of course she did, and mutual recognition was instantaneous. I really wanted to give her a great hug there and then but I absolutely didn't dare, which was just as well since her father was standing right beside her, smiling his greeting and extending a broad hand in welcome. He was well into his seventies, a tall, substantial man with a stoop and a noticeable limp, with long grey hair elegantly swept back from his broad forehead, his face deeply etched with lines but wreathed in smiles for his English guest.

Conversation was limited in the sixty-mile drive across country to the Ingolstadts' village, Herrenbach, since my German was written rather than spoken, and Herr Doktor Ingolstadt understood, or pretended to understand, very little English. So it was up to Hilda, who alone of the family had accompanied her father on the drive, to keep up the conversation and to translate back and forth. This isn't going so well, thought I. I'm too shy, not making a good impression at all, on Hilda or on her father, and I don't know what to do about it.

But I was received with the greatest warmth by Frau Ingolstadt and by Doerte, aged ten, who danced around me with delight at the special bars of chocolate, Cadbury's Fruit and Nut, that I had brought from England. Hilda's younger brother Karl scowled as he slipped past us all without a word and headed off into the village. Frau Ingolstadt sighed and looked pained, and Herr Ingolstadt muttered something under his breath, but the dark mood passed quickly and I was escorted up the front steps, under the grey stone pediment carved with the welcoming phrase 'Gruss Gott,' and on into the house. It was an older home, eighty years old if a day, thought I, pock-marked with dozens of shell holes, some as large as six inches in diameter.

"So you are inspecting all the war damage, are you?" called out Herr Ingolstadt, whose English seemed suddenly to have improved. "It was the Americans did that to my fine home, not the English, not your people. Ha, Ha!" That was a bitter, mirthless laugh, I thought, and I wondered how the War had treated Herr Ingolstadt and his family.

I was shown to my room, given time to unpack and to bring down the presents I had acquired for the family: expensive perfume for Hilda, at which she was delighted; cigars for Herr Doktor, splendidly received; a porcelain brooch for Mutti, to her great joy; Harrogate toffee for Doerte; and a motorcycle belt buckle for Karl, who grunted and smiled briefly when he received his present later in the evening..

Then at Mutti's suggestion, Hilda and I set off for a walk through the village before dinner. Herrenbach is a large, sprawling village, almost a town really since it holds a market every week. There was a tall pitch to the roofs of most of the houses, dark red tiled roofs, with white or cream-colored plaster on the walls front and back, some half-timbered, all attractive though none truly outstanding. And there were still holes and gaps along the street where houses had once stood before the War. An entire new section of the town had arisen in former farmland, however, just in the past few months, to accommodate East Germans who had fled from Russian occupation and who now formed a distinct community that kept itself very much to itself, tolerated rather than warmly welcomed by the old inhabitants who had been heavily taxed to provide homes for their refugee fellow-countrymen. Hilda hurried me through this section, to catcalls of "Hants Up!" and "Inston Churchill!" as Hilda talked in English to me. She explained to me that relations between the two groups in the village had become very strained just a few days ago with the annual election of the Buergermeister: The refugees had stood solidly by the leader of their people, while the long-term villagers had been split between Social Democrats and Christian Democrats, with the result that an unprepossessing, stout and aggressive newcomer, Fulke Grueben, had won the election and now controlled the entire government of the village and district. Hilda and I passed through the orchard belt around the village and emerged onto the open hillside which afforded a spacious view of broad hills and dark forests, clean-cut square fields, tiny, tightly-knit villages and an occasional town clustered round its church. At this distance and in this peaceful country-side there was no sign of war damage. We walked through the countryside for half an hour and then made our way back home.

After a very filling dinner in which I was introduced to hot *Kartoffelsalad* (potato salad), the family sat around reading, sewing and talking quietly, just letting the time slip by. Herr Ingolstadt offered me a small glass of brandy which I accepted gratefully, declining, however, to smoke one of the cigars that I had brought with me from England: I knew my limits. And so to bed...

The next day also passed quietly, with Herr Ingolstadt out in the village with his closest friend, identified to me as 'Herr Loewe' (Mr. Lion). This formidable, tall, bald and angular man with a somewhat skull-like face walked with a pronounced stoop, with one leg rigid and a cane to support him: he was altogether an elderly and severely damaged individual. Hilda whispered to me that he had spent the war years as a Captain in the SS on the Russian front where he had received his wounds. I remembered with a shudder the horrors of genocide committed not fifteen years ago by the SS on Jews and Russians alike on that selfsame front, and wondered how many murders 'Herr Loerwe' would have to answer for when, quite soon now, he should have to face his Maker. Just at this moment, however, the two old comrades were sitting in the sun outside the village café, each enjoying one of my cigars and a first morning glass of brandy.

Doerte was still in school, and there was housework to be done. I offered to help Mutti and Hilda as I would have at home, but I was promptly shooed away: housework was never a man's work. So I sauntered into the village, bought postcards, wrote them to my family, and sent them off. When will Hilda be free, I wondered, and I hope it all gets more interesting than this. They had prom-ised me a drive into the 'mountains,' no more than considerable hills, closely wooded and doubtless very attractive in their way but scarcely mountains, I thought. How strange and somehow disappointing: here I was, physically so near to my dear Hilda, but she was inaccessible, closely bound up in her family, farther removed from me almost than when we had been a hundred or more miles apart, one of us in England and the other in Germany. Stop thinking that way, I told myself, just go up to her and ask for a good long walk, all day perhaps. Germans like to do that, I remembered, 'Wandervoegel' and so forth, their whole country crisscrossed by hiking trails.

So on my return to the house I spoke up, and Hilda was delighted by the offer and the prospect of a day away from the chores of home, out in the sparkling German countryside in springtime. "But I'll have to ask Mutti if this is all right," she told me, and left me standing in the middle of the living room as she went in search of her mother. She came back smiling all across her face. "She says 'yes'," she told me, "but I will also have to ask Vati, and that may not be so easy if you and I go out hiking alone. I think I'll ask Mutti to do that for me. Vati is really anxious for me, you know, and he doesn't want to believe that I have grown up and can look after myself." Once more she left to seek her mother, now deep in the family ironing, but she soon returned with the same enthusiastic smile. "Oh yes," she called out even before she came up to me. "She says she'll sweeten the way – that is correct idiom, is it not? – and when she really sets herself to ask for something from Vati, he cannot find the way to refuse her. Poor Vati!" and she broke off, with barely suppressed laughter.

That evening, however, was less comfortable than the one before. Herr Loewe came to call, which Hilda whispered to me was always a bad sign, and the two old men continued to drink together, steins of beer and chasers of brandy. Hilda's brother Karl lounged in, smelling of the beer that he had spilled down his front, and sat athwart the sofa, one leg hooked up around the arm, and displaying to its full extent the motorcycle belt buckle that I in my naivety had chosen for him.

"Can't you sit up straight, boy," barked his father, "particularly when there are guests in the home? Here's my good comrade Herr Loewe, and here's Hilda's young man from England. Sit up straight, I tell you, now, -- this instant!"

Karl slowly drew himself up, raised himself off the sofa and transferred himself to a large stuffed armchair, where he again spread himself almost horizontal, his battered cowboy boots crossed in front of him.

"Ach, these are not good days, my friend," snarled Herr Loewe. "Remember how it used to be: the Hitler Jugend program would straighten up lads like that. Why, in a couple of weeks you would truly be proud of him!"

Herr Ingolstadt started to look uncomfortable at the mention of the former Leader, any praise of whom was now an absolute taboo, but he volunteered no word of disagreement, which I took as a sign of silent assent.

"Your days are passed, Daddy-o," muttered Karl to Herr Loewe. "But I can see where I am not wanted, so I guess I'll just go look for my friends." And he left the house, the outside door swinging back with a bang behind him. Hilda tried to comfort her mother who had started to dab her eyes with her handkerchief. I just sat silent, looking straight ahead, thinking "Wow, this is some history lesson that I've walked into!"

The evening passed, as evenings do. The next day dawned bright and sunny, with both a chill wind and a sense of the charm of springtime in the air. Perfect for a walk, thought both Hilda and I, as she happily packed up sandwiches of *wurst* and Edam cheese between thin slices of dense black pumpernickel, with pickles, fruit and aerated water for us both. After breakfast, at which we saw no sign of Hilda's father or of Karl, who were both sleeping late after the previous evening, Hilda and I set off in shorts and hiking boots with knapsacks and hiking sticks. She knew the whole area intimately – she had grown up here – and had our route all planned in advance. We would take one of the great hiking trails, sure to meet and greet fellow-hikers, through the woods, past the fields and eventually up to the highest hill in the area, almost a mountain, from where on such a crystal clear day as this the view extended for miles and miles in all directions, almost to the Schwarzwald in the south and to the Rothaargebirge in the northeast. It was all perfect, and I was struck most forcibly, as Hilda had planned that I would be, by the crossing of the broad and well-trodden path we had taken, leading from west to east, with an equally well-trodden one stretching north and south. The signpost read "Nord, nach dem Deutschen Meer – Sud, nach den Alpen – Ost, nach Russland – West, nach den Atlantischen Meer." Now that's absolutely splendid, thought I, beaming at Hilda, how romantic can you get!

And then I did something I had never done before, something completely spontaneous and unplanned: I took Hilda in my arms, lifted her off the ground and gave her the greatest hug and kiss I could manage. Then suddenly I dropped her, certain I had spoiled everything, that she would be furious at my advances and would wish me to drop dead on the spot. But, *mirabile dictu*, nothing like that happened! She straightened herself up, pushed her hair back off her face, looked shyly at me, and proposed that we keep on walking awhile, looking for a place to rest for lunch.

We found the place soon enough, a narrow little valley with a stream rippling fast down the long hill that we were now ascending. We ate in silence, aware that something had happened between the two of us but not knowing what to do about it, or indeed what it really was. Hilda was the older, two years ahead of me, and by far the more sophisticated, the one who knew the world as I did not. So it was for her, she realized, to set the pace, to take control of this fluid situation and not to let it run out of her hands. She was genuinely fond of me, there was no doubt about that, but it was altogether as an older sister cares for a younger brother – and she was afraid that I might be beginning, had indeed already begun, to overstep that line. So she smiled at me, often and warmly, as we ate our pumpernickel and *wurst* sandwiches, trying to keep me close to her in affectionate confidence but not, oh surely not, as the boyfriend of her dreams, the Prince Charming, the dearly beloved that she had yet to meet... But as for me, what fantasies coursed through my mind, all but a few of them very pure and ethereal but, let it be admitted, some of them now physical and unabashedly sexual. But of course I said nothing untoward, just noticed with appreciation the curves of her form. We packed up our sandwich papers and proceeded on our way.

In an hour or so, as the path slanted up the hill ever more steeply, we left behind us the thick forest of oaks and maples first for open birch woodland, and then for the rocky open spaces of the mountaintop, with short dry yellow grass, spring bracken and the first flowers of heather all around them, their wild scents mingling with the clean mountain breeze into the intoxicating air of pure freedom. No one who has not experienced that can understand its joy – or so I felt as I flung myself down at full length on the open summit of the hill, or should one say the mountaintop, with the view clear and unencumbered for many a mile in every direction. I rolled around, whooping and laughing, inviting Hilda to join me in an almost pagan celebration of the glories of nature – and join me she did, albeit in a more restrained and decorous manner. She pranced down to where I lay spread-eagled in the heather and the bracken and sat herself down very close beside me, her knees drawn up and wrapped between her arms as she gazed at me: for the first time she found herself looking at me as a man, not as a younger brother – and I knew it instantly.

I rolled over, propped myself up on one elbow and reached for her, pulling her down on top of me and kissing her face as ardently as I could.

"Oh no!"she cried, "Edward, oh no! This is not right! This is exactly what you must not do. It is absurd, we are good friends, are we not? In my country a girl can never have a boyfriend who is younger than she is, and anyway you're not my boyfriend, not at all. Oh, if only I had known you would do such a silly thing like this, I would never have come out here with you. You are spoiling everything! I wish you had stayed in England, I really do. We were good friends then. Why don't you just go back? Why not?" And I could see that she was starting to cry.

"All right, all right, I see," I said as I scrambled to my feet. "I've made the most abominable ass of myself and gone a good way to killing off the best friendship I ever had in my life. Oh God, what a damned fool I am! But I just lost my head and couldn't help myself. Don't you know how bloody attractive you are? Is that my fault? Goddamit, I've just made a mess of the thing that means the most to me in my whole life!"

"Edward, stop that right now," ordered Hilda, taking command of the deteriorating situation. "You are, and I want you to be forever and ever, my dear good friend, but not in <u>that</u> way, not in that way at all. Now, can we start again, and go back home –it's quite a long way now – and then never say a word about this to anyone?"

And so we walked back, the miles seeming longer on the homeward trek as they always do, without much conversation between us. But as we approached Herrenbach Hilda reached out, gave my hand a special squeeze, and dared to blow me just the tiniest kiss.

Dinner time again, Herr Loewe again, glasses of brandy again… and Hilda out of sight almost all the time, working away in the kitchen with her mother, Doerte in attendance, and Karl out with his beer-buddies, their voices heard yelling wildly up the street every now and again.

"Ja Mutti, meine geliebte Frau, und Hilda, meine geliebte Toechter, kommen Sie hier sofort!" called out Hilda's father once dinner was over, the cigars lit and the womenfolk retreated to the kitchen to clean the dishes. "Come here, both of you!" he boomed. "I want to tell this young Edward Englaender what I did in the War, do you hear? He ought to know, he ought to know, to open his eyes to what I nearly, oh so very nearly, did in his beloved country. '*Gott straf England!*' as we used to say -- but of course we can't say that any more, can we?" he half-whispered with a sly wink to Herr Loewe who was grinning fiercely through his crooked jaw.

I sidled anxiously into the sitting room and took a seat by the window as Herr Doktor Ingolstadt bent down over his desk and retrieved from the bottom drawer a worn cardboard file folder. He slipped open the knots on the old tapes and parted the covers. The file was capacious, but just two items lay in it, a faded photograph the size of a postcard and a torn and bleached sheet of yellowed exercise paper with faint pencil lines drawn upon it -- nothing else at all. Then why were Herr Ingolstadt and Herr Loewe gazing at these scraps with such longing, such fond nostalgia?

"First the photograph," intoned Herr Ingolstadt. "Come here, young Englischer Mann, and let us take a look at this together. What do you see, eh? What do you see?"

'Well, sir," I said politely, "that is a very large building, with columns and carved pilasters all along the front, a really impressive big building in a city, and with a street running next to it and a big open space in front. I can't say I recognize it."

"A big open space, say you? Yes indeed, that's the Champs Elysees in Paris, and my office, my very own office, was right there in the central position in that building!" Herr Ingolstadt exclaimed triumphantly. "And why did I have such an office, you ask? Herr Loewe, you are the one who knows and can remember the truth, yes? Let us have just another little glass of brandy and I will tell this young English boy a thing or two, oh yes I will – and he has much to learn about the great Fatherland, yes he does, the young English boy."

"At the end of the War," continued Herr Ingolstadt, setting down his instantly drained glass, "when the Americans should have been fighting like the very devil himself to stop the Russian pigs from fouling our great capital Berlin, the D*ummkopf* Americans were banging holes in my own dear house, holes I could have filled in by now, but no, I want my family and neighbors to remember how stupid and blind the Americans were, silly little stuck-up Yankee brats, all so proud of themselves. Where was I? Oh yes, the damfool Americans were banging away, and they came and searched my house from end to end, and took away with them everything I had, my medals from *der Fuehrer,* my photographs of *der Fuehrer* embracing me with a smile – how many people ever had that heaven-sent honor, I ask you, how many? -- and his personal and handwritten letter of commendation to me for my work in the great days of 1940, all my medals, the whole row of them, only exceeded in number by Feldmarschal Hermann Goering, Reichskanzler Heinrich Himmler and a whole line of poor, blind generals who never managed to fulfill the Leader's inspiration, his vision of the Greater Germany and the Thousand Year Reich – but they missed two things, the stupid little fools, the dwarfs, the American pigmies. They never found this photograph and they never found this drawing, one of the first I ever made in those days of so very long time ago." And here he could not restrain a couple of tears from slipping down his cheeks.

"Look at this paper, Englischer boy, look at it and tell me what it is. Remember that I was the foremost railway engineer in the Third Reich, *Nommer Eins.* That will give you a clue. Number One I was, the best and most skilled railway engineer in all the Reich."

"Vati, let him be," pleaded Hilda. "Remember, he is our guest, and everything you are talking about was so long ago, another lifetime really, when Edward here would only have been a little baby like me, if he had been born at all."

At this point Herr Loewe began to groan and to dig his elbow into Herr Ingolstadt's ribs, aiming a sneer in Hilda's direction. Embarrassed by his friend to be even listening to a woman, Herr Ingolstadt went on, ignoring his daughter entirely. Her mother retreated into the kitchen, but Hilda stood stock-still in the doorway.

"So, and I was Railway Engineer! The best in the world, no question. *Nommer Eins,* I tell you! And how could I serve my Leader, *mein Fuehrer,* better than by obeying his instincts and doing all in my power to make his dreams come true? But let me tell you," he added hastily, noting the surprise and disgust on my face, "I was not Party Member, no, I was simply forced to do my duty. Like every other German at that time I had no choice but to obey my Fuehrer."

He could see at once that I did not believe him, having been witness to the close bonds of friendship that bound this railway engineer to a captain in the dreaded Schuetzstaffeln. But he went on with his story anyway, quite unable to stop and excited by all the memories that crowded in on his mind.

"So, England stood in our way, refusing to acknowledge our Aryan superiority after the weak and degenerate France, land of Latins, Jewish bankers and uncultured Arabs from Africa, had surrendered to our ever-glorious *Reichswehr.* England had a useful navy, we do acknowledge that, but England stood so very close to the shores that we should now call our own, now that poor pitiful France had seen the error of her ways, abandoned resistance and pledged herself, under her noble General Petain, to help the glorious Reich in her rightful campaign to exert mastery over the lesser races of the world. England could have helped, oh yes, truly she should have, for she was considerably an Aryan nation, but she was pig-headed and led by Jews and Churchill and other *Dummkopfen,* and so she must go to the wall. Why, I was one of the crowd of officers photographed with Feldmarschal Hermann Goering when he stood upon the Gris Nez of France, gazing across to the white cliffs of *verdammt* England! So it was I, it was I, the greatest railway engineer of them all, it was I who was called upon to rebuild all the railway centres in the cities and ports along the south coast of England after the great invasion that would bring the death of the gangster Churchill and the restoration of your true king, Edward VIII. Many railway terminuses in English resort tows or port cities would be severely damaged, either by our noble Luftwaffe and Kriegsmarine in the invasion, or by the cowardly English themselves, blowing up their own railway stations so that the glorious German Army would be slowed down in its magnificent advance upon London. And here is the proof, little Englischer boy! Look at it, and see how your misled nation could truly have followed the path of the great Fuehrer!"

"*Ganz gut,* mine friend, perfect right!" chimed in Herr Loewe, casting a malicious grimace at me, who was indeed paling under the assault of these two aged and unreconstructed Nazis.

At their invitation I carefully took up the paper, which had yellowed with age and had begun to tear apart at its margins and creases. What I saw, when once I had become accustomed to scanning the faint pencil marks, was a simple sketch map of the English Channel, the south coast of England stretching across the top of the page and the north coast of France and Belgium across the lower edge. Black dots with faded names along both coastlines indicated cities and ports, and, sinister indeed to my eye, out of each port in France and Belgium radiated straight lines to all the British ports opposite them, with the distance in kilometers neatly written in, and – here was the point – the main railway lines from the coast to the capital all drawn in, kilometers and all. There were also notes down the sides of the paper, describing the strength and potential for resistance of each English port with estimates of the damage that might be inflicted upon the railway network, but time had erased very much of this. However, it was not hard at all for me to locate my own hometown, Hastings, and to make out its name, still visible after all the years.

My stomach turned over. So this was it! Hilda's father had drawn up plans for the invasion of England in 1940! And still, seventeen years later, in 1957, he and his fellow-fiend 'Herr Loewe' still gloated over those plans and over that document. Why, I swore to myself that I would have bayoneted the pair of them if they had ever dared to show their ugly faces across the Channel, that noble body of salt water that had saved England from the Spain of Philip II, from the France of Louis XIV and of Napoleon, and from the Germany of the Kaiser and of Adolf Hitler! For the moment in my righteous wrath I had forgotten that I had indeed been only a newborn babe in 1940.

I seized the offending paper out of Herr Loewe's hands, and tore it right in half, and then again in half, and again and again, until only little shreds of paper remained. There rose a harsh and broken frothy scream from the throat of the old SS officer, and Herr Ingolstadt rushed to the aid of his friend, carrying him bodily from the room, staggering through the doorway and throwing violent curses over his shoulder at me.

Hilda stood rooted to the spot where she had been standing near the kitchen door. "Quick," she urged me, her eyes flashing, "you must leave the house this moment! Vati will never forgive you, and Herr Loewe will surely kill you if you stay: he has a whole hidden armory of Nazi weapons. Please listen to me! I speak the truth, really I do!"

"What? You can't be serious. This is nonsense. I just can't believe it! Is my visit absolutely over? Where shall I go? I don't know this town. Do I really have to go back to England, right now? Wouldn't the police help me if those two were after me?'

"Don't count on the police," she answered. "No one here much likes English people, and one who served the former regime straight through to the end is something of a hero in their hearts. They could easily arrange an 'accident' for you."

'But what shall I do? Oh Hilda, you have to help me! This is unbelievable. I just can't accept it. But there's no one else but you. Can you help me? Oh Lord, I have got myself into such a mess! Well, I guess I could maybe try to follow that footpath out to the North Sea or east to the Atlantic, but there would be customs officials and all that sort of thing, and I don't even have my passport on me or my clothes or any money or anything...."

"I can help you, but I may be finding myself in terrible trouble for it. This is what you have to do, I am telling you the truth, please God to help me. Hide out in the woods tonight. No one will be looking for you there so soon. That wicked old fool Herr Loewe couldn't follow you there, and Vati couldn't either. And tomorrow just as it's getting light I'll come and meet you with Vati's car and take you to the train station at Grotesheim about ten kilometers up the road from here, and there you can get a train back to Koeln, and then you'll be all right all the way from there. No one will be following you."

"Oh yes, Hilda, you're right! But I just can't believe it! So I really do have to go, and I won't see you again? I tell you, I just can't bear it! But won't you get in the most god-awful trouble for taking the car?"

"After some time has passed and Vati quiets himself, Mutti and I will make him see that by getting you right out of here I will have saved him and Herr Loewe from attacking you, maybe murdering you. That's exactly what that dreadful Herr Loewe would do anyway."

She showed me the way out of the house before her father and his friend had recovered themselves, and pushed me over the wall at the bottom of the garden, telling me to keep to the right and go steadily up the hill until I saw the road and then to wait in the hut on the corner there until she came along in the morning.

So we parted, with only a quick kiss and hug and one fond glance between us. I spent a wakeful night in the old and almost roofless hut on the edge of the woods, where it had begun to rain, a long, chilly spring rain. At first light Hilda appeared at the hut with the car and my hastily packed suitcase just as she had said she would, and I leaped in, wet through and chilled to the bone. Hilda stopped the car for few minutes by another shed farther up the road so that I could change out of my wet clothes, and appear at least halfway decent at the train station.

When we arrived at Grotesheim Hilda jumped out of the car and helped me with my things. "Never, never write to me! Never again in life!" she said, her voice catching. "They will be watching my mail, and I don't think I will write to you either. What's the point? But one last thing, you were absolutely right to tear up that God-damned map and to throw it in the face of Herr Loewe and" – here she sobbed out loud -- "poor Vati! He has been good and loving father to me, but he is wrong about the Hitler days and the War and all that, oh so very wrong! Any time I try to talk about the Hitler days he says that is all gone and forgotten, but it isn't, it isn't! And I am not to talk about the Hitler days no, not ever, ever. He speaks some German idiom – proverb, you call it? – that the grass has grown over everything, and everything will be forgotten until some stupid donkey comes along and eats up all the grass so the history comes right back again. Tomorrow he will be telling to me that you are that *Dummkopf* donkey, and I will be forbidden ever to see you again or even to write to you. I know my Vati through and through, I really do, and mostly I love him. So either I have to obey him because he is my father and the head of my family, or I have to leave my mother, my home and my family, with nowhere to go and no money, and I love Mutti so, and little Doerte, and my silly brother Karl with all his troubles. So, dear friend of all my heart, I haven't slept at all last night, but this is what I have to do. Goodbye, oh goodbye forever in my life!" And she broke down in tears, floods of tears.

"Edward," she said, gulping and collecting herself, "remember this. You became a man last night, a hero who stood up for his country when it was just and when my Germany was very wicked, and I love you for it! God be with you, dearest Edward, dearest friend, for the rest of your life." She turned on her heel, never looking back, and drove away just as fast as she could, blinking through her tears.

I stood transfixed and bereft, and then I waited an hour or two for the local train. I made my way to Koeln and from there to Ostend, by steamer to Dover and by bus home to Hastings, an older and sadder young man. My family was astonished to see me, and explanations were not easy. My father blamed himself for sending his son into a nest of Nazis, but it was not in his nature to apologize to me, emphasizing instead that I had surely learned a lesson that would serve me well all my life long. My father never mentioned Hilda to me again. My mother was solicitous and then deeply thankful that her son had escaped so easily, thanks to that dear, kind German girl. Indeed, the only person to whom I could truly unburden myself was our family friend, Andrew Foyle, who in his many years in the shadow of the police work of his father had become all too closely acquainted with Nazis and the low side of life.

I had an easier task than Hilda, though I suffered enough: but in her lonely sadness Hilda had to live with the knowledge that in one vital part of his being her dear Vati was furious with her, almost hated her, for introducing a serpent into his home and then for helping it to escape. And her Mutti would share in that, ambivalent as she would ever be in her soul between her unquestioning loyalty to her husband and her fondest love of her daughter.

So Hilda Ingolstadt disappeared from my life, and I from hers. Both of us were plunged into sadness, surely sad and indeed more than sad for many years down to the very depths of our hearts. Sixty years later I still think of her and wonder if she still thinks of me.

CHAPTER 7

MCLENNOCH IRON

I was one among a good number of boys who left St. Adalbert's Academy at Christmastime. I had secured my entry to All Saints' College the previous autumn, had served two terms as Head of House, saw no further school distinctions coming my way, and frankly would be perfectly happy to miss the winter-spring football season. About a quarter of the leavers in any school year would depart in December, so my decision was not an unusual one. Apart from a certain boredom, a been-there-done-that kind of feeling about St. Adalbert's, I had a positive reason for wanting out. I would have nine months of the coming year, from January to October, before term would start at All Saints, to do something different, something special, something I had never done before and which I probably would never have a chance to do again. I had practically no cash at all save a little saved-up pocket money, so a life of luxury was not for me. I would not in any way need my father's orders to go out and earn my keep, for staying dully at home for ten irretrievable months held for me no appeal at all.

So what should it be, I wondered? Work my way around the world, principally on ocean freighters? That would be exciting if I could secure leave in the ports-of-call, but there would be a whole heap of dreary bone-breaking toil on shipboard in between. Volunteer for, say, six months for humanitarian, zoological or missionary work in Africa, Asia or Latin America? Now that had real appeal, whole new fields of wildlife being the principal draw. Any disadvantages? It would not in any way that I could foresee help prepare me, give me a foot up, in the career in business that I anticipated, aiming to follow in my father's footsteps as a company director. So, option #3: if after university I were to enter the field of mining or heavy engineering, which was my father's field, then experience of the life of a miner or a factory construction worker might really enable me to present myself after graduation from university to a business corporation as a valuable employee with an interesting background, especially if I chose to study economics or a subject such as chemical engineering at All Saints. So I told myself to be practical, and my father could surely point me in the right direction.

And that's how it happened that on a bitter cold day in January I found myself on a train northward bound from London to Glasgow, from where it was but another short train journey to Clanachan, a rough, unappealing and rather dirty industrial town a few miles east of Glasgow. I had located beforehand the one hotel in the town, and there I put up for a night or two until I could find a lodging house. Winter in Glasgow was a good deal colder than in London, a very damp and penetrating cold. The public rooms of the hotel were heated by generous coal fires, but in my own room there was only a minute coal fire glowing in the little hearth, barely warming a few feet of space around it. That night, after a tasteless dinner of grey meat and wet, over-cooked vegetables, I wondered if I hadn't made a prime mistake in subjecting myself to all this. Oh well, I thought, it's only the first day, and I pulled the limp bedclothes tight over myself, wearing more clothes in bed that night than I had on the street in the daytime.

The next morning I walked over to the offices of McLennoch Iron, where my father had procured a place for me as what amounted to a paid guest worker on the team engaged in the construction of a blast furnace, one of the very last ever to be constructed in Great Britain. The arrangement was that I would undertake any useful work, moving between gangs of plumbers, bricklayers, welders, steel construction men, wherever I might fit in. There was one provision, however: I could not under any circumstances whatsoever perform any task that would fall within the compass of the skills and experience of the working men. The unions were strong and they kept a good eye open for the interests of their members. They did not care at all if I would have nothing to do: I was not one of theirs. But equally they had no objection in the least to my presence on site provided that I did not get in the way of the work. This was not a very exciting prospect for me, but there it was, and I felt committed to sticking with it for a few months at least.

At the office I was met by Mr. Albert McLennoch himself, who spoke to me kindly in a somewhat paternal way and promptly handed me over to Gerry Chuckhill, the head of the construction team that had started to erect the new blast furnace. I rather liked the look of Mr. McLennoch, but actually I never saw him again in all my months on site since he was in charge of managing the whole steel-making enterprise and I would be the lowest man on the totem pole on the new construction job. Gerry Chuckhill was something quite different from the gentlemanly Scot that headed McLennoch Iron. Gerry was well into his fifties but looked older. He was bald, had a really large spherical stomach which was quite impressive in itself, a sharp and enquiring face, a strong and commanding voice, and a wickedly short temper. He peremptorily looked me up and down, and said with a wink "Ye'll do!" Then he took me away to the prefabricated offices and store rooms from which the construction project was handled. "The name's Gerry. Come and meet the others" was all the conversation he had.

'The others' were four engineers with different specialties. Alec Handel was the civil engineer, and he wore a most unlikely cowboy hat and was always singing quietly to himself on a descending scale "<u>Dee</u>dely-deedely-deedely-<u>dum</u> – <u>I am</u> the king of the <u>world</u>." Now what on earth did that mean? Billy-boy Faddingson looked after all the blueprints and other papers of the whole construction: he was in his thirties, a remarkably small man with a bristly mustache, missing the middle fingers of both hands from the time he had fed a broad metal sheet into a press without first drawing down the safety barrier. Taffy Evans, a Welshman of course with a name like that, was the structural engineer, a man with a dark countenance who managed to be both silent and irascible; I kept out of his way. And lastly there was Derrick Crombie, the works progress inspector whose job it was to climb anywhere and everywhere in order to check on the progress and accuracy of all installation. Tall, lank, sallow, with long straight black hair, he was the only one who took any interest in me, the stranger without a proper job to do and without any qualifications at all. Derrick, incidentally, had had his name misspelled in that fashion since neither his parents nor the public registrar in Galashiels where he had been born had known that the name was properly spelled Derek, so Derrick he remained all his life long.

"Derrick, this lad is for you," called out Gerry Chuckhill. "Next time you're out looking at everything, take him along, give him the grand tour. Right?" he roared.

"Aye, and I'll be doing that the noo," answered Derrick quietly. "Come along, Edward – isn't that yer name? -- and we'll fix ye up with overalls and a cap, a donkey jacket for the cold, Toetector boots for the steelwork, and a pair of thick leather gloves. Ye'll not be wanting to be wearing your good clothes on site, I'll be thinking."

Soon the two of us left the set of prefab offices, crossed the broken-stone road and the railway tracks and passed through the gates of the construction site. The new furnace was well over half-way built by now, and steel treads had been installed, or so claimed the construction workers, on all the sets of steps and stairways right up to the top of the entire structure of the furnace some hundred and fifty feet or more above the ground. It was now Derrick's job to make sure that the installation had been completed accurately, and then he could check off the number of each plate on his rolls of blueprints, signing his initials thereupon. As he had suspected, he found that none of the treads on the last, highest staircase had been installed at all, so he had to mark that with a red pencil for further reference and then to move on up to the platform at the top of those missing steps in order to find out whether the treads up there had in fact been installed.

'Noo Edward," he cautioned, "I dinna ken whether ye have a head for heights or nae, and I wouldna be a-scaring you with a demand that ye follow me on high. So stay right here if ye will, and I'll be back – or come along with me if ye like. Suit yourself, laddie." As it happened, I had always had a good sense of balance and an excellent head for heights: I come from a prominent English Alpine mountain-climbing family. So I climbed up eagerly, hand over hand behind Derrick, and maneuvered myself along the handrail of the non-existent staircase, ignoring the hundred and fifty foot drop beneath my feet.

The view from the top was magnificent! There was nothing higher for miles around, and I could pick out the towers of Glasgow on one horizon and rolling hills stretching away up north towards Ben Lomond and the Highlands on another. But it was the view of the building site itself that held me, a really tight site constricted between a major railway line and the range of three old furnaces that were soon to be replaced by this single new one. I knew precious little at all about metallurgy, smelting or iron works, but I could see at a glance that these three blast furnaces were antiques indeed. How had they come to survive so long? They surely belonged in the

Victorian era. They were not built of strong steel plates at all, as all blast furnaces around the world had been for years and years now, and then lined with two-foot thick firebricks that could be replaced at frequent intervals when they had been ground down by the iron ore, the limestone and the blazing coke roiling around in the furnace every day for month after month. No, these furnaces were simply constructed of fire bricks alone, belted with steel bands. At places the furnace walls bellied outwards or curved inwards to a degree I found alarming. The furnaces were charged from above, as all furnaces have been for centuries, but these oldsters still only had single cones, or bells as they are called, at the top of the furnace, not reciprocal double bells as on all furnaces built since who knows when. A load of iron ore or coke is tipped from above onto the cone, which slides down a few feet to allow the material to slide past into the furnace below. If there is only one cone, there springs out, at the moment of opening, an immense rush of blazing gas laced with great chunks of white-hot iron ore and coke, with an immense quantity of dust pouring forth into the sky. If there is a second bell below, it cannot be dropped down into the open position until the top bell is closed, so comparatively little material escapes, just enough to make an industrial town filthy from on end to the other. What was more, these ancient furnaces were all charged by hand. Skips, tall barrows on wheels, filled with iron ore or coke, were hoisted up to a platform near the top of the furnace. There a man would take over, pull the skip back to its point of balance, wheel it forward and tip it over onto the bell, the skip itself being restrained by a transverse bar from following its load right into the furnace. The man had meanwhile smartly stepped away and turned his back in order to save his life from the roaring heat. Outdated? Why, these furnaces were very old, indeed ancient, exactly like the one described so vividly by H.G. Wells in 1895 in his terrifying story *The Cone*, about a murder where the victim was fried on just such a furnace bell.

Derrick and I descended to ground level, with some reluctance on my part since I had enjoyed the height, and Derrick proceeded to give me the grand tour that Gerry Chuckhill had promised me.

"Well, laddie, ye've seen the top," said Derrick, "and that's as good a place to begin as any. So the furnace is this huge strong cylinder where combustion takes place between the coke and the iron ore. Tell me, laddie, why is it coke and not coal, and what is coke anyway? Dinna ye ken at all? Ach, but ye've so much to learn! Do ye know charcoal then? Wood sticks heated awfu' hot without burning, that's recht and all. Well, if ye takes coal and bakes it the same way, coke is what ye gets – and where's the advantage in that, for all the trouble it takes? There's whole acres of coke ovens we have here, lookee way over yonder by the train tracks, see 'em? Coke, and charcoal too for that matter, leaves almost nae ash, nothing to gum up the fire inside yon furnace. And limestone, did ye no ken we use limestone too? Ye canna guess what that's for, so I'll be a-tellin' ye. The slag, that's all the old rock that burns off from the iron in the ore, melts awfu' thick and heavy, like yer morning porridge it is and all.. And for how would ye ever be getting' that goo out of the furnacel, I'ld like to be knowin'? Well, add just the correct measure of limestone and it'll pour out white hot and liquid, it wull indeed. Come on, I see they're just about to open the slag notch on No. 2 Old Furnace, so let's hurry on over and take a peep at it, just for the heck of it."

As we approached the furnace, keeping back a healthy distance however, several men were laying into the slag notch with long crowbars. The notch itself was just a hole a few feet above the bottom of the furnace, blocked by solid baked slag since the last run. A final blow broke through and the slag began to pour out, a thick slurry glowing white hot. A path had been prepared for it across the furnace room floor, so it flowed where directed, between walls of sand that had immediately turned to rough and heavy dark glass. The two of us watched the stream as it approached the back end of the furnace room, and Derrick called to me to watch myself, stay back and keep my distance. Just a fortnight ago, Derrick told me, a man had tried to step over a narrow stream of slag and had missed his footing. He sat down right in the stream. He was pulled out immediately, screaming for all he was worth. He lived through it but lost his bottom entirely and would never do a day's work again all his life long.

Just as Derrick finished this fearful story the burning slag poured over the lip of the furnace room floor, straight down into a deep tank of water. The hiss pierced our ears and a pure white cloud of steam burst up a hundred feet or more into the air.

"Ye canna possibly guess what that's all for, so I'll be telling ye, Derrick shouted. "The slag turns to pellets when it hits cold water, and they pellets goes right into making grade A concrete, that they do and all."

That lesson over, I turned back to my mentor and asked him where all the smoke went from the furnace, because the only factory chimney I could see was maybe a hundred yards away, beyond a row of six or eight great domed rusty steel towers, like farm silos but ever so much bigger, stout and taller, and there were other buildings in front of that row, structures of corrugated steel sheeting concealing whatever it was that took place behind their blank corrugated steel walls..

"Och, and ye're awfu' guid with yer questions, laddie! I'll give ye that, all recht. So you noticed there were nae chimneys right atop the auld furnaces and none planned for atop the new one either, that's recht. Well, the damned auld furnaces surely weren't built wi' nae chimneys at all because the people in those days were awfu' dirty, surely in their work and I'm thinking in their homes too, except maybe they had a guid wife, an auld Scots body, to harass them and make them drop off their dirty clouts out the cottage door.

Listen to me, laddie – here's something for you to do for your education, and that's what this whole dance is all aboot, isna it? Get ye up out of bed on a weekend morning and gang ye away into the country, the fields and the country lanes only a few miles from here to the east, not toward Glesga' but out east, down the wind, ye ken. And what will ye be seeing, I doubt it not? Grey fields, grey woods, grey roads, grey sheep and all, and grey gritty dirt all along the gutters and streambeds, wi' here and there a broad patch of rust. That's what happens to the farmland when ye have nae chimney to the works. A guid chimney, maybe two hundred feet high, would carry the dirt miles and miles away so ye couldna see it in the air, and it would fall where no one would see it, so thin spread, maybe as far as beyond Edinburgh into the open sea, I don't doubt it at all."

"But the pollution's still there, people breathe it, and that's just awful," I interjected in protest at this over-simple solution.

"Clever laddie, clever laddie," Derrick smiled at me. "And I'm recht there wi' ye – and there is an answer, and here it is: Dust Catchers, mon, Dust Catchers! And now let's go see 'em."

I had wondered at what appeared to be four great chimneys emerging from the top of the new furnace uniting first into two and then into one, before surprisingly turning right back on itself, and plunging down into a steel drum-shaped building with a conical roof.

"That's there's the first, Dust Catcher No. 1," said Derrick. "The burning hot gases from the furnace are laden wi' dirt, rocks, iron ore, great lumps of coke an' all! In here they all swirl around, and the heavy rocks of ore and all fall to the bottom, dinna ye see, down a chute and into a skip on the railway track below, and then back to the furnace to be fed into it again through the hopper – nothing wasted. The hot gases travel on by this four-foot pipe here to Dust Catcher No. 2. The gas and any dirt from the furnace, cooling down noo, enter at one end of this building where it is sealed in. It's a tank really, that's all the building is, a bloody great tank, with everything inside sprayed hard all the time by water from above. That heavy spray catches all the rest of the dirt and all, everything left over from Dust Catcher No. 1, and sends it down a chute here, to a tank car on the railway tracks beneath. The skip ye saw before and the tank car ye see now, down on the tracks below the building, both of them go right back to the hopper feeding into the furnace, which we'll take a guid look at presently, but now tell me what happens to all that gas from the furnace, still pretty damn hot and still verra inflammable? Eh, mon, what happens to it, do ye say?"

Well, I had nothing at all to say, my previous comments having made very little difference, just showing up my total ignorance of ironmaking.

"So, did ye never ask yourself what all those towers are for, tell me that now?" asked Derrick, proud that he could explain everything, but just a little irritated that he had been saddled with this ignoramus. He had enough to do keeping track of the progress of the whole building project, noting down every piece that had been put accurately in place and every piece that the work teams said they had put in place but which had not been correctly installed or not installed at all, without the additional responsibility for what he was now beginning to think of as nursery duty.

"No. Derrick, I didn't ask myself anything about them. I haven't even seen them before. Are they for storage? They look like silos on farms, not here in Scotland but in pictures I have seen of farms in America. Is that what they are?"

"And what for would they be storing American farm stuff on a blast furnace site here in Scotland, laddie? Think again, or will I be tellin' ye! Och, I reckon I'll just be tellin' ye anyway. Those are not for storage of anything except heat, do ye understand? Nay? Then I'll be for tellin' ye about that too, won't I now?"

"Look, if this is getting to be a bore for you, let's just can the whole thing, right? I certainly don't want to put you out of your way or make extra work for you."

"Och, laddie, we'll be fighting next if we dinna agree! Nae, nae, I love to show off the furnace and about my part in helping the construction move along as it should, in all the world. We're near three-quarters done with the work noo, after only six months on the job, so let's just go check the stoves, that's what they are, those towers with rounded tops. Stoves. Now where were we? Och aye, the hot gas, still verra inflammable, has been cleaned of all its load of dirt, coke and iron ore, but it's still has to rush along somewhere because there's a whole lot more of burning hot, dirty gas pushing it from behind, all the way from the furnace, which doesn't stop its terrific blasting and burning for anything, not for anything in the whole wide world, so long as it's fed wi' food and ore. So, let me tell you, those towers, those stoves we calls 'em, are filled with firebrick of a special design, great blocks so heavy it takes yer two hands to lift 'em, and they're all perforated with wee holes about an inch and a half across. These bricks all line up so that the holes meet and hundreds of wee tunnels or pipes are formed vertically through the tower. Do ye follow me noo? That's all except on one side, the fire chamber it's called, the side where the gas enters at ground level and is ignited again at point of entry. The flamin' gas rushes up the fire chamber the height of the stove, flips over at the top and pours doon all those wee tunnels. Got it? The mass of firebrick turns white hot, indeed it does, and finally the gas pours out at the bottom of the stove. What do we do with it after that? It's no use to anyone and it's not inflammable any more. It's burnt itself oot, but it' still verra hot. We can't just keep it lying around, with more of it pouring oot from the furnace all the time..."

"So you just blow it off into the air, isn't that right? But the pollution, what about that?"

"Dinna ye see that wonderful great chimney, stands two hundred feet tall? It's lined all the way up with firebrick inside that steel sheathing that you see. The hot gas cools right down to outside temperature by the time it reaches the top, and the higher the chimney the greater the draught, that's the pull on the gas to rush up the chimney and away. And here's the beauty of it. Ye canna see it, no dirty great cloud of smoke. Ye canna smell it either, it's a gas undetectable to humans—unless they're damfool enough to go get several lungsful of it and that would kill ye right off just as lungs full of nothing but nitrogen or carbon dioxide would do. And it just blows away, blows away, and we think no more of it. Isn't that wonderful? This is 1959, and we've come ever so far since Victorian times and all the dirt and filth in the air back in those days, whole cities black as your hat – and, look you, remember how grey everything was all downwind of those old furnaces we are replacing? Isn't modern life wonderful?"

"OK, I get your point. But do you really have all that business about the stoves just to burn up the gases? It seems an awful lot of trouble just for that. And why do you have a whole row of stoves if you only need one to burn the gases?"

"Guid work, laddie, guid work! I'm liking the way ye think. First, we need several stoves because we have to switch between them. When all the firebricks in one stove are hot through and through, we direct the gases to another stove. See all those great butterfly valves down there? That's what they're for. And there's a whole lot more to it than that. Think back to the furnace, will ye? Iron ore, coke and a little limestone are fed in, charged we calls it, through the two bells at the top. But what keeps the fire going? Oxygen of course! Every fire in the whole wide world needs oxygen or it dies -- just like you and me, come to think of it: we'ld be dead in no time flat wi' nae oxygen. So where does the furnace get its oxygen? Didna ye see any great open air holes around the bottom? Damfool question – of course not. Ye remember we saw the slag pouring out of the slag notch, no open holes for it anywhere near there! But didna ye also see the big pipe like a great dough-nut ring circling around the furnace just above head height? And that pipe had smaller pipes feeding down right into the furnace? We calls that great pipe the Tweeyer, that's how we pronounces it but it's spelled something different, something in fancy French, never mind ye that for noo. The tweeyer's full of burnin' hot air being blown at pressure right into the heart of the furnace. Now tell me, can you guess where we get that burnin' hot air from? Ye might just be able to think about that, Sassenach though ye are." This with a cynical smile at me...

"You need air blown in at great pressure, right?" I questioned, trying my best to keep up my end in the conversation, not to appear the complete nincompoop that Derrick seemed to have judged me to be, at least as far as knowledge of iron production was con-cerned – and what else but burning hot air was there to talk about anyway, here in the works, with a complete outsider?

I collected myself and went on, talking in practical, reasonable terms. "So you need high-pressure, very hot air, right? And you have constructed the perfect source for that, haven't you? Those bloody great towers, stoves I mean! And there I was wondering all along, what blessed use could they ever be and you knew all along, but wouldn't tell me! And you must have one hell of a bellows to blow the hot air along, right? OK, that's one up to you, for today anyway."

"Aye, ye're recht," Derrick smiled to me. "I just had to let ye find that out for yourself, dinna ye ken? -- And now lookee, they are getting ready to open the iron notch and let the hot iron flow from Old Furnace No. 2 across yonder. Why dinna we pick up our legs and stride over yonder to see the sight? If ye haven't ever seen it before, it's a sight to be seen and remembered all yer life. Make nae mistake aboot that, I tell ye."

The two of us stumbled in haste across the floor of the unfin-ished furnace room of the new blast furnace, avoiding the gangs of workmen hard at their tasks, and we emerged at the foot of the old furnaces, not close enough to interrupt operations but, sheltered by a screen set up for just this purpose, not so far away as to feel that we were outside observers rather than participants in the drama, albeit at a distance – and drama indeed it turned out to be!

All was set, everyone was in his place, the timing carefully calculated, and at the appointed moment a foundry team stepped forward, clenched their levering irons, and attacked the solid brick wall baked into the mouth of the iron notch. After a great shower of attacking blows upon the solid bricks, the wall gave way and the iron notch opened – which, come to think of it, was the supreme moment in the life of a blast furnace, all that it ever lived to be.

The molten iron shot forth, blazing and unbelievably golden white-hot in the centre, at the sides the brightest yellow like the full sun at midday, and at the extreme periphery red-hot like a sunset. Apart from the hypnotizing beauty and the power and the glory of ferocious molten iron in all its intensity, I was struck by another characteristic of this liquid metal, something for which I was totally unprepared and which struck me as primitive, elemental, magical and intoxicating. This was the fragrance, the aroma, the scent, the odor of molten iron; like a great concentration of maple syrup it was, truly a smell so overwhelming as almost to obscure my other senses. It took me a moment or two to collect myself, to come back to earth from the realms of heaven or hell, from all the fantasy into which my mind had been disappearing. "This is fearful," I thought. "This is glorious, nothing imaginable like this have I ever seen. It is terrifying -- it is godlike -- it is diabolical. I just have to keep my distance, or I will feel like plunging into it in complete insanity!" So step back I did, watched closely by Derrick who knew what effect the close proximity of great quantities of molten metal can have upon a hitherto totally rational being, while blazing sparks arched up fifteen feet and then burst in showers of sparkles like celebratory fireworks. For a brief moment

I thought of Edgar Alan Poe's 'Imp of the Perverse', that devil who tempts one deliberately to take absolutely the worst, most fatal step at a key moment, like jumping off a cliff in order to learn what the experience itself would feel like and to put an end for once and all to the temptation to jump to one's certain death.

The molten iron flowed in a straight and pre-determined stream toward the pig beds where some of the flow was diverted into comparatively small channels leading off from the main channel – hence the name of sow and pigs, with each 'pig' weighing two hundred pounds at least. A great deal of the molten iron was despatched in metal ladles, the great wheeled bowls that transported molten iron along the train tracks, splashing a little here and there, from the original ironworks of McLennoch Iron to their newer subordinate company, Clanachan Scottish Steel, which maintained a plant across the town for the conversion of molten iron into steel, principally by the well-established Bessemer process.

With that, the one truly exciting experience that I had encountered so far in my day at McLennoch Iron, the tour was over – and it was time for lunch. There was no real cafeteria for the construction workers and the office team, and no possibility at all of finding a café in the grimy industrial town of Clanachan, so the management of McLennoch Iron had taken over a disused school assembly hall down the street from the industrial site. Tables and chairs had been placed there for the construction workers, and another set for the office staff up on the stage of the hall. Rooms of one kind or another at the side of the hall had been primitively converted to kitchens and store rooms for the operation of the cafeteria. The food was frankly lamentable: overcooked, nearly identical sodden dark green vegetable matter served every day, with round, white and tasteless potatoes and slices of dark meat hard to chew but optimistically pronounced by the cafeteria staff to be prime steak. In charge was a stout and not quite clean matron, a

Glaswegian of rugged proportions, of stentorian voice and, to me, of an incomprehensible accent. After a few days I did manage to catch on that by the cry of "Thah-hyew!" with the first syllable in a bass tone and the second a high alto whistle, she meant in fact "Thank you!"

The rest of the day I spent sitting at a trestle table in the construction office, transcribing Derrick's red and blue hieroglyphic marks on blueprints to a ledger or progress account of the pace of the construction of the blast furnace. "The tour was wonderful, and Derrick is quite a character," I thought after a couple of hours, "but the job itself had better get more interesting than this. Right now, this afternoon, I am simply wasting my time here. I may be marginally useful to the company, but I have yet to learn the first thing about the working man, which is why I came up here in the first place. Oh well, patience, patience..." But I had little.

After work I followed up on a lead I had noticed that morning. A card on a bulletin board outside the newsagent's shop drew my attention to a room for rent, with breakfast and dinner prepared by the landlady, only a few streets from the furnace. So I went over to explore, and ended up by signing on. It was a rather grim little place and my room was dark, sparsely furnished and in no way appealing. But there was a gas fire in the grate, and the one armchair proved comfortable enough. "Good place for reading Gibbon," I thought as I settled in, "no distractions." My landlady, like the house itself, was plain, serious, straightforward and heavy-set.

The next morning on my arrival at the works I was met by Gerry Chuckhill, informing me that the pipefitters' gang had agreed to take me on for a few days so that I could see how their work was done and what was the need for it. I remembered the constant spray of water at high pressure that washed the hot gas in Dustcatcher No. 2, perhaps a useful thing to know but hardly the subject of all the work the pipefitters would be doing for the next several weeks. Here's how it went. The great steel trunk of the furnace, its 'bark' or shell a good many inches thick, constructed of the strongest steel though it was, would, if untreated, be worn down after a few months, and the furnace would have to be 'fired down,' let out of commission at a considerable loss of profit. But to replace all the steel plates would really be to rebuild the entire centre of the whole smelting operation, so that would have to be avoided if there were the least possibility of doing so. Actually this could in fact be accomplished, if banks of massive fireproof bricks were set up to protect the steel plates from the turmoil of the roaring and tumbling rocks of ore and limestone within the furnace, and the great masses of coke that gave the furnace its fuel. It would be less expensive to replace heavy, bulky and complex firebricks than to build up the furnace again from scratch. Of course the hotter the firebricks grew, the faster they would wear away. So they had to be kept as cool as possible, glowing yellow hot rather than white hot if that could be achieved. But how to cool them down? The answer was that each brick, three feet from front to back and two feet high, far too heavy for one man to handle, had been baked with a strong steel pipe weaving its way hither and yon through the brick. The ends of the pipe protruded from the back of the brick as it was set against the inside furnace wall, and there piercing that wall were holes of exactly the size to accommodate the pipes. Cold water would be piped up to the top of the furnace, and every firebrick would be attached in series to the water source so that water would flow through the firebricks until it reached close to boiling point, when it would be piped out of the bricks and back down to the water tank below, losing most of its heat as it descended into the dark depths of the reservoir. The experts, the designers of the blast furnace, knew very well that the cold water would very soon reach boiling point, so a given injection of water could only serve a handful of bricks. Consequently there would be a mass of piping required, a steel web stretching from head to foot of the exterior of the furnace with every pipe necessarily labelled with bright colored symbols, letters and numbers, so that sections could be replaced with a minimum waste of time should any section crack or burst under the strain. Well, there was indeed plenty of work for the pipefitters! And I was there to join them.

Their leader James Cruikshank was known universally as Wee Cruikie or Jim the Wee Crook since he stood barely five feet high, with a wizened and creased face that broke into the most disarming of broad grins at a moment's notice.

"Welcome aboard, Laddie!" he called out. "And I'll be callin' ye Laddie all the time. Dinna fash yesel' o'er that – it's just me way, that it is and all. Ye just hang around wi' the rest of us and watch what we do. Ye ken, dinna ye, that we canna give ye any useful work to do, not even a wee stretch? That's recht agin Union rules, that it is, recht and all, and anyway I wouldna want fer ye to be gettin' yer pretty hands dirty, now would I?"

The gang carried up on their shoulders from the back of the site next to the railway tracks thirty-foot lengths of two-inch piping, and laid them down carefully, never bringing forward more than they could install in one day. Before they touched it at all the pipe had been the responsibility of the transport workers, but after the fitters had so much as laid one finger on it, it was theirs, and pipe of the required strength and endurance was very expensive, but also easy to cut up, steal and sell far away from the furnace site. And it was surprisingly fragile too, as I learned out when one member of the gang tripped one day and let the pipe slip off his shoulder. My, did he ever get a tongue-lashing from Wee Cruikie!

It astonished me that no plan had been made beforehand, here on site or back at Head Office, of precisely how and where each length of pipe should be fitted so that it did not crowd its neighbors or interrupt the strong flow up of cold or down of steaming hot water. Each length of pipe, hundreds in all, had therefore to be individually fashioned, and no two pieces seemed to be alike. Wee Cruikie was an expert in managing the strands of all this pipework, planning outside access to every single pipe. It was, I was told, very hard to foretell when one pipe might crack or break under the strain – and a furnace out of control could be a mass killer indeed, no exaggeration. So Wee Cruikie would take a steel rod, a thin rebar from the concrete plant, and have his men pump it in a pipe-bender to just the right angle and design of the next length to be installed. Then it would be threaded at each end and nuts added so that it could be fitted tight to the head of the pipe already embedded in firebrick. The other end would be led down the outside the furnace in a veritable web of pipework to the great tank next to the water main, close to the hydrant that would deliver the water in the first place. I marveled at the skill and stamina of the pipefitting gang, and at the way they worked so knowledgably in the streamlined process that they had evolved in their many years of teamwork in heavy construction. Other places around the site needed piping, yes, but none had such a dire need of true expertise as did the mighty blast furnace itself.

So I just stood around and watched, stood around and watched, chatting when I could with Wee Cruikie and the members of his gang, but conversation was difficult and unsatisfactory: their accents and vocabulary were too different from mine, and they were working too hard to give much time to conversation; Cruikie kept the pace moving along smartly since they were all paid on piecework; and actually I found I did not have much to say to them, so different was my life from theirs. It was all fascinating for an hour or two, fairly interesting for another hour or two, but increasingly monotonous after that. By the end of two days I had had enough, so with great deference I approached Gerry Chuckhill and asked whether I might move on, particularly into something more constructive than just standing around and looking at working men concentrating fiercely on their task at hand. Gerry, well, he just stared at me, and turned away.

I served my second tour of duty, as I named it, accompanying a team of welders. Welding fascinated me: the blazing white light of the welding rod transfixed me, just as on an infinitely larger scale the blaze of molten iron had held me suspended in awe. I longed to weld, and begged to be allowed to do so. There was no question at all, naturally, of whether any of my welding might be incorporated in any way into the building. Naturally nothing could possibly be done about that, nothing at all: I was not a certified welder, which was vital to management; and I was not a member of the Union of British Welders, which was of prime importance to labor. There was no way in which I could set myself at variance with either of these bodies, union or management, and I certainly did not want in the least to do anything like that. Anyway, all I wanted was simply to have the experience of using welding equipment for a few minutes. Well, a problem arose – of course it did. Who would pay for the powerful electrical current and who would pay for the two or three welding rods that I would surely use up in my (useless and unnecessary) welding experience? There was a standoff, and my hopes collapsed. But then something small but rather lovely happened. Union and management actually got together and agreed, they actually found that they could in fact agree. Just as long as none of my welding would be in any way incorporated into the structure of the blast furnace or its supporting buildings, I could be allowed, after a day or two, to try my luck with a welding iron and to learn how it would feel to wield this tool with which skilled men earned their living wage. Management would kindly supply the equipment and pay the costs, and no worker would lose time.

The welding itself was fun, I really had to admit, hunched down beneath a vast welding helmet, total darkness all around me until I made the contact between the welding rod and the steel before me, and then the whole screen, the little dark window half the size of an envelope, lit up in front of me. Clinching a new welding rod into place, I drew it across two steel plates with the rod melting as it flowed along while the raw steel felt the heat too, so that the whole mass melted together, completely, and set into one single united piece of metal, not a blend. And then, at the end of a passing stroke, I lifted up the rod and the contact was broken. The universe grew totally black again to me, and remained so until so further contact was made – but already I overheard the voices of the professional welders:

"Here, Eddy me laddie, ye'll be puttin' all of us oot of a job, so give it here, will ye noo? There's a smart fellow! But, by Jasus, ye havena never welded before anyhoo, have ye noo, or been to a welding training program, have ye noo? Why, that there seam o' yourn wouldna last but five minutes on the furnace, and then where would we all be, wi' the whole damn blast furnace tearing doon upon us? We'ld all be burned up to Kingdom Come, that's where we'd be, make no mistake aboot it!" And that was how, amid such jocularity, my short and totally undistinguished welding career crashed to an end. It had not been an unparalleled success, I was compelled to admit to myself, but I had certainly enjoyed the taste of it.

A few days later, however, when I was beginning to get seriously browned off, having no work at all to do and next to no chance to get to know on a personal basis any of the construction workers since they had no interest in seeing me after hours, Gerry Chuckhill announced to me that they had contrived to create a job of great responsibility for me to work on. Chuckhill made much of this, emphasizing how this was the way in which I could repay the company for its goodness in taking me on, at the risk – what risk I wondered? – of jeopardizing its good relations with the unions.

"Here's what ye'll be doing," announced Chuckhill. "We have a ton of these 'ere firebricks comin' in, all for lining the stoves what

Derrick took ye up to see 'tother day, and for linin' yon tall brick chimney – get it? Recht noo, a couple o' goods trucks o' them bricks have been unloaded up yonder at Brae Head, way up past the furnace works. We dinna ken if they're good enough in quality for the work we need to get out of them, and we've had in some bad loads recently, so that's where ye comes in, Edward, sir, wi' yer skills and yer power of observation. [Some sarcasm here, I thought] We'll set ye up recht enough, wi' all the required measurements, internal and external, of them bricks, and calipers and all, and ye'll be checking every tenth brick as ye moves along. Ye'll need to check the wee tunnel holes through the middle of each brick as well as the overall size of the brick, mind ye, and note down the cracking: non-existent, verra slight, noticeable, borderline acceptable, failure, etcetera, etcetera. Recht, me lad, got it has ye? Then come along o' me, and we'll get ye started the noo, recht and all."

Brae Head was a cold windswept piece of land, once upon a time good rich farmland like so much of Lanarkshire but more recently a site for the storing of great stacks of iron ore, coke and suchlike. So it had degenerated into simply empty barren land, grey or rusty all over, desolate indeed. Along one side ran a spur of a single railway track, and next to that stood two piles, maybe forty feet long and six feet high, of furnace firebricks. These specialized bricks were hexagonal, each one several pounds in weight, with hard sharp edges. Along each of their six facets was scooped out a half cylinder, so that when two bricks were placed together a circular passageway was created between them. In addition, a similar circular passage penetrated each brick from top to bottom. It was easy for me to see how they would be employed in the stoves, a perfect design.

I wore my own heavy clothes and company overalls over them, plus a thick donkey jacket like a naval pea jacket but even heavier, and a sturdy tweed cap – there were no hard hats at an industrial site at that date, 1959, no one had ever heard of them, would have dismissed them as effeminate --, and I was also equipped with heavy-duty leather gauntlets since those heavy firebricks had sharp and unforgiving edges. Dressed like that I was set to work, with a clipboard and paper on which to record the dimensions and qualities of every tenth brick in these two long, extended piles. What a god-awful prospect, I groaned to myself. How long can I keep this up?

I set myself to do it, however, and do it I did. I struggled on for a whole day, with no company except for the time when one of the blokes from the cafeteria brought me a couple of sausage rolls and a Scotch egg, plus strong lukewarm tea in a thermos with a loose lid, calling that dinner.   The young man and I tried hard but could manage very little conversation, for a host of reasons: first of course, we came from such different worlds, Edward Brackenthwaite the Southron, the Sassenach, a man of education, and Jock McGinty, Glaswegian Irish, an industrial laborer from the Gorballs; secondly, our accents were so alien to each other as to be mutually all but incomprehensible; and thirdly, poor Jock McGinty, having complained several times of toothache and having missed several days at work on that account, the local dentist, working within the National Health System no less, had extracted every single last one of Jock's teeth, telling him that this was the one surefire way to make certain he would never suffer from the toothache again in all his born days – and the National Health would give him false teeth for free all his life long, once his bleeding gums had settled down enough to accommodate them. I could not possibly conceal my horror at this, but young Jock merely attempted a wan smile with quiet resignation in his deeply painful condition, muttering that that was just the way the wurrld was: he wasna the furrst and he wouldna be the lasst. That picture of poor suffering Jock McGinty was one I simply could never get out of my mind, for years after the whole McLennoch Iron experience was over and done with for me.

Just one point of relief came to me when I was on the point of throwing in the towel, calling it all a day, and returning to England as soon as ever I could, even if I would be running away with my tail between my legs. Far off, close to the far end of the field of my vision, I could descry a pair of lapwings, tumbling together across the sky, far, far off, way beyond this industrial wasteland, over real country, real grass, real fields. I drunk this all in, and managed to go on working, at least for a few hours.

The next day I told Chuckhill that I simply could not carry out research all by myself any longer, that I simply had to have human companionship at least for part of each day. Gerry Chuckhill looked me up and down, scowled in deep disappointment, and said that since he had not been the one to employ me, he could not be the one to terminate my employment – but that he would feel constrained to report to higher authorities on my inability or unwillingness to cooperate.

Then, with perhaps a malicious gleam in his eye, he made another proposal to me. "Ye ken that great factory chimney, the one as stands a couple o' hundred feet high above all the furnace site? Does ye ken that, at all? Well, that chimney is lined wi' the selfsame firebricks as ye were workin' on, dinna ye ken, and they needs inspection too! If ye canna stand working all by your lonesome on the surface of the earth, as all of us here in the office had wi' considerable trouble to ourselves, mind ye, set up for yer own personal and individual benefit, what would ye be a-thinkin' o' scalin' them heights and checkin' o'er the firebricks in the throat of the chimney, way up there in the sky, eh, Eddie me lad? They say the view is grand from up there, grand and all, make no mistake about it!"

And he rubbed his hands together, remembering that the only way to scale that chimney, two hundred feet high, was by an outside ladder, every rung of which was welded at each end to the steel shaft of the chimney, safe enough never to detach itself whatever

the conditions. But outside those rungs there was precious little, just vertical strips of steel a couple of inches across all the way
down the chimney, separated about nine inches apart and each
one welded securely to a horizontal hoop of steel three feet in diameter that itself was welded to the chimney, some dozen feet from
its neighbor up and from its neighbor down. So a climber might
find relief in bracing his back against the band or loop of steel behind him, but it would remain a fact that up to two hundred feet
of empty air yawned directly beneath his feet.

Now in fairness one must admit that it was in no way at all
Gerry Chuckhill's aim to cause physical harm to me, let alone to
bring about my demise, God bless us no, but it is a true fact that
Gerry would feel a certain satisfaction in embarrassing this young
neophyte – not that Gerry would ever, ever have volunteered to
climb those rungs himself: he had no head for heights at all, and
he was altogether too bulky to be able to haul his person more
than twenty feet up any ladder in the world. He imagined that I
would agree to undertake the task, would start out full of brash
confidence, and then, thirty or so feet up in the air, realize what
an extraordinarily threatening position I was in and fold, climb
down quietly and unobtrusively, in defeat, and slip away into the
background. So, Gerry Chuckhill would be vindicated in his poor
assessment of me.

"Right, I'm for it!" I called out sturdily. "Got any good gloves,
ones that won't possibly slip off my hands and that will be guaran-
teed to grasp firmly all those cold steel rungs? I can't go up without the best gloves in the world! Just let me have the measuring
equipment, please, the ruler and the calipers, the notebook and
pencil, anything else I might need."

"Look ye here, laddy," said Gerry, "I didna mean for ye to be
takin' me that serious. This is a job for an experienced steel construction worker, those fellows ye sees walkin' out along those high
open beams in the new casting house by the furnace. It's not for

the likes of ye, Eddie, oh no, not at all! I surely takes me hat off to ye for yer courage, laddie, but, noo, this is nae a job for the likes o' ye!"

My dander was up. "Yes, it is a job for me! It really is. I'm taking it, and that's that, so please just let me have all the stuff I'll need. And I'll take all the responsibility on myself, so that's all right. You didn't make me go up – I chose to do so, of my own free will."

"Well, if ye really means it…. It's up to you, ye know. But I still thinks ye shouldna, I really do, swelp me God."

So, a short time later, I started up the climb that might indeed cost me my life – and I knew it. But I stepped forward nonchalantly, grasped first one steel rung and then the next above it, and was gone in an instant. I climbed on, carefully setting my feet and hands in place, never moving forward until I was sure of each rung, testing each one in turn for rust or decay, concentrating on hand-over-hand, one-foot-then-the-other. I told myself that if I could only remember never, never, never to look down, then all would be well. My Uncle Digby and my Great Uncle Lionel had been notable mountaineers in the golden days of that sport in the Alps in the early 20th century, and my first cousin Ted climbed whenever he could in the Himalayas, in the Atlas and in the Hindu Kush. But could I in fact match these mountain gods of the family in this most industrial and urban of environments? Doesn't imagination take over at such times, I wondered, and wouldn't the presence of this ever-deepening hole of empty space growing steadily beneath my feet become the overwhelming reality in my entire universe? And might it not be better simply to make my way down, quietly and sensibly, concentrating on that one straightforward task and not on my imagination, until the happy moment when *terra firma* would once again be set in its rightful place beneath the soles of my feet? Humiliation would surely be nothing compared to that most profound relief.

Two hundred feet of emptiness all the way down to the ground when once I had reached the top -- I just couldn't prevent myself from thinking about that. And what about the wind? Might it not be strong enough at that altitude to blow me loose, particularly since the steel rungs were cold to the touch and so my fingers, growing numb in this northern winter, even through Gerry Chuckhill's prime gloves, were slowly losing the strength of their grip? I certainly couldn't be blown far away from the chimney, but I could plunge all the way down to a deathly embrace with Mother Earth at the base of the ladder. Oh dear God, what to do? Solid commonsense ordered me to drop this whole line of thinking, don't you dare take this up as a personal challenge, for God's sake for what idiocy are you risking your entire life? Climb down while you can -- forget this whole damn business. It's madness... But then a sense of adventure overtook me, that feeling familiar to so many young people, that the whole world stands in front of me, inviting me to prove myself, and it was up to me, to me alone, to seize the day, never to slink back in cowardly retreat.

So up I climbed, upward and ever upward, two hundred feet in all, rung after rung, pausing for breath every now and again, but never, ever looking down. I didn't even allow myself to look around, certainly not upward to see how many rungs I might yet have to surmount in order to arrive at the peak.

And then suddenly I was there! No more rusty iron chimney stood in front of me blocking my vision, just sky and the endless, endless view all around. I breathed deeply, lungful after lungful, stood back on the rungs of the steel ladder, and marveled at all I saw. The sky itself stood out above all else, for it stretched not only from one horizon to the other, north, south, east and west, but it seemed to lap right in on me, to tell me that I was above the measure of the earth and therefore could actually look down, yes, down, upon the encircling horizon. I was living right up there in

the sky -- I was a denizen of celestial eternity. This I had never expected. Truly it was a miracle!

At last I understood a familiar passage in *Paradise Lost* that had
puzzled me since I had first encountered it a year or two ago. An
angel had descended from Heaven to visit Adam and Eve in the
Garden of Eden and had floated down on a sunbeam, comfortably riding the ray of light all those countless miles from Heaven
down to Earth. Well, he conversed pleasantly with Adam and Eve
in the garden for a while, and then he politely took his leave and
headed back to Heaven, once more choosing the easy journey of
a ride on a sunbeam for his travel back through interstellar space.
By this time, you see, evening had approached, so the angel could
catch a ride on a convenient sunbeam that slanted not downwards
from the heights of Heaven toward humble Earth but rather aslant
the Earth at sunset, inclining gently back down in the reverse direction, from the Garden of Eden high on the land down to the
horizon out at sea. It works out, I thought, it really works out,
transfixed as I was by all that I saw – a new vision of Heaven and
Earth – and a new insight into Milton.

"All right? Are ye all right?" a faint voice reached up to me
from many miles below. There, far away beneath him, stood Gerry,
Derrick and a whole crowd of construction workers and engineers,
all amazed, desperately anxious and aghast at my foolhardiness --
and astonished at my equanimity.

'Fine, fine! Never felt better in my life," I called back. "Come on
up, and let's have a party! But first I've got to check these goddam
bricks, and for that I'll have to get right up and go around. Hold
on, hold on!"

"Dinna ye dare go on up nae farther!" That was Gerry
Chuckhill's voice, as full of command as he could make it. But really he was quaking in his boots at the responsibility he would have
to face if this stupid boy should fall down and break his precious
little neck. Oh God, he would lose his job, his reputation would

be shattered, he would face God knows what kind of a lawsuit from that idiot boy's family. Oh God, please bring him back down safe! And *then* I'll give him what for! Oh yes, I surely will!

But it was too late: it always had been, ever since I had set my first foot on the first rung of the ladder, and even before that, ever since I had accepted Gerry Chuckhill's challenge to climb up to the very top of that blessed two hundred foot chimney and check out the firebricks in the top few ranges of the lining.

So I pulled myself up to the point where my waist was at the level of the top of the chimney, and then with scrupulous care swung one leg over the top so that I now sat comfortably astride the very circle of the chimney wall. Mercifully it was a clear sunny winter's day with only a slight breeze: the thought of lightning never occurred to me. I took from my breast pocket the small clipboard with the notebook and pencil attached by a chain, and tucked them beneath my thigh. "Should have tied them around my neck," I thought, "but too late now, can't go back down just for that!"

I leaned forward until my chest almost lay along the coping of the chimney and glanced across at the opposite side. I took notes on the condition of the surface of the brickwork over there. "I'll call that Brick Number 1," I thought, "and I'll mark the brick this side that I can reach and measure but cannot see since it is down the chimney, this one I'll call Brick Letter A. So when I'm finished every brick will have a letter and a number, and when I'm back in the office I can match them up and see what comes of it. That damfool Chuckhill, how the devil did he think I would be able to look right into each bloody brick and at the same time measure the kinds of cracks it has? He's the one who's cracked, if you ask me, not the goddam bricks. And he's got a surprise coming, when Head Office learns that he sent the son of the construction company's Managing Director two hundred feet up a chimney just to look at bricks he couldn't really look at anyway. But then if Chuckhill hadn't sent me up here, I would never have had this glorious experience, higher than the angels, higher than the top of the world. Whoopee! So why should I get that poor idiotic devil into trouble? He's probably terrified enough as it is."

So I eventually came to the end of my trip around the chimney top, and tucked away in my pocket the notebook, pencil and clipboard. I sat straight up, threw my arms in a sweeping circle about the heavens and the firmament, and yelled at at the greatest pitch of my lungs: "Oh God, I love You! I love You! God bless You and all this Heaven I see!" (Down below, they hardly heard that at all -- but then the voice of God is often missed by people on earth.)

It was time to descend, which I managed to do, hand over painful hand, foot after cramping foot, concentrating mightily all the time until with a jolt there was no step farther down to be taken, and I had finally arrived back on *terra firma*. It was Derrick who dashed forward first.

"I thought we had lost ye, laddie, lost ye afore we really got to know ye! And now I'm a-crying, damn fool that I am." And he swept me up in a great hug, whereupon the construction workers assembled from all corners of the building site crowded around, clapping and cheering.

"Ye're now an honorary member of the United Construction Workers Union, me lad, and make no mistake about it! No dues, an honorary member!" And everyone cheered and cheered, while I stood there, numb and disoriented.

"Golly, thanks everyone, thank you so very much. I only did what I was asked to do, and it was fun! You ought to try it some day!"

"Not I," cried one. "I'm a married man and I dinna want to make me old lady a widder-woman, no Sir! And there's the wee bairns too." Everyone laughed and cheered again.

And then Gerry Chuckhill stumbled forward. "Dinna ye ever go telling yer Dad I ordered ye up there, there's a good laddie, recht?

I didna order ye up there anyway, not in a month of Sundays – I only allowed ye whenas I couldna stop ye, an' that's the truth, ain't it?"

"Oh forget it, Gerry," I said with a grand dismissive gesture. "No one's blaming you, and I had a perfectly wonderful time, didn't I? Now just let me make up my report on those blessed bricks, what I could make out of them anyway, and we'll be done with the whole thing."

But that wasn't really the end of the incident, since the steelwork construction workers, those who walked nonchalantly out along the steel beams, took it upon themselves to make much of me, to follow up on making me an honorary member of their Union, on condition of course that I undertake no for-profit work on the entire blast furnace building site, or indeed on any other. They needed the income that they were earning, and they were jealous of the rights that they and their predecessors had secured at the expense of management over lo, these many decades. But they were very friendly to me, invited me a few times to share their lunch, explained to me what they were doing in their line of work, how the United Steelworkers' Construction Union was organized, and even asked me once or twice to meet them after hours, to share their company at the local pub where they downed much whisky and beer, one retired member even boasting of his accustomed fourteen pints of Guinness of an evening of celebration, and that's the truth. Poor toothless Jock McGinty went so far as to invite me to accompany him to the one-night appearance in concert in Glasgow of Louis Armstrong and his All-Stars, a totally unforgettable occasion, in the spring of 1959. We went in together, and I have kept the program of that concert to this very day. I swore to myself that I would never forget poor old toothless Jock, and I never have.

But after the great chimney climb and subsequent celebration very little more happened to lighten or brighten my overall experience, especially my desire to become acquainted, from the inside as it were, with the British workingman. My lodging proved a sad disappointment: here my landlady barely ever said a single word as she brought in my supper, tea she called it, upon my return from work: two pieces of toast, two slices of ham or black pudding, or a couple of sausages, or even two eggs, with margarine, jam and two cups of tea, and that was that. She was a large, stalwart woman and simply did not want to talk, at least to me, about anything at all. Her husband was a diminutive creature with sunken cheeks who glanced furtively around the sitting room door from time to time, smiled brokenly, and disappeared. After a few more weeks of this, interrupted only by one three-day weekend in which I took myself off to Loch Lomond, boarded the ferry at Balloch, stayed the nights at the small hotel in Rowardennan, and scaled Ben Lomond, happening to my great delight upon a small herd of red deer only a few yards from me on the upper slopes. Back at McLennoch Iron I was nevertheless getting fed up, fed up good and proper.

And then one day, I suddenly upped and made my decision: I was going to leave, that very day, stay one last night in the dreariness of my lodging house, and then take the train from Glasgow back to London early the next morning. I would say nothing beforehand to family or friends: I was sure my father at least would try to dissuade me, and I didn't need that, so I didn't tell him. So when the five o'clock whistle blew and the men downed tools and left for home, I strolled over to Derrick Crombie and Gerry Chuckhill, two of the only three people whom I had really got to know, and to their surprise shook their hands warmly and bade them farewell. Gerry I could see was rather relieved that this unwanted visitation had so suddenly come to an end, but Derrick, well, he had to turn his face away and brush his cheeks briskly with the back of one rough hand as he clasped me with the other, and, staring deep into my eyes, wished me joy and success for the rest of my mortal days. And Jock McGinty? I stood around and waited for him at the gate of the construction site, but he must have left early for some reason, and I didn't know where he lived. So I missed him, and was sorry for that.

Back in London, I sat myself down at home and pondered how to spend my time for the several months in front of me before the opening of my university career. What to do? No more exploring the common man – no seaman's toil around the globe – no anything else that looked deceptively attractive and appealing. "I know," it suddenly came to me, "the Alps! That's the ticket! Climbing that chimney was splendid, and now I have a notion that I've inherited the family skill and delight in rock-climbing. So off we go to the Alps, I do believe, on the little money I was paid at McLennoch Iron. Yes sir, yes sir!!"

Well, forty years later, in 1999, after my career had taken me to a life many miles away from Scotland, and after I had acquired a family consisting of a wife and three 'wee bairns,' as I began to describe them to myself, I found a chance to return once more to Clanachan. The family and I could pass through Clanachan on our way to a summer holiday in the Highlands. There would be time for a visit to the ironworks since we planned to spend a night at Stirling, not so very many miles north of Clanachan and the gateway to the Highlands. Then I could show off to my family with some pride the great blast furnace that I had built, single-handed of course, and the two-hundred-foot chimney that I had scaled to the wonder and amazement of the local citizenry. But once we had arrived by car in Clanachan I was, to my great surprise, completely unable to find my way to McLennoch Iron; the hundred and fifty foot new furnaces, the bulky stoves and the towering chimney were nowhere to be seen! Not a single person at the local Post Office could help, so I called in at the Carnegie Library – no enlightenment there either, which was very strange. Close to giving up in frustration and filled with bewilderment, I turned to an old man sitting in the sunshine on a park bench just outside the library, 'bearded as the pard,' relaxed with the gentle passivity of old age, looking at nothing and at no one, lost in the thoughts of a misty long ago.

"Excuse me, sir," I began, "if I am not disturbing you, do you happen to know the blast furnaces of McLennoch Iron, here in Clanachan? I had a job there, many years ago, and I would surely like to show my wife and children the site where I worked for many months back in 1959."

"McLennoch Iron, did I hear ye say? Noo, that's a name I havena heard for many a year altogether noo. I used to work there mesel', aye indeed that I did and all, but noo I'm retired these many a year. But I do ken where McLennoch's Iron used to stand, I do that. It's all gone these many years, that it is and nae mistake aboot it. It's all gone, sir, all gone, and all the people who built it and worked there, they're all gone too, I doubt me not, away oot o' this life altogether, all but me and mebbe a few other lingerers, till the good Lord calls us."

"All gone? All gone? But it was a terrific furnace, a great new blast furnace forty years ago, when I worked in the building if it, to replace a row of three ancient Victorian furnaces, almost a hundred years old at that time. It can't be all gone now, it just can't be! Why, I want to show it to my family. So where is it? – Do please tell me."

"Verra guid, sir, and I'll be tellin' ye everythin' as what I can. Over yonder, way doon past the railway brig, ye'll be seeing a great open space, like twa or three soccer fields or more, wi' nowt on it noo but mebbe a passle of them containers, great boxes for goods trains that come in off the cargo ships from Japan and Koree and places like that – and that's all ye'll be seeing of auld McLennoch Iron. Gone it is, nae iron nor steel made around here any more. They say it all comes from Poland and Roosha and Koree and places like that, but I dinna ken, it's not for me to say. But it's all gone these many year noo – gone, I say, like me own poor wee tooths sae long ago."

I gulped, stared, stood stock still, and gasped out loud. "Poor wee tooths!" That did it, the dam was broken, memory flowed in.

"Jock McGinty, is it? Jock? After all these years? I just can't believe it, I really can't! Jock McGinty, for God's sake! Why, I'm Edward Brackenthwaite, the wee English lad you brought dinner to, years and years ago, when I was measuring those goddam bricks up at Brae Head, and you, poor lad, had just had every last tooth in your mouth pulled out by some bastard dentist – may he rot in Hell! Do you not remember when I climbed all the way up to the top of the great chimney, just for a dare? And we went into Glasgow one evening together, to see Louis Armstrong. Don't you remember that now?"

"Aye, aye, sir, noo I kens who ye are," mumbled out Jock McGinty in his odd whistling voice. "That's all sae long ago, that it is and all. Well, life took us awa' on different tracks, didna it? But we canna go into all that, because I'm a-forgettin' most of it, and that's probably a mercy anyways. I barely remembers you, sir, but I surely wishes well to you, and to your lady and them bonnie wee bairns there in the back of yon smart motor car. Ye'll be coming fra London, I take it. And life's been guid tae ye, I can see that. Well, well, God's blessing upon ye, and fare ye well...," and Jock's mind wandered off along the paths of fading memories, and he no longer knew that I was present. I turned away, blinking, and left him to his reveries.

"Well, that's that," I said to my wife and children. They had been waiting patiently until I should come back from my journey to my teenage years, and I explained what had happened. Now we could all move forward to our promised holiday in the Highlands, to the Cairngorms and even to Lochinver and Suilven in the far northwest. "First it's on to Stirling, not so far away," I announced. "There the Royal Hotel awaits us, a good overnight there after a

140

first-class dinner, and then it's up, up and away to the Highlands and a real family holiday!"

"Hooray! Yippee!" they all echoed – and Clanachan slipped away behind us. But in my bed that night I could not help myself blinking back a silent tear for all I had known at Clanachan – the dirt, the cold, the bleakness of it all, the sneers of Gerry Chuckhill, the slow, gentle warmth of Derrick Crombie, the sadness of Jock McGinty, the entire life of a vigorous, lively but now completely scattered and vanished community.

"God bless you all, you poor dear people," I murmured to myself as I slipped into sleep.

CHAPTER 8

LEANTHE ONE DAY

I allowed myself far too much time to walk from college to the train station. I know I always do that and I always arrive everywhere much too early, but this time particularly I wanted to be there in plenty of time, to collect myself, to straighten my tie, brush my hair and in general make myself presentable. This meeting was going to be important, would not be easy I felt sure, and would mean a great deal to the three people closely involved. So when I walked into the station I sat down on a bench in the waiting room, carefully rehearsed the most important elements of the meeting, and tried to clear my mind of all other thoughts, everything else that might intrude and preoccupy me. Well, after a bit I couldn't just sit there for the half hour and more before her train from London was due, so I stood up and walked out of the station building onto the one immensely long platform that constitutes the train station at Cambridge. Why, I wondered, had the LNER never built a second platform across from the first, to shorten the length and make the walk easier for passengers, particularly the elderly and those burdened by suitcases such as every last one of the students returning to the university after vacation? But I drove these speculations from my mind and returned to concentrate on the business at hand. I paced the long straight platform from one end to the other, slowly, four times, trying hard to stay focused.

The time passed, and at length I caught my first site of her train steaming north from London and pulling slowly into the station. Would she really be there on the train, I wondered? Might she have changed her mind, or might Sterling Rigaude, who had carefully engineered this occasion, have had cold feet about the value of this meeting for him, for Leanthe and for myself? I will admit that I was full of trepidation, knowing that Leanthe, properly Lady Leanthe DeBecque, had reveled in the honor of being the premiere debutante of her season and was, by every account and by all the press photographs I had seen of her at charity balls, clearly a young lady of the most astounding beauty, poised and utterly at ease in the midst of fashionable gatherings. And there was I, a bookish undergraduate of no particular interest, who happened, by the chance of boarding school experience, to be the closest friend and confidant of the young man to whom she had, at least by his account, lost her heart. Would I recognize her? Well, that was a silly thought. Of course I would, the most dazzling person who could possibly be on that train. I was growing anxious and I could feel it in my palms, for no reason at all – at least, that was what I told myself.

With a hiss of steam the train drew to a halt, doors flew open all along the coaches, passengers descended. Staying in the centre, right by the way out through the ticket office to the street, I stood, scanning first to the left and then to the right – until I saw her, and the breath fled from my body. Leanthe was indeed spectacular, truly radiant! She stood taller than I had imagined her, with long blonde hair tossing on her shoulders, and she wore a bright lemon-yellow suit, jacket and skirt made of some light-weight but substantial material, looking almost tweedy – and she was the cynosure of every eye on the platform, a situation which was clearly familiar to her for she looked completely at ease and unselfconscious, as her eyes roved back and forth in search of the young man to whom Sterling Rigaude had entrusted her for the day. She saw me, looking straight at her from twenty feet away, and she beamed her welcome at me through the crowd, like the rays of the sun parting grey clouds.

"You're here," I stammered as she moved forward. "I was just wondering if you really and truly would be here, I mean, well, it's really terrific, isn't it? – and Sterling has told me all about you. By the way, I'm Edward Brackenthwaite – that is, of course that's who I am. How could I be anyone else? Ha, ha!" Well, I was revealing how completely nervous I was, making a fool of myself even before she and I had even spoken together or begun to get to know one another, and all because I was so afraid she would be disappointed in me, would have preferred 'Edward Brackenthwaite' to be any single one of the good-looking young men from the university who crowded the platform, rather than this unexciting and very ordinary fellow who confronted her in his old tweed jacket and grey flannels.

"Edward Brackenthwaite, oh Edward, I am so very glad to meet you! I have heard all about you from Sterling, and we really do have a lot to talk about, don't we? Sometimes I just don't understand Sterling at all, and other times he is clear as day. So you have absolutely got to help me there, haven't you? Sterling said you would do all that, and I really need to know some answers. But I am going on much too fast, aren't I? I am always so silly that way, can't help myself, just go running on and on!"

She paused for breath and gave me the widest of smiles, her beautiful white teeth gleaming in her long oval face, and her dark blue eyes batting at me. I was so stunned by the reality of her presence that I had not even moved to walk with her off the platform, and we were almost the last to do so. Beyond the ticket office we were fortunate enough to find a taxi, almost the last in the line. The expense would be monstrous for me but taking a taxi was clearly the right thing to do. Everyone else was walking along the road into town, except the few who were lining up by the bus stop.

"Oh, do let's take a bus, Edward! Or I'll pay for the taxi, I can't let you do that. As it is, you're offering to give me your whole day and that's quite enough. I know how penniless students are, quite romantic really, the artist starving in his garret and all that, but fearfully impractical. So the bus it is, right, or we'll walk like everyone else."

Walk, I thought? No, not on your dear life, my dear, not in those delicate white sandals with their inch-high heels. And I don't see you sitting in an airless bus, with every eye turned on you in envy of me for the chic of your person and the gaiety of your laughter. So a taxi it will certainly be, and I can eat out of hall all next week.

So the taxi it was, and she bestowed on me another of her doe-eyed smiles as she climbed in. I pointed out the landmarks as we rode to my college -- Hobson's Conduit, the towers of King's College Chapel, the medieval gatehouses of Trinity and John's -- with Leanthe cooing and glancing in all directions as though she had never been in Cambridge before. Perhaps it was indeed all new to her, perhaps she had not been here before, but most people seem to find themselves in Cambridge at some time or other, and I was far from being able to tell how much joy and curiosity she was truly feeling inside herself at being in the heart of the university, or how much she was simply putting herself forward in every way she could in order to win my approval, even my friendship, so that I could at the right time and with the least embarrassment help her with answers to those questions to which she had somewhat cryptically referred in our first conversation.

We left the taxi at the porter's lodge of All Saints' College and walked across Founder's Court to my rooms, which looked down from the second floor onto the cobble paths and the lawns of the courtyard. To tell the truth, I was floating on air and hoping that every single person I knew in college was aware that I was the one who was squiring this vision of light golden loveliness, that it was me, Edward Brackenthwaite no less, who was privileged to walk through the College in friendly personal conversation with this glorious angel.

By now it was close to lunchtime, so I knew that she and I would not stay long in my rooms. There would just be comfortable time to sit back and relax from the train journey, the taxi ride and the walk through the college. I offered Leanthe a glass of sherry, South African I was ashamed to say because of the inferior quality, but those were the days of *apartheid* and most of my set would never buy anything South African, but S.A. sherry was the cheapest and that was the one preprandial libation we allowed ourselves, whiskey and such being quite out of reach. No, she demurred, anything like that would go straight to her head and she would feel silly, giggly, and then sleepy. Actually I rather liked the prospect of all that, but Leanthe's face was now beginning to take on a serious cast, anxious, worried, gloomy: flippancy and sparkle were fading, and that set me back. The shadow of a cloud had entered the room, and I remembered distinctly why it was that she had chosen to set out alone from London, away from all her set of lighthearted and joyous friends, in order to spend the day with someone she had never met before and with whom she might find she had precious little in common. All we had in fact were our two close but vastly different relationships with Sterling Rigaude. She sat staring silently out of the window, deep in her thoughts and with a frown crossing her brow every now and then, and even a tear at the corner of her eye. It would have been intrusive of me to have said a word, so I didn't do that and we shared our silence for several minutes on end, each one seeming to me longer than the one before.

"What a perfect beast I am, and how heavenly you are!" she suddenly exclaimed, sitting up straight and turning right around to gaze at me. "Here you are, giving up your whole day and your studies and whatever else you might be doing, just to walk around with me, and now I am letting you down by behaving abominably, ignoring you totally for hours and hours on end, thinking all the time of someone else and of my own troubles, instead of making even the teeniest little effort in the world to do something for you, to make it worth your while to give your whole day to me. A perfect beast, that's what I am!" And now she was very close to tears in earnest.

"I say, steady on there, steady on!" was the best that I could offer, for I had no other words. I wanted to add "<u>dear</u> Leanthe" or even "old girl," but I didn't dare. So I just looked at her, feeling that devoted love was starting to rise in my heart, together with sympathy for her and with anger at Sterling, since I knew perfectly well that he and his ways were at the bottom of all this. He had told me, he had warned me, and he had asked me to help him out of this trouble that he had himself created – without a doubt the first time he had ever asked anyone in the world to help him in any personal way. I had been immensely flattered, for there was something truly unusual, special and spectacular about Sterling, which Leanthe and everyone else had seen – and it was I, Edward Brackenthwaite, whom Sterling had chosen to be his closest friend and confidant. I must not let him down, and now I must look after this gorgeous Leanthe too.

"Leanthe, dear Leanthe," I said slowly and distinctly, feeling I was taking my life in my hands in daring to call her 'dear.' "You have come to Cambridge to talk about Sterling and what's going on inside him which would be very hard for anyone to understand and infinitely harder for you to take, that is, if you have any idea at all in the whole wide world what the whole blessed thing is all about."

I was getting tied up in my words, and this was most emphatically not the way I had planned so very carefully way back there- about a million years ago on the station platform about how I would broach the topic, so delicate it was, and so incomprehensible and completely unforgiveable it must seem to anyone who did not know Sterling Rigaude as closely as I did. I knew Sterling as Leanthe did not. I had to stop thinking about all that and try to rescue the conversation.

"But is this the time for the great discussion?" I blundered on. "Look here, enough's enough. I think we're both hungry and lunch isn't even in sight. You know as well as I do that I want to talk with you about Sterling, that's what this whole day is all about. But I'm jolly hungry, and I bet you are too. I mean, I'm sorry, I think I'm being too familiar, and you must think me the most terrible God-awful ass and all that. But why don't we go out and find some lunch first and then we can talk all we want to after that? What do you say?"

"A perfect beast and a God-awful ass – I think we are very well matched, and I love you for it!" And she rose from her place by the window, crossed the room to me and gave me on the cheek a quick kiss wet with her tears.

"Now, just let me take care of my face -- I must look a fright. And then yes, let's go for lunch, dear Edward."

We walked out of All Saints and across to Market Hill where we stopped at Willett's, the new and elegant sandwich stall that had recently opened for the season. I should have said that this was early May and Cambridge was looking delightful, her freshest and best. We chose sandwiches (smoked salmon for her, prawn salad for me), two water ices, and a bottle to share of sparkling but non-alcoholic cider – ideal. We wandered past Great St. Mary's, crossed King's Parade, entered King's by the decanter-and-wineglasses gateway, and made our way down to the Backs where we took our leisure and enjoyed our picnic on the sloping lawn beneath the willow tree. The scene was perfect, the colors serene: Leanthe aglow with her blonde hair and her lovely yellow suit, the acres of immaculate lawn as green as ever green could be, the Chapel and

King's Fellows' Building magnificent in their grey stone facades, and all set beneath the bluest sky of a radiant day in May.

"Punting! Oh, how delicious!" she squealed. "Oh, how absolutely what I've always wanted to do, all my whole life! Just look at them all out there on the river! Can't we do that? Oh <u>do</u> say yes, dear sweet, sweet Edward, do say yes! Please, pretty please!"

So of course we rose, crossed King's Bridge and walked out along the Backs, past the Mathematical Bridge at Queen's and across Silver Street to the Anchor, where we rented a punt for an hour. Poor Leanthe's feet in her elegant sandals were beginning to give her grief by this point, so she was very happy to lie down and take her ease in the bows of the punt, leaning back in her seat and gazing up at yours truly. Now I was never very much of a punter but at least I met with no disaster, did not fall into the river, nor lose the pole, but managed to stay upright with the punt floating along generally in the right direction. I must say, this is one of the greatest delights that this whole God-given world has to offer, to punt successfully on the Cam along the Backs on a sweet afternoon in May, looked up at with adoration (or was that my fond imagination?) by the most dazzling of all the heaven-sent young girls in their elegant summer dresses who graced the river from one end to the other on that glorious spring day. Well, it quite went to my head and I could not resist telling Leanthe about the broken-down old punt owned jointly by several of my friends and myself.

"Well, we had to find a name for the poor run-down old thing. So what do you think we came up with? Can't guess? 'Messalina', after the Roman empress of scandalous reputation, because she was possessed by so many people and because she couldn't sink any lower!"

Well, oh Lord, that did it! What a god-forsaken fool I was! I thought I had lost all the ground I had made with Leanthe because she shuddered and turned her head completely away from me. But after a moment I saw to my relief that she was quaking with laughter rather than disgust.

"Why, I never thought you had it in you, you wicked Edward! Whatever can I do with you?"

"Well, yes," I said with relief. "I can tell you what you can do, or rather what we can. We can take this punt back -- time's up anyway --- and then go to King's Chapel for Evensong, and there I can say my confession. The service is at half past three, and the choir, as of course you know, is absolutely the best, number one in the world. Vienna Boys Choir puts up a struggle, but my vote is for King's any day of the week. And you know, that might just set us into the right frame of mind for that down-to-earth discussion that we really have to have, yes we do. Not looking forward to it very much, to tell you the truth, but that's the name of the game and I absolutely can't let you down."

Well, it's King's Chapel that can't ever let you down, such a *tour de force* it presents to everyone entering it. The sheer size and height of the last great Gothic building constructed anywhere in the world bring peace and tranquility to all diminutive people walking quietly around inside. We passed through the great screen, a magnificent piece of dark Renaissance woodwork, and took our seats in the sub-stalls, gazing up at the vast array of stained glass windows above and on all sides.

'Storied windows richly dight,
Casting a dim, religious light,"

I murmured to Leanthe, so glad to be close to her and in such a setting. "That was Milton, you know, and since he was at Cambridge it's a fair bet that this is exactly what he had in mind."

Leanthe leaned forward in order to whisper something to me, but at that moment the organ started to play and we were both lost in the sweep and fullness of that great instrument. The choir processed in and stood at their desks behind the row of lighted candles that provided the only man-made lighting in the Chapel. Evensong took its lovely and stately path through the canticles and psalms, through the lessons and prayers, to the anthems and then to final blessing.

With the rest of the congregation we moved slowly down the length of the Chapel and out into the late afternoon sunshine. Only when we were outside, back in the world of everyday life, did we realize that we had unconsciously been holding hands ever since we left our seats in the sub-stalls. We gave each other a quick, almost nervous glance but we did not drop our hands. Without either of saying anything, we both knew that the time had come for the discussion we had to have, and that made both of us anxious, even a little afraid, she because she did not know what might be coming, I because I thought I might lose the charm of her company, the sparks of love that I felt warming my heart. Where to go to talk? The obvious answer was my rooms, so we walked back past Clare and Trinity Hall and took the little hidden passage that opens up into the glorious vista of Trinity Great Court. From there it was but a short way along Trinity Street and past John's to All Saints – and there we were, back in my rooms, she sitting again a little uneasily on the sofa by the window as I set a kettle on the gas ring for tea.

"Well," she said decisively, as she opened her eyes full at me, "we've got to start somewhere, so I'll go first. After all, I'm the one who has come to see you, and you have right to know what this is all about."

Actually of course I knew all too well what it was all about, because Sterling had pleaded with me to have this meeting and to explain everything to Leanthe in the gentlest way possible, so that she might learn and understand his position without bursting forth in righteous and unforgiving anger at him and at all that he had so thoughtlessly, even hard-heartedly, brought down upon her head, if not indeed upon her heart.

"The thing is," she started, and I could see the courage it took for her to say this, "I met Sterling first when once he came to our home soon after joining Daddy's company, and I really liked him. Not love at first sight or anything crazy like that, but I just liked him. He was so much fun to talk to, and he used to make me laugh -- oh, how we laughed! But I don't have any idea what he saw in me, because I just listened and that's about all."

"Oh, come on," I interrupted "Don't tell me you don't know how beautiful you are, and that any man in the world would give his eye teeth just to be the centre of your attention!" You can see how far I had come, from my nervous introduction to Leanthe on the station platform to this moment when I was frankly discussing with her the effects of her astonishing beauty. This is also the moment when I might mention something else highly relevant, that 'Daddy' was none other than Neville DeBecque, the Right Honourable the Earl of Goddesdown, former Chancellor of the Duchy of Lancaster, and now Chairman, Managing Director and God-knows-what-else of the Bank of London, in short one of the most prosperous and successful captains of finance and industry in the country with close personal ties to the Prime Minister and cabinet.

"Oh, please don't say things like that," she answered me. "It makes it all so trivial. And it wasn't like that at all. I mean, Sterling was really nice, just fun to be with – you know, there's something so very likeable about him, almost magnetic. Everyone seemed to feel it. Daddy and Mummy were quite taken with him, he was so respectful and he knew instinctively all the right things to say and all that. Oh Edward, Edward, do you have any idea at all what I am talking about?"

Yes, I did know exactly, and I proceeded to tell her all about Sterling Rigaude at school. He was universally popular -- charismatic would be the word -- and he was good at cricket and football, not truly gifted athletically but always in the front rank of boarding school society for his enthusiasm and for the passing jokes he would toss around. In the boarding house Rigaude, as we always called him (surnames being the only ones we knew in most cases and anyway the masters all called us by our surnames as if we had no other) had friends of every age, something highly unusual in that closely stratified atmosphere, where the oldest boys were demigods and the youngest little slavies.

How was it that I had come to know him so well, I who had no stature of any significance in the boarding house, who was thought of as too fond of the schoolbooks and not fond enough of the rough and tumble of the playing fields? The truth is that Rigaude and I shared one abiding interest that was of no concern and only the slightest appeal to anyone else in the house – birds. Yes, birds, <u>Birds</u>.

I had, from the age of six or seven, always known that birds would have a fascination for me all my life, and the joyful observation and the scientific study of birds have occupied many hours of my spare time. Biology was my special subject in those last two years of boarding school, with chemistry close behind. I adored birds as the free and spectacular spirits of the air, the fields, the woods, the sea shores and the open ocean that they are. Of course I reveled in the sight or 'scoping of a rarity, marking as red-letter days in my diary those on which I had seen a new species, but that was always subsidiary to the general delight of the whole. It didn't matter how many simple Goldfinches I saw, each one would make me catch my breath, and the same goes for each wheeling Fulmar at the cliff face, each stilting Redshank on the marshes, each House Martin skimming by the eaves.

But Rigaude had a different approach: he reveled in birds for the simple number of their species and the great variety of their forms. Why, the very walls of his room at boarding school were covered from end to end with photographs and paintings of every size of birds of all kinds, but most especially with maps of the world, countless maps, of this scale and that, of entire continents and of tiny groups of Oceanic islets, perhaps the only home of one little species. Once seen, a bird became for him a statistic, not the delightful message from God that each bird truly was to me.

And it was precisely here that we discovered not at first but slowly and surely in the days and months that passed in our last couple of years at boarding school, how profoundly we differed in our pursuit of birds, how eagerly we had at first agreed in a common pursuit, and latterly how solitary and far away we each became to the other as we peeled down together the layers of our enthusiasm. Here is what I found out, not all at once but progressively, bit by inexorable bit: Rigaude, with his driven personality, his determination to succeed where no other birder had gone before him, saw the whole world of birds, when the facts were laid down in front of each of us, as something quite different from what it was to me. Rigaude simply <u>had</u> to see with his own eyes every single species of bird on the planet, every single last one of them. He was a driven man. This total fixation was later recognized by the medical profession at the end of the twentieth century as a form of monomania, something that could take over and indeed destroy a person's life, but its insidious danger had not been established when Rigaude and I were young and when it was brushed off as something comic: the poor fellow will grow out of it, just give him time, and so forth. 'Ornithomania' it would later be labeled, and it has proved to be no joke but a consuming passion for its thankfully small number of devotees, a passion for which, without altogether realizing what they were doing, they would gladly sacrifice career, friends, family and all. Truly it is an affliction of the mind, but Sterling and I had no clear idea of that at all, although we did know that he would never grow out of his burning enthusiasm: it was a central part of the very essence of his being. So, once schooldays where behind him, he was compelled, absolutely compelled, to find the wherewithal to pursue his overwhelming goal. People could wait, people did not count for all that much, it was just that he <u>must</u> see his birds. He really and truly liked people, he reveled in their company; and he was not the least averse to the awakening allurements of the sexual life, but he stayed true to his vision: birds first, people as the extra, people as the the icing on the cake.

Well, in our schooldays Rigaude and I would delight in anything new we had discovered about birds, any aspect whatever, and we celebrated, almost worshiped the joy we had in common. And slowly from this grew a close personal intimacy, the product first of some occasional spontaneous remarks about family, politics, world affairs, what-have-you, and then progressively into a revelation of each to each of his own self, his hopes for his life, his plan and method of seeking and acquiring whatever it was that he most desired at that time. We ranged in our conversations far beyond birds into other common fields of our everyday life, but that was still the principal element in the long run. In short, we grew to know each other better than anyone else knew either of us. This is how life-long friendships are forged.

And I learned something else about Rigaude, something almost unique and not a little sinister: all the time he was climbing, climbing, climbing. This was not so much in order to reach any particular goal as the working of another integral part of his character and personality, a force driving him remorselessly on, always upwards, indeed he knew not where. He confessed to me that he recognized that people found his company pleasing, so he used that, and he sharpened his social skills: he did not enjoy sports, which constitute the very centre of life in a boarding school, for the sports themselves at all but for the camaraderie that he could exploit, in his movement upward, always using people for his purposes. Schoolwork was of precious little interest to him – he was no natural scholar at all – and he saw no way in which book learning or the approval of the masters would be of any use to him. So he turned to me for help, especially in his Latin, which we all had to learn and which he found fatuous in the extreme.

All this I described to Leanthe, and she took it in very carefully, nodding in recognition. She knew something about the ornithomania that Sterling and I shared, he being far more deeply infected than I, and she smiled patiently at what she took as merely a quirk of character. She also knew that Sterling had used me for my somewhat higher than average skills in Latin and in written English, and she added that surely I had used him reciprocally for his social skills compared to my innate shyness, and I freely admitted that she was perfectly right in that. So far, in all the account of the schooldays that Sterling and I had shared, Leanthe and I were truly in accord.

But then, two years ago, I had come up to university, while Sterling, having no use for book-learning or fine arts, had turned his back upon further education and entered the world of commerce and business in the City of London. To be perfectly frank, he wanted money, wanted money desperately, so that in the course of time, just as soon as he could drive time along, he would travel to the great tropical rainforests of the Amazon and New Guinea, to the remote highlands of the Peruvian Andes, to the beetling and frozen cliffs of Novaya Zemlya or Patagonia and to everywhere in between, to anywhere in the world where birds in all their multiplicity might find the means to survive. His love of birds had indeed metastasized into a mania in him, and to satisfy this thirst he absolutely had to carve for himself a successful and eminently profitable career in business.

His father, who had died while Sterling was in boarding school, had during the War been a colleague in war work and friend of a man of notable family but some years younger than himself, the Earl of Goddesdown. A couple of years before leaving school Sterling had set himself to cultivate the earl as someone who could be invaluable to him when the time came for him to embark upon his career in business. So Sterling turned all his considerable social charm, his charismatic appeal, upon the earl at their first and each subsequent meeting, so it was not long before Lord Goddesdown offered him a place as a junior member of the Bank of London whenever he should wish to take it up. The bank had offices in a great many cities around the world, and Sterling made up his mind to win for himself the best place he could. His lifelong goal, as might be imagined, was not to serve the Bank or to rise to the commanding heights of world finance, but to be the one who amassed the longest life list of species of birds in the world, no matter how he might do this and no matter how much it might cost. He would do it, he <u>would</u> do it, and he would use every means, every person he could in the pursuit of that ambition. The Bank of London would take him around the world, and he would travel there as the personal representative of its Chairman, the Earl of Goddesdown.

"Enter the Lady Leanthe DeBecque, daughter of the noble Earl," I said. Leanthe gulped, leaned forward and fixed me with what I can only describe as a most hostile glare. "I can see where you're going with all this," she hissed, "and let me tell you, you're lying, you're lying through your teeth when you insinuate that he would use me, use me, my foot!" Her voice almost rose to a scream.

I thought she would leap out of her chair and leave the room that instant, dash back to London with nothing accomplished, her troubles even greater than before, and my attempt to help both her and my friend completely in ruins. "He's not like that, not like that at all," she went on. "You may have known him as a boy, but I know him as a man, a real man, a far better man than anyone you describe. I just won't have it! You've got it all wrong, and I wouldn't be surprised if that wasn't all because of jealousy, yes, plain old-fashioned jealousy. *You* can't have him any longer as a schoolboy, and you don't want *me* to have him at all as a man. So there!" And with that she flung herself back in her chair and continued to glare at me through the tears which had sprung in anger to her eyes.

What was I to do? I sat very still for several minutes, and it is very much to Leanthe's credit that she did exactly the same, nothing more. We both knew that hysterics and fury could only hurt, not in any way help. She needed desperately to understand the man who was Sterling Rigaude and the boyfriend that he might or might not be, and we both knew that I was the only one, truly the only one, who held the key. She had come to me for help since Sterling had asked her to do that, and I stood there to offer her all the assistance I could since Sterling had begged me, in sincerity and in the name of our deep friendship, to do just that. So she froze herself into silence and waited for me to explain. As for me, I could not help but wonder, silently you may be sure, whether perhaps she did not very privately recognize some small uncomfortable worm of truth in my description of Sterling Rigaude as a driven man, charming to one and all, to men, women and children of all degrees, yet at heart, when the chips were down, out for himself alone. And yet, that would in fact be only a superficial delineation of this complex fellow: there were secret depths to him or I would not have loved him, and he was caught in a mania from which neither I nor anyone else had any idea how to rescue him.

"When first he met you," I began again, gently and hesitatingly, "he must have recognized, as we all do, that you are a perfect vision of feminine loveliness." Here she tossed her head in irritation, as though that were irrelevant. "And he was scared out of his wits because you held the upper hand. He knew people were drawn to him, were always drawn to him, but now he had met someone who could draw people to *her* far more strongly, by her wonderful loveliness and by the transparent kindness and sincerity of her character. He had never known competition before, and he didn't know what to do with it." By now Leanthe was staring at me wide-eyed, all her hostility subsiding. And I, remembering how tongue-tied and maladroit I was in the presence of any girl, was utterly amazed at myself, my daring and my forthrightness in confronting this whilom debutante, the toast of London society, with the intoxicating consequences of her radiant sex appeal. I clenched my jaw, pushed all that right behind me, and took up the story.

"So he stuck to his guns," I went on, "and proceeded as he had always done, in the only way he knew how to proceed. He courted your father, if I may use the term, made up to him in every way that occurred to him, subtly and thoughtfully, for Sterling is no fool, and the consequence was that he secured employment in the Bank of London, but of course only on the bottom rung of the ladder – not an office-boy, you know what I mean – but as a junior trainee at the foot of the long, steep ladder. He was appalled at the prospect of long years in a totally subordinate position, having, in his simplicity, envisaged that his father's friendship with the chairman would set him up on the fast track, the very fast track."

"Are you trying to tell me that that's why he made a play for me?" she interjected. "Because if you are, your heart is black, black as pitch, and I simply won't sit here and listen to such nonsense. He really does care deeply for me, you know!" And the tears ran down her cheeks again – and I, I almost broke down too.

"Dear, dear Leanthe, do please let me try to tell you what I am certain has happened, what I believe and know with all my heart. Sterling may first have looked at you as an entryway, an ally if you will, who would if things went well lead him closer to your father and to the goal that he had set for himself. At first he may have looked at you that way – in fact I think he did. No, I am <u>sure</u> he did. He has as good as told me so. He had never cared deeply for anyone in his life. I was closer to him than either of his parents, I knew that from the outset, but he didn't really need me, or indeed care about me in the very depths of his being. He was just getting along in the world, moving ahead along the pathways he had chosen for himself, so easy, so smooth, on account of his charismatic appeal to one and all, that he really knew no other way of looking at life. No one, no one at all had ever really touched the essence of his being or come anywhere close to doing so.

Now I have to tell you something about his parents. They were surely devoted to each other when they married, right after the war. I knew Professor Cedric Rigaude, Sterling's father, only slightly since he died when Sterling and I were in boarding school. He struck me as a lonely and disappointed man. He had been an archeological scholar of some note and great promise, an Orientalist, and he wanted oh so deeply to spend years at a time in the Far East, but his wife's health failed her, I don't know why or how, and she just could not be removed from the care of her doctors in London. So, in his loyalty to her, Sterling's father felt compelled to stay in London too, and to set himself to work not among the remote peoples of the world but in old and musty libraries of academic institutes, frustrated and finally deeply embittered that someone, albeit someone he loved very deeply, had brought uselessness and irrelevance to his life. Sterling resolved even as a child that he would never, never, never follow that road -- No Sir! No love would ever hold him back from the desires and goals of his life, whatever the cost might be.

And then you appeared, dear Leanthe. That's what I meant when I said that half an hour ago, but I spoke so clumsily and of course you had no idea what I meant -- how could you? Oh, Sterling had had a date or two along the way and I expect there were a couple of kisses, but I don't think that there had ever been anything more. And then, as I say, you came into his life, first as a means of approaching the Boss, so he turned on upon you all his charm with its customary overwhelming effect --"

Here she stiffened and I thought we might have another outburst, but before that wave broke over us, I rushed on.

"And then he fell in love! Head over absolute bloody heels! He had had no intimation at all that anything like that could ever, ever happen to him: it just wasn't in the game plan. But it did, oh my God, it surely did! And at the same time your affections for him, my dear Leanthe, took a turn in the same direction, oh yes they did, and you can't deny it. He has told me all about that, indeed he has. He saw the light in your eyes, and he of all people almost started quoting poetry."

At this Leanthe smiled a shy smile behind the tears that were drying on her cheeks, and oh, I wanted so much to kiss them away, but I had more sense than to reach for her.

"So now we've come to the end of the road," I said. "Sterling is panicking for the first time in his life, and for the first time in his life he is reaching out to another person for help: he's venting to *me*. He is so afraid for you, of what he might in his clumsiness do to you, how deeply, irrevocably he might hurt you, that he has asked me to try to explain everything to you. He is terrified of any personal commitment -- I have never seen anyone so terrified. He wants to get back to how things were a few months ago, when you and he laughed together and both your parents approved of his presence around the house now and again. Let me tell you, my dear, my very great dear, that I have absolutely no idea of how you thought your time, days or years, with Sterling might pan out in the end. Perhaps you dreamed of marriage one day, a home and a family. Well, let me tell you this, Sterling would take his own life, I verily believe that, before he would ever tread that road. Travel, money, birds and a fast life with a death years before the first signs of old age make their appearance, that's what he envisages, and, believe you me, that's exactly what he'll do. Yes, he will! He will certainly do just that.

And my job -- oh Lord, dearest Leanthe, it's so difficult -- is to try to ease the path for you. He really does care for you in his own way, he really does, I've said that, and your beauty and sex appeal really are overwhelming. Every man in the world would lose his better judgment in your presence, you know that, it's just the way things are – and it's wonderful, because here I am, spouting forth all kinds of nonsense, looking right into the eyes of the most beautiful girl I have ever seen anywhere in the whole wide world – and now I think I'll just go away and die because I don't think I am making any kind of sense to you...."

Leanthe had cried so much and so hard that she simply couldn't cry any more, so she burst out laughing and flung herself across the room at me, and gave me a long, long hug. There was really nothing more to be said by either of us after that, so neither of us did indeed say anything at all. We just hugged. I felt that I had failed altogether, that I had not in the least helped her to face her future, or helped that rascal Sterling Rigaude to come to terms with the sin he had so thoughtlessly and blindly committed, and that therefore I had failed utterly in all the offices of friendship, both to my lifelong friend from school and to this newfound most glorious Girl.

And then it was time to be thinking about that train back to London. Leanthe and I had created in just a few hours such a good heartfelt friendship between us that neither of us wanted her to go, but life has to move on and she did not want to be late home. So we pulled ourselves together and walked over to Market Hill to find a taxi back to the station. On the long platform we just stood in silence for the most part, Leanthe, always a vision of perfect loveliness in her golden aura, sobbing softly from time to time into her handkerchief, and I looking out past her to the horizon, doing all I could to hold myself back from joining her in that exercise.

Puffing and wheezing, the train from the North pulled in, and we stood and looked each other deeply in the eye. We both knew that this was a real goodbye, that her life in London and mine at Cambridge really had nothing in common, and that her friends and I, and my friends and she, would never mingle. The train stopped, the steam hissed, the doors opened, the guard called out, the whistles blew.

Suddenly Leanthe was in my arms, all over me, her head turned away from me across my shoulder. "Thank you, thank you, my dearest, dearest dear," she whispered, "but God only knows what's going to happen." And then she embraced me, such a strong hug, such a strong hug! But never a word more, never a word -- and she was gone.

A week or two later Sterling let me know that he and Leanthe had 'drifted apart' (his words), so I knew that I had done my duty to both of them in my sad role as Anticupid. Naturally I never saw Leanthe again in my life and I have never heard a word from her, but she still lives in a secret corner of my heart where I cherish her, and I send her my blessings whenever I think to do so – and that is very often.

CHAPTER 9

SUMMER AT THE
CARONSON INSTITUTE

I t was evening on the first day, in June 1975, of the first Caronson
Summer Institute, that creation of the banker Samuel J.
Caronson, designed by him to perpetuate the memory of his dearly loved twenty-five year old son Simon, killed in a mountaineering
accident the previous summer. Now the celebration of the opening
of the Institute was behind us, the grieving and emotional speeches
of Mr. and Mrs. Caronson appreciated by the staff, by the Director
of the Institute, Jonathan Dunkerley-Jones, and by the sixty young
people, the first participants in what was sure to become an annual institution, the Student Study and Mountaineering Program.
Then the Caronsons and their friends and family members drove
away in their long sleek black cars, back to Aspen or Denver, and
Jonathan Dunkerley-Jones settled down to the business of introducing himself and his colleagues to the young people. There
were twenty-eight adults in all, teachers for the mornings of study,
members of the athletics department for the afternoons and weekends of mountain sports, two registered nurses, the chef and his
kitchen staff, secretaries and handymen. Of course the students

would play their part too, with cooking, cleaning up, and maintenance work indoors and out. It was part of the ethic of the new institute that no job was too high for the lowest peon not to play a part in it, and no task too low for the mighty not to give their share.

Jonathan -- all were on first-name terms -- announced to the students that there would be an assembly first thing tomorrow morning to go over the academic side of things, to give each student his or her schedule and to allow for all the changes that anyone might wish to make. The classes were all to be directed toward the life of the mountains: geology, botany, zoology, ecology, and conservation; the life of people who made their living in the mountains; and local, state and federal law. There was a buzz of excited anticipation among the students at the prospect of all these attractive choices.

This evening the students were invited to make their selection of mountain sports, knowing that this would be a commitment for every afternoon for four weeks and for every weekend with camping out on the Saturday night, whatever the weather. These were the choices: rock climbing, white water kayaking, horseback riding, and mountain hiking. Again there was an excited buzz. There would be one or more adults in each group, depending on the number of students who signed up and the availability of resources: clearly ten people could not ride eight horses, for example.

There was a moment of suppressed laughter when the adult leader of the mountain hiking group, Rodney Tregannet, introduced himself: he hobbled in on crutches, with one leg in a cast. In his embarrassment he apologized profusely, explaining that a car had hurtled downhill altogether too fast, driven by a young man who had never even been in the mountains before, and who now sat in jail at that very moment after he had run down and killed a hiker. Before that disaster he had forced Rod Tregannet's car off the road on a hairpin bend, where only the guard rail had saved Rod's life. So alas, with a broken leg he could not take on a group of mountain hikers this summer. All this had happened just three days ago, and there had been no time to find a full-time qualified replacement. I am Rod Tregannet's nephew, Edward Brackenthwaite, and I had been expecting to work hard through the summer to complete my Ph.D thesis but was glad to take over the hiking group on the weekends. I could not afford to give up my weekday afternoons as well, so the hikers would be apportioned out among the other sports groups on those occasions. Presentation of my thesis could wait until October, but I could not delay it later than that. The students gave me polite applause, but it was immediately clear that mountain hiking would not be the first choice of many of them.

The students themselves were a mixed group, decidedly a mixed group. Samuel and Rachel Caronson had made it a cardinal principle of the Institute that, first, no young person who was already experienced in mountain sports should attend since the whole purpose of the Institute was to introduce young people to the Rockies in a most responsible way, and second, that they should be selected – a process in which the Caronsons had played an active part themselves – on the basis of their widely differing backgrounds, in order to bring forward another principle of the Institute, namely, taking the young out of their familiar circles so that they would learn to cooperate with and depend upon people of their own age but from very different backgrounds. The Institute would gladly provide full financial support for the students wherever necessary. So there were present some from the 'St. Grotlesex' prep schools of New England, some from overseas (English, French and Mexican in this first year, but the field would surely widen), a good number from inner-city public schools, farm boys from the corn belt, fundamentalist Baptists from the deep South, and the sons and daughters of factory hands. The only qualifications had been enthusiasm and skill in presenting themselves as people who would contribute something of good solid worth both to their new community, the Caronson Institute, and later to the school and social environment to which they would return, -- and then beyond that, they would have to demonstrate that they possessed some special spark, highly individual and greatly to be desired by the Institute. The students did tend to look at each other warily that first evening, each seeking out one or two companions from backgrounds not too remote from his or her own. As anticipated, however, after only a week or two all that unfamiliarity had disappeared and they all, or almost all, took with delight to the strenuous life of the mountaineering institute.

Each group leader in turn explained the nature of his mountain sport, its challenges and its rewards. Once that was done the students signed up for their choices in order of preference. Well, as might be expected, white water kayaking took the lead, except among those few who had a natural aversion to water or who had encountered in some form a drowning or a near-disaster back at home. Rock-climbing appealed to the huskiest of the boys, and also to some of the most lissome of the girls, a combination that the staff had not altogether foreseen. Horseback riding was greatly over-subscribed, partly because of that fine natural affinity that some young people, girls in particular, often feel for horses. But poor mountain hiking came a cropper: only three people signed up in the first round, one a tall lanky lad, Alexis Lenglen, a stalwart youth with a faraway look in his eyes who seemed already to be striding forth among the mountain peaks; the second a gentle and good-mannered youngster from France, Pierre Delarue, who felt anxiety at what seemed to him the ferocious nature of the other sports except riding, but he had never known a horse; and the third Meg Suffern, at fourteen one of the youngest members of the institute, pale, somewhat overweight, shy and self-effacing. How had she come to be selected for the Institute, I wondered? I realized that I would find out soon enough when the time came for me to take over responsibility for the group.

Jonathan Dunkerley-Jones and Bud Tamerack, the Sports Director, put out an immediate appeal to anyone who had even contemplated mountain hiking to make that his or her choice at this time. No one stepped forward. "Wouldn't anyone like to join up?" asked Jonathan. "You would have great influence in this little group, have things go the way you want, like choosing which peak to climb, a level of choice you might have not in one of the large and popular sports, and we would all be grateful to you for fulfilling the spirit of the Institute. Any comers, then?" After a moment a tall, poised and graceful girl stepped forward, Caitlin Kennedy. One could see that she was efficient and had a capable and kindly disposition. "Thank you, Caitlin! Thank you, Caitlin!" he said, and everyone clapped.

"Well now, let's see," said Jonathan, beginning to perspire. "Where do we go from here? You know, I really would like to put in a very strong good word for mountain hiking. It's actually in lots of ways the best of all these sports. You may not see that at first, and I surely don't blame you there, but listen to this. You're in Colorado, right, slap-bang in the heart of the grand old Rocky Mountains. Splendid! Will you ever again in your life get a chance to see the world-sweeping view from one 14,000 foot peak across all the miles to another, with all the wonders of whole ranges of mountains and valleys spread out before you – if you are riding a horse up a steep, stony trail in the woods below-- or if you are inching your way roped to your friends up the face of a precipice -- or if you are way down below the mountain peaks in the canyons, your face awash with spray as you navigate at breakneck speed past one great boulder after another? Think of all you'll be missing! Why, I bet when we all get together on the last day of the Institute and tell all the stories of our adventures and expeditions, there will be lots of you just wishing and wishing that you had opted for the peaks rather than the saddles, the rock faces and the kayaks – not that they aren't all wonderful, they certainly are that, oh yes absolutely, but let's hear it for mountain hiking! Any volunteers now, or shall we take our chances with ballots? I hate to say it, but we really have to even out the numbers. So anyway, let's go to round two of the voting and see where we stand after that."

The students took back their voting slips and crossed their first choices out on Jonathan's instructions. Then they turned the slips over and listed their choices anew – and indeed there were changes. First, and somewhat surprisingly, the numbers for the three most favored sports evened out to a large degree, with the pleasing result that almost everyone would with gladness have his or her first choice, and second, no fewer than five students had now marked mountain hiking as their first choice! They had been won over by Jonathan's eloquence, and they also realized that the visits every weekday afternoon to the other sports would give them a smorgasbord opportunity that none of the other students in the Institute would experience at all.

"Yeah, man, that's really cool!" exclaimed Duke Sutton in a voice that carried clear across the room. "I sure can dig seeing all them mountain peaks around me! Wait till I tell the folks back in the city what they's all missing!" Duke Sutton came from Harlem, and his teacher had helped him with his application for the Institute. She had not quite written it for him but had helped him to express his eager enthusiasm in words that another could read. And enthusiastic he surely was, eager to take his chances in standing out, far away from his familiar urban environment.

Aaron Blankenstein was a tall, slender boy with owlish glasses and a scholarly mien. "There will be poetry in the silence of the mountain peaks," he said, "and I would dearly love to listen to that. So I'm for mountain hiking."

"How interesting -- and that fascination with nature appeals to me too. Listening to poetry? Oh yes, I will listen with you too!" said Iris Singleton, soon to be a senior at Miss Porter's School in Farmington. She stood up, an elegant figure in her loose purple shorts and lavender sleeveless top, over which her long black curls were spreading.

"Oh what the heck," exclaimed Rosie Durrindale, "I never saw a mountain yet, 'cos there ain't none in Chicago where I come from. But I'm game for it and I'll get myself swinging round them peaks like nobody's business."

So there it was, the group of eight mountain hikers complete:

Alexis Lenglen, the tall, well-built boy from Marin County, California, eager to hike, to conquer the mountains; an original volunteer for the sport.

Pierre Delarue, the young Frenchman, anxious to be accepted and to fit in, but no real hiker. He had been one of the first to sign up, but that was in good part because he did not know horses and was somewhat in fear at the prospect of kayaking or rock climbing.

Meg Suffern, the youngest member of the group, pale and chubby, looking as though she were filled with trepidation, as indeed she was, but one who had been quick to sign up since she thought hiking would be the least demanding activity.

Caitlin Kennedy, athletic, good-looking and graceful but with a somewhat superior manner. She came from an old family in tidewater Virginia, and attended St. Margaret's School in Tappahannock.

Duke Sutton, from Harlem, African-American, gregarious, tall and loose-limbed, eager to be the centre of attention, with a loud voice and a way of flinging his arms around and shouting aloud.

Aaron Blankenstein, tall, gentle, dreamy and self-effacing, a lover of poetry; the son of a nationally known rabbi in Washington, DC.

Iris Singleton, from Canton, Connecticut, a trim young lady with a sense of fashion, self-contained, a successful student of the history of art at Miss Porter's School in Farmington.

Rosie Durrindale, an easy-come-easy-go, cheerful and boisterous, up-for-anything kind of a gal, ready to laugh at the world.

Rod Tregannet turned to me and slapped me on the back. "Look here," he said, "we gotta thank Jonathan for this. He's some great guy! And then let's go meet the kids. Look, they're introducing themselves to one another right now."

So Uncle Rod and I crossed over to join the group, and general conversation ensued. The next day the academic assembly and the signing up for courses would take up the morning, and then in the afternoon Rod planned to explain in some detail to the hikers what would be involved, and how they would be distributed piece-meal among the three other sports for the weekday afternoons. He would be working that out with Jonathan and the other instructors this evening before going over it with the hikers tomorrow afternoon. For the latter part of the afternoon tomorrow he would send them off on a short and easy hike, no more than an hour or two at most, with no packs: it would take some little time to acclimate them to the high altitude, for them to grow used to their stalwart new boots, and to wearing packs which when stuffed full could weigh up to forty pounds.

⇒╬⇐

The first of the four weekends arrived soon enough. Uncle Rod explained to me that I would drive a farm truck with all the hikers in the back, to the foot of Grayson's Fork, a stream in a wooded valley that sloped down from the mountains, and hike from the end of the dirt road there up to the timber line at the head of Grayson's Creek. There we would set up our overnight camp, each hiker having carried in his or her backpack a sleeping bag, mattress roll and plastic tarp to keep out any rain that might fall, plus food for the evening meal, for breakfast and for lunch the next day. It was hard to keep all of that under forty pounds, but already Duke Sutton and Alexis Lenglen, the two largest and strongest of the boys, had offered to help the less stalwart girls by sharing part of their loads. I was particularly glad of that: it showed how even at the start, before the first mountain hike, the group was beginning to coalesce into a team, not just a string of students.

That first serious hike, uphill along a rocky path, was hard going for Pierre Delarue who was not a strong lad but who was ashamed to admit that he had any difficulty. Meg Suffern stumbled along gamely, encouraged by cheerful banter from Rosie Durrindale. Alexis Lenglen and Duke Sutton strode out together but did not at all welcome my firm orders to them, never to go ahead so far that they were out of my sight. They seemed to resent that, or rather to resent the slow pace set by Meg and Pierre, so I had to take them aside at our first rest stop and let them know in no uncertain terms that they were not individuals out here going wherever they wanted and however they wanted, but that they were members of a special and privileged group and it was their duty to serve that group. They responded well, and offered to take the sleeping bags and some other items of the lesser brethren so that we could all proceed at a little closer to the pace that they would have set for themselves. Then it was lunchtime, and after that the forest began to thin out as we climbed higher and higher. The creek tumbled along next to the path, and we all filled our canteens. Caitlin, Aaron and Iris accepted the high-altitude pills that I offered: after all, this was their first strenuous activity at a noticeable height above sea level.

We pushed on steadily after lunch, and conversation had indeed flagged by the time I called a halt for the night, having set ourselves to make our campsite several hours before nightfall. Uncle Rod had told me of a clump of ten- or twelve-foot high jagged boulders, an outcrop from the mountainside just below the tree line, and that was my objective. The rocks would provide some cover, shelter from the wind if it should chance to blow although nothing significant was forecast, and a measure of privacy for the girls when it came time to bundle up for the first time in our sleeping bags. The site was easy to find, and I called a halt.

"Phew," gasped Duke. "I thought you was never going to let us stop! What's with you, man? Here you are, driving us all over the top of the mountains."

The others slung their packs off their backs, and leant against them, their heads back and their feet straight out in front, doing nothing but looking up at the pine trees and easing their aching legs and backs.

Soon it was time to think about dinner. Lunch had been easy, sandwiches brought from the kitchen back at the Institute, but dinner would need cooking, even though it was only hamburgers with lettuce, tomatoes, crackers and fruit. The boys unpacked the frying pan and griddle that they had been carrying, together with the meat patties in an ice pack, and the rest of the food. Unconsciously – it seemed natural – the boys scattered to look for firewood while the girls assembled the dinner. On any other occasion it would not have been a meal that any of them would have relished, but they had exerted themselves for a good many hours now, and so it tasted pretty darned good and not one morsel was left for the squirrels, the chipmunks, the jays, the crows or the nutcrackers.

After dinner and after sitting in a circle around the campfire, some of us were soon thinking of turning in for the night while others were determined to stay up to see the brilliant mountain moon and the myriad stars that are always so sadly obscured for the much-to-be-pitied urbanites below. Before any of that, however, we had to establish our nests for the night, and again I was impressed at the spirit of cheerful cooperation that had taken such a good hold of the group. At this early stage in our acquaintanceship the girls wished to be separate from the boys, and the boys respected that, perhaps with a wink and a sly, sidelong glance but with never a single reproachable word. So we stretched out long, sturdy cords and fastened them to clefts in the rocks or to forks in the tangled low trees, and from one to another of these lines we slung our sheets of heavy plastic, thereby creating a simple slanting roof that would shed any rain that might be thoughtless enough to disturb our slumber. In short order nine such canopies were spread between the branches and the clefts, and waterproof bed-rolls and sleeping bags were laid out below, each with its owner's backpack nested within and a bundle of clothing, rain poncho and towel amassed to serve as a welcome pillow.

When night fell the wide-awakes gazed, gazed and gazed again in open-mouthed awe as stars of all sizes and brilliance seemed to burst towards us right through the heavens, so that there was scarcely space for the midnight black of the sky to assert itself between the myriad, myriad points of light. Pierre came into his own at this point, quoting from memory line after line of French poetry in praise of the heavens. He would not tell us the author, becoming suddenly abashed when asked, so we surmised that it must have been his own verse, but he would not admit to that. And then, surfeited with awe, the young people splashed their feet in the mountain stream that tumbled past our campsite and screamed happily at the icy shock until I had to act as the adult in the group and to urge them to be quiet, first for the sake of those who needed to sleep in order to regenerate their strength for the morrow, and secondly, I dared to express, for the sake of the life of all the wild denizens of the mountains, so many of whom only venture forth at night, perforce shunning the day and its host of predators. How would these creatures feel at the raucous distur-bance of their primeval environment, the only home they could ever know? So the boisterous students crept off in silence to their little shelters, maybe blaming themselves and each other as the disturbers of Eden.

"Morning has broken, Like the first morning," sang out Iris in a clear, strong tone. That was how we were awakened some hours later, so we opened our eyes, grasped hold of where we were, stretched our limbs, and soon sat upright, blearily taking in our surroundings and realizing that breakfast would not of itself come to us: we had to go fix it.

Soon we had that behind us, oatmeal and tea or coffee, so we bundled up our packs and set off once more up to the shoulder of the mountain where we would cross over on comparatively level ground, skirting the great rocky mass and the highest peak above us in a long three-quarter loop that would bring us to another trail back down from the peak – Mount Grayling, just over 12,000 feet – and thence to the spot where we had left our farm truck.

I had been warned of a possible snag, however, and had come as well prepared as I could be, with a good length of rope and an ice-axe. The group had been eying these, some askance and some with happy anticipation of excitement to come. Well, this was the situation: on the slope of the mountain that we were to traverse, the northern slope, there might well still be snow lodged in the deep, steep gullies that ran down the mountainside. 'Corries' they would be called in Scotland, I told the group. "Yippee, real snow!" yelled out the irrepressible Duke Sutton, dashing headlong past everyone else in order to be the first to freeze his hands, to taste the snow and then to pelt it at his companions.

"Shut up, you goddam fool!" I shouted after him, "and get right back here this instant. You slip on that snow and you could be hurtling right down the mountain so fast that no one and nothing could save you. You would crash headlong into the broken rocks at the bottom of the tongue of snow. Why the devil can't you do a simple thing like listen and wait for instructions? Better people than you and I have met their death on these mountains. Don't you remember how Mr. Caronson told us how his son Simon, who was just a few years older than you, had been killed, yes, killed dead, stone dead, right about here in these mountains only last summer? Now look here, I'm the boss here, the only boss, and you damn well better remember that – not because I am any big shot or anything like that, but I do know mountain hiking – and you don't!"

That did it, or rather, I thought that did it. Duke slunk back, and then had the good grace to come right up to me and apologize. He's a good lad at heart, I thought, as I gave him a quick slap on the back, just about a million miles from his home and background in Harlem.

We approached the steep slope of frozen snow, no more than fifty or sixty feet across, but at least a quarter of a mile long down the mountainside, and we had encountered it halfway along its length. The narrow path across the rocky scree had been whitened by the boots of many of our predecessors, and we could dimly make out the trail starting up again on the opposite side of the corrie.

"I think the sensible thing to do," opined Iris Singleton in her clipped New England accent, "would be to make our way carefully down to the bottom of the snow – 'corrie,' did you call it? – and then climb up the other side, and pick up the trail again."

"Yes, yes, I'm with you," called out Meg Suffern, whose wide-eyed expression betrayed her anxiety. "Yes, count me in too," echoed Aaron Blankenstein. "I really don't have the best sense of balance or head for heights."

"Oh, for goodness sake," broke in Alexis Lenglen. "Didn't we all come here to get the most out of the mountains and everything they have to offer? How are we going to get anywhere at all if we chicken out and turn back at the first challenge? I'm all for challenges. That's why I'm here at the Caronson Institute and I did kind of guess that all of you were too – but I guess I guessed wrong. You just want to stay in the parking lot all day."

"OK, enough sarcasm," I interjected. "Maybe you'd all like to have a vote on it. That's ok with me, but like I said, I'm the boss, so if there are eight of you I have nine votes all to myself."

Silence. "I have hiked for three summers around here" I continued, "and I do believe I know how to do it. If you will all simply listen and do exactly as I say, we will all get safely over that lick of snow, which I have crossed a couple of times with groups before, and we will all stand ten miles high for having done so. Right? Anyone for turning back, or for grinding all the way down to the tip of the corrie and then heaving ourselves up again? That scree is pretty steep you know, and those stones are all loose and sharp."

Silence again. Good, I thought, we're on our way, with only one ego slightly bruised. So I tied one end of the rope securely around my waist and gave the other end expressly to Duke Sutton, murmuring to him quietly "I am counting on you," and then also to Alexis Lenglen, the other strong young man in our group, "You too, my friend."

"Now listen carefully, all of you! There are no second chances here, and no fooling around, absolutely no fooling around, get it? I'll go over first and cut out steps all the way in the frozen snow with the ice-axe that I have brought along for exactly this purpose. That should be easy because I know another group passed this way only two or three days ago, and we haven't had any rain since then, certainly not enough anyway to glaze over the frozen snow and make it slippery. I promise you, I'll cut out good, deep steps with a firm flat footing so that all of you can easily follow along. The only thing is to concentrate on what you are doing, to look at where you are placing your feet. Never look up! Never look around! Never look down! You can do all the looking around you want right now, taking in these incredible mountains, but when crossing an ice corrie, no sir, no looking around at all. You'll need your best balance. When I get to the other side, with all the steps neatly cut out, I'll untie the rope from my waist and have Duke and Alexis haul it in for the next person to cross, and they will tie each of you in. Duke and Alexis will wind the rope about themselves and brace themselves firmly just in case anyone slips. Then the worst that could happen would be a short slide down the hillside for the length of the rope. I checked beforehand and Alexis has been a Scout for years and years, so he knows his knots. Right, Alexis?"

"Yes sir, yes sirree!" sang out Alexis, proud to have the responsibility cast upon him.

"Duke, you go second last, got it? Alexis ties you in and you cross like all the others. Then we toss the rope back to Alexis, throwing it well across the corrie. You and I, Duke, will end up tied together at this end, and Alexis will be the last to come across. Right. Now has everyone got an idea of what he or she has to do? Questions? No questions, that's ok. If we play it right, this will be one big thrill to go into those letters home after this weekend!"

Everything started well. With the rope tied firmly about me I made my way across the frozen snow, cutting out deep steps as I moved along. I reached the other side and tossed my end of the rope back, and one by one, some with confidence and some with the jitters, the others followed me. Finally I was about to heave a sigh of relief, with only Duke and Alexis to bring up the rear. Alexis started to make his way across when I realized with wide eyes that I had ordered him to be the last, preceded by Duke. That was a mistake all right! Now who was to check that Duke could tie a good strong knot around himself for the final traverse? The Boy Scout had gone ahead. Well, there was nothing for it: Alexis could not turn around half way across, so narrow and deep were the steps. And if I were to make him go back and then take last place, why, Duke would be so humiliated that he would surely try something stupid like crossing with no rope at all. So Alexis crossed over and tossed the rope back to Duke, who did try to tie himself on securely, but I couldn't see the knot. Oh what a goddam fool I am, I thought, please God let him make his way across all right. Why the devil hadn't I gone back after Alexis crossed over? What an idiot! As Duke started out I realized too late that for certain sure Alexis or I should have gone back to inspect the knot, but now it was too late for that. Then Duke made a complete ass of himself. Right in the middle he stood up to his full height, let out a whoop and flung his arms into the air in triumph. Of course he lost his balance, of course his pitiful knot slipped, of course he plunged right down the steep snow slope! But a miracle happened – God was looking after him. He managed to keep himself aimed true, flat on his back, his head uphill and his heels downhill. And he was lucky that when he landed at the foot of the long slope he managed to brace himself and somehow to avoid a twisted ankle or broken bones. He called up at us with a wave and a laugh, and clambered up the rocky slope. He was tired, quiet and subdued by the time he reached us, and we were all cold with waiting in the freezing mountain air.

What could I say? We had both been idiots in our different ways, and if he had hurt himself, conceivably had killed himself, his blood would have been on my head – although he did not know that. So I said nothing at all, just glared at him and shrugged. Off we set again, as I offered up a silent prayer of gratitude and thanksgiving.

We circled the steep shoulder of Mt. Grayling and began our long descent through open rock, half scree, twisted dwarf trees, stunted pine woods, and finally the mixed forest of the lowlands. There was just one swift, fast-flowing river to cross, the South Fork of the Grayling River, and then we would soon be back at our truck, driving home to the Caronson Institute. But it was not to be as simple as that.

We made our way steadily around the shoulder of the mountain and down the long steady slope of the trail that would lead us to the truck. Just a mile short of where we had left the truck there was a gorge to traverse, a gorge cut out by the river and in itself quite impossibly steep and rugged for this group of tyros to climb down. There was just one way across, just one, and that lay by way of a wooden bridge across the South Fork. Well, there should be no real problem about that, I thought. Sure, there had been a really heavy downpour a few weeks ago, but any floodwaters would have abated long ago and we ought to be able to cross by the old log bridge with no trouble. No trouble, did I say? Oh Lord, the severe storm had washed the bridge out, or rather left it dangling in position at a most hazardous angle! My mind raced: what to do? One: attempt the bridge and risk lives – not such a good idea. Two: look for a way down into the gorge and across the river – but the jagged crags and the swift flow of the icy water made that impossible. Or three: climb all the way back up the mountain, retrace our steps over the snow corrie, and return by the path along which we had ascended yesterday – but we would never complete that by nightfall, and we had no more food for supper tonight or breakfast tomorrow. So, once again, what to do?

I took a closer look at the bridge, and took Alexis, Caitlin and Iris forward with me. They could help me decide. The bridge had been built across the river from level ground to level ground, with a thirty foot vertical drop to the roaring river beneath. Two strong tree trunks had anchored the sides of the bridge, stretching across the gorge, and shorter trunks and straight branches had been lashed or nailed to them at right angles, making a corduroy surface to the bridge itself. But one of the great tree trunks had dislodged itself at the far end and now hung down at a 45 degree angle, twisting the branches to which it was attached into a quarter spiral. The nearer end of this trunk and both ends of the other trunk still held fast, or certainly looked as though they did.

So there was really nothing for it but for each of us to take turns to cross, tied securely round the waist once again and anchored by two of the strongest of our number on the open bank this side, and to a nearby pine tree on the other side. There was no question here of cutting elegant footholds in frozen snow. We would be treading on rough logs, horizontal where started but each one at a steeper incline until the slope grew close to 45 degrees down to our right at the far end. Could I be justified in risking young lives or limbs with this challenge? If anyone slipped and had to be hauled back up the log slope, wouldn't he or she be so shaken and deeply scratched by that experience, probably bleeding from snags sticking out from the logs, that he would have even less chance of a successful crossing the second time? And how were they to keep their balance? We only had the one rope so there could be no handrail.

"There's only one thing to do," said Alexis. "Your ice axe has a decent grip at one end where the tines point out front and back, and it has a sharp point at the other end. Couldn't we use it as a hiking cane, with each person using it, holding it by the comfortable grip between the base the tines, and then tossing it back across the bridge for the next one?"

'Great idea, Alex," said Caitlin, "but some if us, particularly the younger girls, may not have the strength or the skill to throw it all the way back. We might lose it entirely, tumbling down the river!"

"So why don't we all just take off our belts and use the cords we have to tie up our waterproof sheets. These together ought to be strong enough to make a line for the ice axe so we wouldn't lose it. And we could make a short loop right by the handle so we could put our hands through and not let the ice axe slip out of our fingers."

"OK," I agreed, "you're right. But boys – and this means you, Duke, more than anyone else – no fooling, absolutely no fooling about pulling at the girls to tease them about dropping their bluejeans now they have lent us their belts. Got it? Anyone does that, I'll report back at the Institute, and if he or she isn't sent right home, I'll quit this job and I'll tell Mr. and Mrs. Caronson exactly why, with names and all the details. And think what that would mean! What report would go home to your schools and families?"

So it was decided, and so it happened. I sent Alexis across first, and it was easy for him, and then Duke to get him on the other side and out of the way, then the other boys and lastly all the girls, with me bringing up the rear. To my delight and infinite relief it all worked like a charm: no one panicked, no one lost his or her balance, everyone used the ice axe properly as a hiking stick, and everyone behaved in a most mature and responsible way about lending their belts to the group. A terrible obstacle had faded away beneath our feet.

Before we set out for the last mile back to the truck I called all the group around me, looked each one in the eye, shook their hands and thanked them all for their stalwart efforts and flexibility under trying circumstances.

"This day you have all become real, qualified Mountain Hikers," I concluded – and they all glowed, particularly Rose and Meg, and Pierre, who had been consumed with fears right up to the moment of trial.

"Edward, I believe I would try Holy Cross if I were you, I really would," said Uncle Rod Tregannet to me a couple of days later when we were starting to hatch plans about where I might take the group for a different and really worthwhile mountain hike the next weekend.

"It's a splendid mountain" he went on, "one of the very grandest in the entire Rockies. Looking up from the valleys and low country miles and miles away you can see the great white cross of snow that clings all year long to the North Face and gives the mountain its name. Mind you, scaling that particular face is utterly impossible for you people, completely out of the question. It's ice-bound all year, it's pitched at almost ninety degrees in many places, and there are zero paths or hiking trails anywhere near it. Keep off!

It's a killer, and has indeed seen the death of many a skilled and experienced rock climber. They say that's what the white cross is all about, to mark their graves."

"Then, sweetest Uncle of mine, why are you recommending it to us? Have you a death wish for your dear nephew? I never suspected that – indeed I thought we were actually quite fond of each other, but now I can see I had better take good care."

'Oh come on, dear boy," he laughed, "you know what I mean! There's a few good strong trails up the opposite, southern face of the mountain, steep yes, and rocky, but certainly accessible and good, strong fun if the wind is blowing. And then when you reach the top and look out over all that mighty precipice falling away at your feet, miles and miles away to the horizon with no comparable mountain to obscure your view, why then you feel like the King of The World! God, I wish I could come with you – but this damned leg, and that bastard driver, God rot him."

So we decided, and Holy Cross it was to be: a long slog first through forest, then up onto an open, thinly wooded saddle where my uncle half-remembered that there used to be and still might be a stone shelter – it was worth knowing about that if the weather turned tricky. And from the saddle we would follow a long steep trail up the back of the mountain to gain an unparalleled view and a real sense of achievement once the summit had been reached. Sounded good to me, and I was sure my team could do it, if the weather was kind: that was always a big If.

So off we set on the Saturday morning with our backpacks, our sleeping bags and food for a couple of days, headed for the formidable and renowned Holy Cross Mountain. The primary ascent was indeed, as promised, a long slog, a long steady hike uphill through the close-set trees, some aspen, some maple, mostly pine. Pierre had never encountered mosquitoes such as those who found us, not even in the Carmargue or by the mouth of the Loire, so we all plied him with Wild Woods Off and kept on up the hill.

Meg found the going hard, and we all sympathized with her: she weighed a tad more than she ought to have, and we split up most of her pack between us, Iris Singleton from Connecticut as usual taking the lead in looking after those who had need of assistance. Iris was admirable, full of friendly and maternal solicitude without ever being in any way condescending to anyone. Her background at Miss Porter's gave her *noblesse oblige*, thought I, and I was surely glad that she was one of the group.

The air grew thicker, the slope grew steeper, our backpacks grew heavier; and the slight and hesitant breeze slipped quite away. The humidity began to get the better of us, so we all felt the need for a break even though we had been walking for less than a couple of hours.

"Time out!" I called, "Time Out! What do you think? I say we all need a break." Never have I seen gratitude break forth from so many countenances at the same instant! Nine backpacks thumped to the ground in unison, and bodies sprawled upon them and upon tree stumps lying here and there.

Yes, it was indeed time for a break, and for the first time that afternoon I began to wonder if we were not in for a classic Colorado bone-drenching thunderstorm, so close and humid had the atmosphere grown. Well, if so, what to do about it?

Option #1: Call the whole thing off, head back for the truck, get good and soaked or not soaked at all on the long way back, depending on the time of arrival of the storm, forget the wonderful promise of Holy Cross Mountain, drive back down the valley to the Institute, and sit there alone and shame-faced all weekend long, with no one around except us cowards, who would then face surprise and derision on Sunday evening when all the other groups returned. The other students at the Institute could hardly help but feel scorn for my team, and my own students might feel the same for me, that I had truly let them down, and this would in all likelihood would bring down upon me the severe disapproval of

Jonathan Dunkerley-Jones and Bud Tamerack, and of Uncle Rod, for my utter spinelessness.

Option #2: Press on to the end, pretend that discomfort and misery do not exist, cheer my young charges on with cries that our skins are waterproof so what are you worried about, we are going to damn well hike up Holy Cross as far as we can, maybe to the timber line but no farther if there is a very real chance of lightning, and then, utterly soaked to the bone, ourselves *and* our packs, we would search around for somewhere to stretch out our plastic sheets to prevent even more water flowing in where there is already water, water everywhere – No, that wouldn't do at all. On thinking it over, that was not a good option, not a sound decision taken by a responsible leader of a group of neophyte teenagers, some of them by no means the strongest young people you have ever known. And what would they gain out of it? Streaming colds and sickness maybe, nasty resentment at all they had been inveigled into doing, scorn for the heartiness of the Institute, and yes, quite likely, honest-to-god homesickness.

Is there an Option #3? Yes there is, and we'll take it, by golly! Press on just as far and as long as it looks feasible. No false bravado. And then turn back if that is truly the wisest things to do. No place for false pride here, I kept telling myself: I have the less able students to consider. I knew that saddle we had to cross between the mountain and one of its shoulders was not far ahead, and I told myself that we would at least get that far, where the real climb began, and make a decision at that point. So, having discovered that people will go along gladly with almost anything if it is explained to them and if they have some voice in the outcome, I called the group together and went over all three options. In all seriousness I told them that we would decide by vote at the crossing of the saddle and that this one time I would not exercise my nine-vote prerogative.

By the time, half an hour later, that we reached the saddle, rain had begun to fall, first in light drifts but before long in earnest, and then within minutes in sheets so thick that even our view of the forest all around was growing obscured. There was no need to take a vote: we would absolutely turn around, and exert ourselves to the utmost to get back to our truck before nightfall. That was a gloomy prospect indeed, and I was so glad when Rosie Durrindale of all people decided that this was the time for a cheerful outburst of song. "Oh what a beautiful morning, Oh what a beautiful day!" she belted out, pirouetting all around us, her poncho and back-pack whirling. Laughter drove away our flagging spirits, and in no time Caitlin Kennedy sang out "You are my sunshine, my only sunshine," and boy, did we all laugh, each one of us searching in his or her memory for songs of summer, sunshine, blue skies and what not. I was so proud of them all. "Summertime, and the living is easy…" That was Duke Sutton and Louis Armstrong!

After a few minutes of tom-foolery we calmed down, faced our dreary future and shrugged our heavier-than-ever packs back onto our shoulders – and I remembered Uncle Rod's half-storied recollection of a putative small stone shelter, like those on the Appalachian Trail way back east, right about here somewhere, near the crossing of our trail on the saddle with the stream, now a torrent, flowing down into the valley.

"Stop!" I called out. "Everyone to me, now. I've just had the best idea in the whole wide world!" And I told them that we would split up and search for a stone shelter that might or might not exist but would certainly be concealed in the brush and un-dergrowth in this drenched and darkening forest, if indeed it was anywhere at all. "Here's what we do," I said. "Line up right now in alphabetical order by your last names as I call them out" – puzzled looks all around, coupled with some resentment at this seemingly childish game – "and take note to who stands before you in the alphabet and who behind." I counted the off Aaron Blankenstein, Edward Brackenthwaite, Pierre Delarue, Rosie Durrindale, Caitlin Kennedy, Alexis Lenglen, Iris Singleton, Meg

Suffern, Duke Sutton. "Now form a wide circle with each of you by the guy or girl next to you in the alphabet, up and down the alphabet, and Aaron Blankenstein links up with Duke Sutton at the end of the alphabet. It's a circle, right, got it?" They all got it, and moved into position in an open circle. "Now face outward and move out away from the centre of the circle, searching for the old stone lodge while absolutely without fail always keeping in sight of your two buddies, one up and one down the alphabet. Sing out if you can't see one or other of your buddies. That's the most important thing of all! We can't have anyone getting lost in this forest in the rainstorm now it's beginning to get dark. OK, everyone? Now git!"

And git we all did, with fast and eminent success. No one lost touch with his or her buddy: the system worked exactly as it should, and in no more than five minutes Pierre had located the stone cabin, now greatly overgrown with weeds and vines, and with just one narrow path twisting through the bushes to the door.

"Bet you it's locked," said Rosie. "That would be a rare laugh on us: the only shelter in the world for miles and miles around, and the door's locked. Shall we even bother to try it?"

"Oh please, do let us try!" exclaimed Pierre, taking her seriously. "We can't just walk away without trying."

With a look of silent authority Caitlin stood forward and set her hand to the door. No good. It wouldn't budge. "Oh Lord," she said. "Well, here goes again." And this time she really set her shoulder to the door, shoving with all her weight, and this time it flew open with no resistance at all, poor Caitlin flying in behind it and landing in a tangle of limbs with, good grief, someone else beneath her on the other side of the door. She leapt to her feet with a gasp and a scream and hurtled back out, breathless and indeed frightened not a little by the grasping hands of whoever that Other was. A man's laughter reached our ears from behind the closed door. Now it was clearly my time to look into the situation. Cautiously and well prepared to jump back if need be, I approached the door, knocked firmly and called out that we were simply looking for refuge from the rain, so could we please come inside?

The door swung open and through the murk inside I could see that the cabin was almost full of hikers who had taken the same refuge that we now sought. There was only one window, small and unglazed, but there was a fireplace with the bright embers of a fire glowing in the grate.

"Come in, come in," called out a friendly and welcoming voice. "How many are there of you? Me and my gang, we almost fill up the place, but you're mighty welcome to make yourselves at home with us. The name's Alan, and these here are Bud, Jenny, Eddie, Sarah, Lincoln, Meg, and Bella. Now mind you all get the names right. Folks round here are mighty sensitive." He laughed, his companions did too, and then we all joined in, each of us volunteering our names in turn as we trooped into the shelter and out of the rain. They explained to us that they had started their climb earlier than we had and they had made it right to the summit of Holy Cross before turning around and coming down as fast as they comfortably could, closely pursued by the storm that from they had first seen miles away, approaching from the north ever closer and closer. They all had backpacks, but pretty skimpy ones: if they had to spend the night in a stone cabin several thousand feet up the flank of one of the tallest mountains in the Rockies, in a cold rainstorm no less, they would surely feel the chill long before morning.

"Well, we thought of that," Alan went on, "and as soon as the rain began we hauled in here all the brushwood and branches we could lay our hands on. It was getting dark already, what with the storm and all, and we didn't have a mind to try out that steep trail down the mountain in the dark. Sarah here twisted her ankle on the way down from the summit, and it's beginning to swell."

"And hurts like the goddam blazes," added Sarah, pale but smiling stoically.

"Tell you what," I said. "We have a couple of ace bandages with us, and those plastic chemical bags that act like regular ice-packs when they're squeezed and twisted. Iris, aren't you the one carrying the First Aid kit right now? Would you mind getting it out for Sarah here?"

In no time the two girls had become good friends, Iris an upcoming senior at St. Margaret's, Tappahannock, and Sarah a junior majoring in psych at the University of Colorado at Boulder. Alexis solicited help from Bud and Eddie in pulling together the campfire in the grate, and boy, weren't all those college kids happy that we had brought plenty of matches along! They were down to their last two and were growing anxious. It made my team feel useful, equal inhabitants of the stone cabin with the group that had already established prior ownership by squatters' rights. Duke loved hefting the pine logs around, and he was good at it, showing off his muscular dexterity to the girls, both our own and the college gals we had encountered.

A dark afternoon turned to a dark evening, and it was time to think of dinner. The rain did not let up at all. We all had our meals carefully packed with us, but the other eight had precious little between them, having fully expected to make it back to their base camp before night set in. The storm and Sarah's ankle had put paid to that expectation, however, and none of them had any intention of tackling the tricky downward trail in the dark, a really damfool thing to do even if they had had the aid of moonlight. Of course there was no moon at all tonight, only sheets of rain, and blustery wind to knock you off your balance..

"We're OK, we really are," insisted Lincoln and Jenny, who made up something of a couple. "This won't be the first time we've missed a meal and it won't be the last time either. Why, we didn't eat anything for a day and a half a couple of weeks ago when we

189

were hiking over in Estes Park and lost our way. God, were we idiots, no maps or compasses, can you believe it? So we deserved what we got. But please, don't mind us. You've been carrying all your food right up the mountain, and you deserve to eat it. Please!"

"No, that really won't do. It won't do at all," insisted Iris, Aaron and Caitlin together. "I am sure we have more than enough if we pool what we have," said Iris. "There are no two ways about it. It's an order, so there. Come to think of it, you had first dibs on this cabin and you shared it with us, squatters' rights and all."

Aaron started to sing quietly, and soon the cabin was rocking. We were laughing as much as singing as we made our way through "This cabin is your cabin, This cabin is my cabin. This food is your food, This food is my food," and I was grateful to Aaron, whom I had thought quiet and dreamy, for his initiative and his courage in starting the singing. All differences between the two groups were soon forgotten, and we all looked and acted as though we had been bosom buddies all our lives long.

So we sat up by a blazing fire, cooked our dinners (soup, rolls with butter and cheese, sliced ham and chicken, and cookies). Water the boys brought in from the stream, and we boiled it good and hard before drinking any of it, with tea, coffee or juice crystals.

After dinner we continued to sit around, listening to the rain which did not give up until close to midnight, and we told 'The Gang from Boulder,' as we named them, all about the Caronson Institute, who we all were and how very different our backgrounds were, even our leader (yours faithfully) being a foreigner, a Brit no less, staying for the summer with his maternal uncle in Colorado, and they told us about their life in Boulder, their families and homes. As often happens among young people brought close together in straitened circumstances, the conversation moved across without hesitation to such topics at the basic nature of existence, the eternal verities -- even whether the universe truly exists at all, a line of thought initiated by Pierre, cynical Frenchman that he was, who insisted that the whole blessed thing is a nothing but a nightmare of God's, from which He would awaken one day. This was solemn stuff, and after a measure of friendly scoffing it was not long before eyelids grew heavy.

The Boulder Gang had no sleeping bags with them, good grief, and the night was growing chill. There were lighthearted jokes and glances, blushes even, at the suggestions from various people, some not so very oblique, about who would share his or her sleeping bag with whom. It was agreed in the end that all our bags should be unzipped all the way down and spread out, each a thick blanket for two people. By good luck we had an equal number of guys and gals (except for me), so we all paired off, two guys or two girls under each blanket, with no 'Boulder' sharing space with any 'Caronson.' There was much proximity and maybe a stolen kiss or two but, I felt certain, precious little opportunity at all for anything more significant than that, so propinquent were we one to another. But I did stay awake nearly all the night long, just thinking and listening.

After a makeshift breakfast in the morning we parted with affectionate hugs and exchanges of addresses all round, and we Caronsons took our slow descent down the trail that in the night had become a watercourse back to our truck, while the Boulder Gang, with poor Sarah still hobbling along with a makeshift crutch, took a different path, one that wound north round the base of the mountain to the spot where they had left their van the day before.

Finally, as we drove back to the Caronson Institute, I felt proud of my group and immensely pleased with how everything had turned out. Inside ourselves we felt no sense of defeat in getting turned back by the storm -- rather, we congratulated ourselves on our sturdy commonsense, and on our skill in making the best of disappointment, driving regrets away in an evening of companionship among new and welcome friends.

But oh, did I ever fail to anticipate the atmosphere that awaited me back at the Institute! Rod Tregannet was standing around in the front hall together with Jonathan Dunkerley-Jones and Bud Tamarack. And did they ever tear a strip off me! "Whatever was in your mind?" they asked, insistently and with anger in their voices, one after the other, "How did you ever know you could trust these young men and women that you spent the night with, and you didn't even know their names, for chrissake? Why, I bet that if we made enquires at this moment, no one around here would have ever heard of them!"

"That's just ridiculous!" I replied, fast losing my temper. "Look, here we are way up the blessed mountain, and we take shelter from a real corker of a storm. So I was wrong to have the kids look for shelter rather than face down a mountain storm, is that it? Is that what you really think? Or should I have asked all those other young people from Boulder to leave if they didn't have with them personal certificates of good behavior, to ask them politely to get the hell way out into the storm, gale-force winds and pelting rain in the dark, one of them with a nasty sprained ankle and all, just because I had a passle of vulnerable little darlings with me, is that it – *and* they had found the shelter way before us? Or should I have fought them, driven them out by force? I certainly did have my ice-axe with me, but it would have been only one of me against eight of them, so here you are, thinking those odds would have been just fine with me, ok? Or perhaps you mean that I should have turned around back and forced our Caronson team right back out into the stormy night down the long mountain trail through the forest in pitch darkness, let alone the rough weather and our path turning into a mountain stream, is that what you would have wanted? And what if all my kids simply refused and went back to the cabin without me, eh? Can't you see, godammit? As it was, I stayed awake the whole blessed night long, listening in case anything went wrong

-- you know what I mean – and then thanking my lucky stars that everything was just fine: the good God Almighty took care of us, *yes He did,* and He lent to us for the night the companionship of some sterling young lads and lasses. So why in Hell's name are you all so bloody angry with me? You should be thanking me, yes thanking me, for handling so well what could have proved a very rough situation indeed if there had been no stone shelter or if we had been prevented by your goddam tender scruples from asking for admittance and a roof over our heads in a terrific mountain storm. I'm just fed up with the whole bloody thing, I tell you, and I have a damn good mind to just quit here and now, and then go tell all the kids exactly why, *exactly* why! And then where will your blessed brand-new Caronson Institute be, I'ld like to know? Well, I bet it would have a new Director next year, if ever it had a next year -- and I don't think it would!"

Silence all round. Silence. And then they were at once at me again, only this time singing a different tune, a very different tune.

"Oh I say, calm down!" said Jonathan. "It's not as bad as all that." The others followed his lead.

"Well, actually, you did do a good thing. It would have been awful rough on the kids to stay out in the cold rain." That, at last, was the voice of my fond uncle.

"Sorry, Edward, I guess I did go too far. I was just anxious about the kids sleeping out there right alongside strangers in the same beds, young people no one knew anything about." That was Bud Tamerack, honest and eminently likeable, but not always the brightest bulb.

"Yeah, Edward, I'm sorry too. I guess I got carried away as much as anyone. Tell you what, we'll put our heads together and see if we can't come up with something really special for a hike for them next weekend, right? It will be their last but one. And after what you all went through we should really sit down and plan something special." And that was the final word from Jonathan, the Director, the man who was looking toward next year as well as to the completion of this.

So sit down we did, that evening, Rod Tregannet, Jonathan Dunkerley-Jones, Bud Tamerack, and I. It was Uncle Rod who played the trump card after we had all given voice to our opinions about what might be the close-to-perfect hike.

"I'll have to call some friends over at the ski lodge in the area," said Uncle Rod slowly and hesitantly, "but I have a feeling that Mount Elbert might be the perfect quarry for your group to slay. It'll be a long, long slog, the longest you'll ever have, make no mistake about it, and the air gets awful thin up over 14,000 feet, but for those kids to find themselves right on the very top of the highest mountain not only in the State of Colorado but in the whole damn Rockies from one end to the other, the entire mountain chain, well if that don't give them the thrill of a lifetime, I'll fetch each and every one of 'em a smart kick in the seat of the pants, and that's a promise."

"We had better be pretty damn careful about this one," said Jonathan. "I reckon we got off lightly with Holy Cross. Suppose Edward here had not had the good sense that he did in fact show, but had told the kids that they were all going to go all the way up to the peak, we can't be defeated by any old mountain, forget the storm, the path is marked, and all that jazz... Well, some of the less athletic kids, and believe me there are some sad cases in the group, well, some of them might not be able to make it, and what then? Have Duke Sutton and Alexis Lenglen and Edward Brackenthwaite here carry them down? In a terrific storm? Maybe lose the path in the dark, and end up right on the steep north face where the snow hangs like a cross all summer long?

Edward, I really owe you a big apology. Please forgive me. I mean it, I truly do! Please forgive me. I shouldn't have lit into you as I did. That was inexcusable and I kick myself for it. I was so goddamn disappointed that you had not given the kids a peak, that you had all turned tail and seemed to quit, and then took the chance – yes, I know you had no option – of spending the night sleeping with strangers.

Anyway, to get back to the point, I believe Mount Elbert is on the cards for you, yessir I really do, I do indeed, but we had better, all of us, and I mean *all*, take on every bit of research we can to find out about weather, the condition of the trails, crags to be avoided, rocky rivers to be forded, everything, everything we can possibly learn about Mt. Elbert-- got it everyone?" And they all agreed. So there it was, it was set. Mount Elbert for us!

By Thursday, two days before we would be due to depart for Mount Elbert, research was complete. A fellow at the ski lodge had taken a group, adults not teenagers but indeed people barely conditioned to hiking at high altitudes, right to the summit just two weeks ago. This group had set out in the dark before breakfast from a makeshift camp not far from the base of the mountain, took food and water with them, had hiked as fast as they could, and had returned after nightfall. These people were strong young adults, not teenagers of various strengths like my group. We all would have to start around midday on Saturday after a long, long drive from the Institute in the morning, would have to sleep out a good way up the mountain, probably without water nearby, and then would have to complete the climb and be back at our starting point well before nightfall on the second day, the Sunday. We learned that the going was as easy as it ever could be in these mountains, with no harsh gradients, no unmarked paths, no roaring torrents or snow-covered corries. The challenge lay in the many miles to be covered, all uphill of course; in the fact that the long last stage was well above the tree line with every hiker fully exposed to all the winds in the heavens and to any sudden storm; and in the nature of the path itself at that altitude, all sharp and broken stones, no gravel, no rounded rocks for us to hop on from one to the next. But the reward would be spectacular indeed, a panorama of mountain peaks stretching far in every direction, 360 degrees around us, and every single one of them lower than the one upon which we would be standing. Yippee, a thousand times Yippee!

I drove over to the Institute on Thursday evening and called a special meeting of the hiking group. I explained the whole situation in detail to all of them, not glossing over anything but also informing them that they would be achieving something that probably no one else they would ever meet in their entire lives would ever experience -- let alone the rest of the gang at the Institute, with their horses, their kayaks, their crampons. We would have to carry our packs up to wherever we spent the night, but could then stack them there well off the trail and in the hours before dawn make the final climb unencumbered, just when not only would the oxygen be pretty thin and so exhaustion lay only just around the corner, but also when the air itself would be freezing cold since we would have to start our final approach to the summit before there was any warmth from the sun. Oh my, were we all excited, challenged and a little frightened!

"This'll just show 'em!" then shouted out Rosie Durrindale. "They've been teasing me about us all being quitters last time, lying all comfy in a warm hut out of the rain with a bunch of fellers and gals from Boulder, all of us girls in the arms of handsome young men sharing our sleeping bags. Phooey! I tell you, I just want to show 'em, that's all, and I don't care if I do die my death of cold, frozen goddam stiff, right there on the top of the highest mountain in all the Rockies! I'll show 'em, I tell you, I bloody will!" We all laughed and clapped her on the back. Hurrah!

Saturday morning rolled around, with our group all feeling a special excitement hard to conceal from all the other members of the Institute, but we told no one what was afoot, not wanting to count our chickens before they hatched, and anyway if bad weather chose to intervene, why then the whole damn thing would just be another shameful flop that we would wish to hide from everyone anyway. So none of us in the hiking group had mentioned Mount Elbert to anyone, to anyone at all. The weather forecast was set fair all right, something we had checked and rechecked time and time again. So off we set for the long drive, the gang hunkered down in the back of the truck and me in the driver's seat up front. Iris Singleton had taken an extended family trip to England and Ireland the summer before, and I was pleased to note that she came out of her gentle reserve to lead the group in singing "It's a long way to Tipperary, it's a long way to go!" Splendid, I thought: how good that she's coming forward and that kids as different from her as Duke Sutton and overweight young Meg Suffern are really taking a shine to her. That's what the Caronson Institute should be all about, I thought, at its best, and Samuel and Rachel Caronson would be proud of us.

It was late morning by the time our truck rolled into a meadow and came to a halt on the edge of a grove of cedars way down in the valley beneath the mountain peaks. Indeed, no peak was to be seen anywhere: they all loomed out of sight behind their broad and rounded shoulders. "Ah, mon Dieu," sighed Pierre, tongue in cheek, "the Mont Elbert, he does not exist. All is a dream of the good God, as I told you last time on Holy Ghost Mountain, was that not so? Well, we will see, n'est-ce pas?"

Well, ontology had only limited appeal to the rest of the group after more than two bone-shaking hours in the back of a truck, so no one took Pierre up on his challenge. With a self-effacing shrug he looked away, and like everyone else gave his attention to the stowing of all his possessions in his backpack. And then off we set, walking along the grassy river bottom flats to begin with, and then up a gentle slope through deciduous woodland until conifers began to predominate and it all began to feel like the mountains again. Slog on we did, as we had been told we would have to, for hour after hour, with only the briefest of pauses along the way. By this time in our common hiking career we had really begun to act as an integrated group of friends: Duke had cast aside his boastful frivolity; Alexis, Caitlin and Iris had emerged as the solid, dependable, eminently likeable and efficient centre of our group; Pierre and gentle poetic Aaron had paired off together; while Meg and Rosie, the youngest and most vulnerable members, had found something of a home under the care of Caitlin and Iris. Especially pleasing was the way that Duke and Alexis had taken it upon themselves without even the slightest hint from me, to shoulder virtually the entire backpack loads of Meg and Rosie. As for myself, I could not have been more pleased with how everything was going, just a trifle anxious though I was at the audacity with which we had dared to tackle a truly long hike, mile after mile, up to where the air was thin and where there would be no shelter at all if things began to go wrong in any conceivable way. Well, no use to worry about that now – we had made the decision and we were on our way.

As we finally approached the tree line which straggled obliquely across our path, the evening light began to fade. The handsome sunset lost its radiant glow of orange and copper set against limpid blue, and the gnarled and twisted dwarf trunks of pine trees stood out in stark silhouette against the paling sky.

"Time for camp?" asked Alexis as he moved up the line to walk beside me for a stretch. "Some of us are beginning to think so, anyway."

I turned and called out to the troop: "See that great rock hunched over, up the mountain over there across from the trail?

It's not such a long hike up from here, and I can see there are low trees beneath it on the southern slope, so we might find shelter and even some fresh water. What do you think? How's that for a camp site?"

The group was unanimous: the air was growing thin, our legs were indeed tired, and the evening chill was coming on apace now that the sun had almost set. So we covered our last ascent of the day and then scrambled down some twenty yards from the trail to find ourselves on a level patch of broken rock beneath the great stone – perfect for a campsite with low bushy trees around for some measure of privacy and to give us branches and stumps from which to hang our plastic tent sheets. Dinner was straightforward and simple: no one felt in the mood to cook, which was just as well since Duke, Alexis and I had conspired not to carry the necessary pots and pans all the weary way up the great hill. But we did manage to build a fire from pine twigs gathered by all of us, and then the night came on suddenly, surprising us with its rapidly lowering temperatures. Meg and Rosie first of all, but one by one all the rest of us progressively thereafter, took up our sleeping bags and wrapped ourselves in them as we sat, looking at each other in a wide circle around the hearty fire. "Anyone for a song?" No one actually was; we were all awed at our remoteness from civilization and at our rash courage at confronting alone a night in this lonely mountain fastness. I prayed that the weather forecast, taken so many times just a few hours ago and always promising that all was well, would hold. A storm out here, way up here, would be merciless – and I would be the one responsible for the welfare of all these young people. No use to worry now. Time to turn in…. but it was early by the clock, not past nine. How could we sleep? And what to do if we didn't sleep? It was Pierre of all people who came forward with the answer.

"So, you say, le bon Dieu rules the mountain and wishes well to all of us. Let us pray that that is so. But what would He want from us in return, if He is so good to us that He preserve us? *Hein?* What indeed? My friends, I think you all know the answer to that, no? It is that He wants us to worship Him, to give Him praise for His creation and for His goodness in keeping us alive, we who are so foolish and rash as to risk ourselves to death of exposure, to terrible storms, avalanches, abominable snowmen and all kinds of terrors! No? Am I wrong? Who is there here to say No to me? *Hein*, I thought as much. No one, not one of you…. So, my friends, therefore we are all agreed, and here is exactly how we must worship Him even if we do not know le bon Dieu, even if we are unbelievers. Let us arise early in the morning, even in the late hours of the night, and creep by the light of the stars that God will afford to us, right up to the very summit itself. I have looked at the map with Aaron my friend, and it cannot be more than one kilometer away, probably less. What do you say to all of us lying down in our sleeping bags now, even dressed as we are, and then arising before the first light of the morning and marching up to the peak to greet le bon Dieu as He rises out of the east in the sunrise? That will be our thanksgiving and prayer. So, so, what do you think of that, my friends? C'est une bonne idée, n'est-ce pas?"

Aaron was of course the first to answer, and he took up the tale from Pierre. "Listen to the voices of the mountains," he said. "They all urge us onward and upward, urging us to drink in to ourselves, to our spirits, the mountain experience to the full, to the fullest extent possible. Can't you just hear the voices speaking to you? Listen, everybody! Just stay silent for a moment and listen to the voice of God."

So we all sat and listened, and in the magic of the moment we found ourselves thinking unanimously. "Let's go forward as Pierre says," Caitlin volunteered. "He's really got it right."

"She's got it right too," chimed in Duke. "That chick sure knows something. We just gotta go on. Wow, seeing the stars and the moon from the top of the highest mountain in the world, that's ultimate cool, man!"

And everyone else agreed, their voices all chiming in together. The excitement and enthusiasm just delighted me: my job, an essential one, would be to keep the group together in the moonlight of the small hours, and have us all move forward slowly and steadily – slowly in the high thin air so as not to stumble on the loose rocks that abounded, and steadily, so that we might reach the summit by sunrise, if not by the dawn's early light.

So we set the campsite in order and bedded down in our sleeping bags just as we were at a very early hour in order that we might catch what sleep we could before rising soon after midnight to make the final push for the summit. I was glad that I had been told that the last mile or so was a very gentle gradient from this direction though steep and craggy from all others. I would have to keep the very sharpest lookout that we stray not a whisker from the one and only hiking trail.

Frankly, no one slept very much during that short night, deeply tired though we all were from the long haul up from that green lowland meadow so very far below. I sat up at half past one and called out everyone's name as a roll call so that I could be certain that the gang were all awake. We pulled on our boots, emptied our packs of everything save our canteens, a little food, flashlights and first aid supplies.

"I'll take the lead and set the pace," I said. "And it will be for me to keep us all on the track. It won't be easy to see it all the time, I'm guessing, so Iris, won't you please come right behind me and act as a second pair of eyes? We can't afford to go wrong, you know, so you and I will have a heavy responsibility. Caitlin, would you please keep an eye on Meg and Rosie? And you two, stay right with Caitlin. Duke, may I ask you to carry Meg's pack, and Alexis, carry Rosie's and you, Duke, come next in line? You can stuff all their gear in your own packs if you like -- it would be really wonderful if you don't mind helping the whole group in that way. Then Aaron and Pierre, you stick together next in line, one behind the other, and Alexis bring up the rear. When I call a break after a while people can change places if they like, but let's please just accept things as they are for the first stage. This is one heck of a responsibility we all have, you know, and if things go wrong, I'll be paying for this with my bloody neck, make no mistake about that. I don't need to tell you there's to be absolutely no fooling about, no horseplay, on this night hike. I don't think you'll want to talk much because you'll need all your strength for the hike at this altitude – we must be up around 14,000 feet by now – but I'll not make any law about silence. Quite the opposite in fact: sing out, sing out for God's sake, if anything seems to you to be going wrong: if we are walking too fast, if you really need a break, if you drop something, whatever. Just sing out, ok? And keep in your places in line. Let's pile up all gear that we are not going to take with us up to the summit, right here behind this large boulder, so that no one else who might be coming along might think it has been abandoned and is therefore fair pickings. All right, my good friends, all right? We're on our way! 'Marchons, marchons, pour la Patrie!' Pierre, n'est-ce pas?" He gave me a pitying look for my misquotation, and then we were off, up, up and away.

It was a long, long curve we had to travel, up and around a great flank of the mountain, but the slope was gentle and with the dark grey rocks whitened here and there by the boots of hikers before us, so it was not too hard to find the way. The air was clear, the wind was mercifully gentle and at our backs, -- and, oh, the moon and the stars! Only Alexis, Pierre, Caitlin and I had ever seen the Milky Way before, so polluted has the sky become over great reaches of the United States and the industrialized areas of the world, so there was a constant cooing and singing out in pure delight at the glory of the heavens. Truly, at that altitude there seemed to be almost more points of light in the sky, of differing size and brightness, than areas of blackness between them. It was all magic, pure magic, like our first night together back on Mt. Grayling, but even more spectacular. It was tempting to look too long at the sky and therefore to miss one's footing on an uneven rock on the path.

"Oh, I was so scared about coming to Colorado," called out Meg. "I thought I would be left behind and not keep up with everyone and so miss all the fun, but this, oh this is the most wonderful thing I have ever done in my whole life! And my Lord, this sky, I just didn't know at all that it could look like that. It's a whole different sky back home. This is heaven, pure heaven!"

"I'll say so," agreed Rosie."This sure ain't Chicago, no sir! That's my home town, in case you didn't know. Back there, the sky's just dirty orange-brown at night, and you don't see no more than two stars."

And then the voices trailed off as we gave ourselves over to the serious business of hiking uphill, with uncertain footholds, in the dark, in air so low on oxygen that we all needed to breathe deeply and evenly, pace by pace, step by step, each of us hunkering down deep in our own thoughts. That is how it was for the first hour – and then I called a rest. Five minutes squatting on the rocks, a pull at the water bottle, and we were off again.

Another hour or less, and the summit drew near! The sky had lightened in the east, and it was clear to me at any rate that we had missed "the dawn's early light," but that didn't really matter so long as we could catch the sunrise. I thought of urging the team on to a faster pace, but a quick look back showed me that that was simply not to be done. More than one hiker was approaching the end of his or her endurance, including, of all people, the tall and lanky Duke Sutton. We were a long way from Harlem, and this experience was like nothing he had ever encountered, physically or in any other way. So we plugged on steadily, and I tried to conceal my anxiety.

And then, at last, we were there! Ye gods, we had made it! We stood, tired beyond tired, exhausted beyond exhausted, triumphant in our success but staggering slightly as we reined ourselves in and told our weary limbs that they did not need to pull us uphill any longer. They told us they did not want even to stand upright any more, so we lowered ourselves slowly down onto the great rocks that covered the summit of Mount Elbert or onto the flanks of the six-foot tall stone cairn that marked the 14,440 foot summit of the highest mountain in Colorado, the highest peak in the entire range of the Rockies. We looked at one another, and we grinned. Oh my, how we grinned! But we were too close to exhaustion for the victory dance that we had promised ourselves, almost too tired to take in the Glory of God revealed all around us. After a few moments, however, we drew ourselves to our feet, still staggering a little, and made a point of each of us fulfilling the traditional responsibility of hikers to the summit of any mountain: adding a stone, however small it might be, to the pile that comprised the cairn on the topmost peak. Cameras emerged from parka pockets, and countless photographs, individual or group portraits, recorded our moment of magnificence.

But then, oh for Heaven's sake, just look, look all around you, far off into the distance to the East! For there rose the Sun, there rose the Sun, in such splendor as none of us had ever seen in him before. First, before he was visible at all, a bright point of light illuminated a far-off peak whose name was completely unknown to us, miles and miles away to the east: the morning Sun had struck it, and it had come to fiery life. Then glowed another bright point, and another, another, more and more in a long, steady, gentle procession as the Sun rose and illuminated peak after peak, the brilliance creeping closer, ever closer to us. And at last lo! we ourselves, each of us, were impaled by the first sunbeam of our day, no warmth in it at all, only a clear bright blaze of piercing golden light. Of course it was Aaron who had the poetry for us:

"Awake! For Morning in the bowl of Night
Has cast the stone that puts the stars to flight,
    And lo, the Hunter of the East has caught
The Sultan's turret in a noose of light."

"You just can't beat old Omar Khayyam," he said. "So don't you even try."

Not only was there was no warmth to the sunlight, but rather we felt an increased cold, for our emergence from the slight shelter afforded by the flank of the mountain had deprived us of a shield between our poor selves and all the winds of the heavens. Thank the good Lord that was a mild morning, for the breeze stung us like a finger of ice. A storm at that moment could have killed us, every last one, yes indeed it could. But all we did was to rejoice in the glory of the mountaintop: at that moment there was nary an atheist nor an agnostic amongst us. We cavorted around, taking little curving runs in order to keep the blood flowing, but clearly it was time to go, before we grew seriously cold. Looking over to the west we could see peak after peak struck in turn by the selfsame Sun, farther and farther into the grey distance beyond us– and suddenly we realized that the stars had hidden themselves, unable to face the competition, and even dear Lady Moon looked pallid and out of sorts.

So we turned away and headed back down the mountain, waving farewell to the cairn and the summit of Mount Elbert as we dropped back down the long shoulder up which we had so recently climbed in the darkness. In our descent we collected our packs, our sleeping bags and all our gear, sat around the cleared campsite for a brief breakfast, which was something of a sad occasion since the excitement, the drama, had all been completed, and nothing more awaited us than several hours of steady walking downhill. So trudge along we did, trudge along and along, most of the time in silence as we took into our separate selves the whole experience, as we recalled and relived the emotions, and all the details that we now did our utmost to compel ourselves never to forget. We were a sober group, introspective and dog-tired, when, many hours later, we finally traversed the long green meadow on the valley floor, and found our truck standing patiently where we had left it in the shade at the head of the dirt road, oh it seemed weeks and weeks ago. The students heaved themselves up into the back and I took the wheel, and we all headed home down that long road to the Caronson Institute. I heard afterwards that they all slept virtually the entire way.

At one point there was a long straight stretch of road down the valley, and I noticed that a farm tractor with a load of hay had just turned onto it at least a couple of hundred yards away. I thought nothing of it, but then -- it seemed in that selfsame instant – the tractor roared past us, and I realized with an almighty jerk that for a minute or two I had fallen asleep. Oh what a mercy that my Guardian Angel had had his hand on the steering wheel! Otherwise it would have been a very different story that the folk back at the Institute would have learned of our expedition, oh my Lord how different! I have never told a soul about this fearful experience until now when I am writing these words. I felt myself trembling all the way back along the miles of our three-hour journey. Of course I knew – long after the event – what I surely should have done from the outset of the drive home: require one member of the group to stay up front in the cab with me, talk to me constantly to prevent me falling asleep since I had had only two hours of sleep the previous night, and change that person every half hour or so. But we are all wise after the event, aren't we?

Delighting in their triumphant return, the hikers never knew how closely the wings of the Angel of Death had brushed past them. He ruffled their hair with his wings, and they thought it was only a breeze.

Tumbling out of the truck back at the Institute we were greeted with incredulity. How could these poor little people, the waifs of the Institute, those who had had to take shelter from a little trickle of rain a week ago, possibly have conquered the King of the Mountains? That question, and all our several answers, filled the evening, and the Mountain Hikers were enthroned in the minds of all as the princes of the day. The heartiest congratulations of Jonathan Dunkerley-Jones, Bud Tamerack and Rodney Tregannet warmed all our hearts. Never had I felt such pride in all my life – but all the time my mind conjured up another picture entirely, one almost as real as the true one, a picture of agony, death and desolation along the roadside, the farm truck overturned, and I, dead or alive, solely responsible for catastrophe.

There was only one more weekend left for us at the Caronson Institute this summer, so how should the Mighty Hikers spend it? With scores of peaks all around us, this should have been an easy question to answer, but that was not really the case. We had experienced the ultimate, one might say, in mastering Mount Elbert. Literally as well as figuratively, we could climb no higher. So the problem facing me was how to avoid a sense of letdown, of anticlimax, among those valiant young people who had come so far from our first excursion in our circle around the shoulders of Mount Grayling.

Bud Tamerack suggested that we cut loose from the Rockies as such and head west to the Red Sand Hills, but I wasn't so sure that would be such a good idea. Those hills are just that, hills, not mountains at all, wild and unspoiled country for sure, beautiful pinewoods with slopes and scree of loose rock – and, a real potential danger to the more adventurous of our group (for some reason or other it was Duke Sutton who sprang to mind, I wonder why) for the temptation of cliffs to scale, hand over hand up the steps of a cliff face formed by layer after layer of ruddy sandstone. But all that rock was friable in the extreme, and never would I allow myself to become responsible for the safety of young lives on a cliff face of crumbling, rotten rock. No, sir, there would be no Sand Hills for us!

Rod Tregannet began to speculate about caves, a good source of excitement but also another source of real potential danger. I could just see plump young Meg Suffern caught and held fast in some tight opening – and in the dark, what's more. And anyway there just weren't so many caves to choose from, for this was granite country, not limestone at all. Sorry, Uncle Rod. Any other ideas?

It was Jonathan Dunkerley-Jones who saved the day. "Tell you what," he murmured confidentially as he leaned forward in his chair and took a puff at his pipe. "Bud's idea that you strike out into new country and leave the Rockies behind for a couple of days has set my mind thinking. You know, the great desert country of the Southwest isn't so far away, and you could all hike for miles there, out in the open desert if you take care about water and the midday sun and things like that. I'm not suggesting you set yourselves to scale some Hopi mesa or other – again, much loose rock, maybe twisted ankles and worse – but you could hike right up to one or more of those great sandstone arches and along the rim or the foot of a canyon or two. Hey, wait a minute! Why, you could all explore those ancient Indian cliff dwellings! Two or three are real tourist traps, Mesa Verde, Betatikan and a couple of others, but with some research I bet you could locate something maybe not as spectacular as those, but remote and unvisited by any save the adventurous – and that, my boy, is you!"

Excitement began to fill the room as Uncle Rod, Bud Tamerack and I looked at each other with widening smiles. Jonathan, however, had not joined in the round of mutual congratulation.

"I'm afraid I've just thought of a snag," he said, "and this is it. Every single one of our groups – rock climbers, white-water kayakers, horseback riders, and you all – want to take out a truck next weekend for a great final experience of the summer. Four groups, and we have just three trucks. How do we get past that one? Anyone have an idea?"

"There's Menannah Lightfoot lives right up the valley from here, and he farms a spread," suggested Bud Tamarack. "I've seen his truck out in the fields from time to time. Maybe he would let us borrow it for a couple of days, for a consideration. I've gotten to know him pretty well. Why don't I give him a buzz?"

That worked out just fine, and Jonathan assured us that even though the Institute's tight budget could hardly cover the cost since Menannah Lightfoot was known to strike a tight bargain, yet after the event Samuel Caronson would surely come up with the wherewithal, particularly if it were to support a group with the spunk to defeat Mount Elbert, at sunrise no less. The old Indian's truck suited our needs admirably, and we kept with us the couple of spades and shovels we found in the back, thinking they might come in handy, you never knew, and anyway they took up practically no room. I wasn't so sure about a five-gallon can of gasoline, for which I could foresee no use at all, but there was nowhere easy to drop it off when we came across it at the last minute just as we were setting our backpacks into the truck, so we took it along.

And so our plans were laid. Research yielded good results. It would be another long drive, like the one to the foot of Mount Elbert, but the kids were used to that and would surely be all fired up at the prospect of hiking in the desert, viewing the great sandstone pillars and arches at Horseshoe Bend in Glenmeade Canyon, and discovering for themselves the seldom visited ancient Indian cliff dwelling of Deltatikan.

The drive was long indeed, some three hours all told, as far as to the foot of Mount Elbert, and the heat of the sun was growing fierce as morning slid toward noon, but at least our route lay along blacktop roads almost all the way, and the students, bless them, had grown used to making the most of the meager comforts of the back of a farm truck. We stopped by the roadside at one point to stretch the canvas roof over the back of the truck. It might grow close inside, but at least no one would be burned by the midday sun. At the appointed spot I drove off the metalled road onto a dirt track that led into the desert. This was fine for a mile or so, but it soon degenerated into a ragged track of sizeable rocks, often following the dry bed of a watercourse. The bouncing in the back of the truck soon grew fearsome, so I pulled up at the side of the track next to a grove of low scrub pines. We stretched ourselves, eased our bruised bones, and climbed down.

"Well, we've got the afternoon ahead of us," I announced, "so let's go find Deltatikan down in the canyon. The rim of the canyon should be no more than a couple of miles due west of this point, if I read the map aright. But lunch first. And then when we come back we can make a fire and cook dinner, and set up our campsite right by these pine trees. OK everyone, everyone on board with that?"

And so we set out, in the noonday sun, all well protected with lotions and hats of various kinds. The hike itself was a joy, not above two miles, which meant that we did not have time really to grow tired but we certainly did have time and distance enough to feel we were well and truly off the beaten track, off any track at all for that matter, as we made our way carefully around the thickets of prickly pear and past great bare boulders hot to the touch.

Duke – of course it had to be Duke – found a long and strangely curling stick, so he picked it up and wrestled with it all around his body, crying out "This damn rattler, he's got me! Jesus holy Christ, I'm not going to let him bite me! But how can I put him down? I have him by the neck, but he's wriggling, he's wriggling and, oh, oh, he's breaking free! Watch out, all of you!" And with that he tossed the stick at three of the girls who had crowded together in horror at the presence of a maddened rattlesnake. The girls screamed – of course they did – and Duke burst out into gales of laughter, doubling over in his delight. Well, it took quite some time for me and everyone else first to calm down and reassure the girls and then to have it out with Duke. Say what we might, he was congenitally unable to see that fun can be carried too far and that terrifying young people of the opposite sex is no way for a gentleman to behave. We couldn't just let him get away with it, him feeling not an ounce of contrition although young Meg had screamed her heart out and even now stood stock still, staring round-eyed at nothing at all and gasping hoarsely all the while. So it was the decision of the group that Duke must pay a price, and this is what it was: he had to carry two girls' packs as well as his own, all day, to make up their campsite in the evening, and tidy up the whole campsite after we were done with it and were ready to drive back to the Institute the next day. With his strength this was really no great burden to him: he saw it as the price to be paid, and cheap at the price. So was our punishment condign, or had we simply shown that we had no sense of humor?

From the rim of the canyon the bright orange sandstone cliff curved over and plunged down vertically a hundred feet or more to the almost-dry streambed below. I was just barely able to keep everyone back from the lip by the authority of my presence, while I sent Alexis off in one direction and Aaron and Pierre in the other to explore the canyon lip for a crevice or steep path by which we might descend to the valley floor. Duke was told to sit still by me, while Iris, Meg and Rosie pulled themselves together after the shock of the 'snake attack.' I was impressed that after five or ten minutes of sitting there together, the three girls rose as one up and came over to Duke, apologizing for having screamed to such an extent that he had been punished for what he had only meant as a laughable trick. That turned him completely around, and he shook hands with each of them as a form of apology and his appreciation of the innate decency of these three young ladies. People just weren't like that back home, he said. No one would ever have come up to him the way they did. He really had a lump in his throat.

Back came Pierre and Aaron, fast friends by now, eagerly announcing to us that not so far along the canyon rim there was a steep cleft, even with steps cut into its walls, presumably by the ancient Deltatikans, and down that path we could easily descend to the bottom of the canyon. Indeed Pierre and Aaron had done just that, in order to find out if the route held good all the way, which it did. So we hallooed for Alexis and he soon came loping in, having explored all along for half a mile or more with no hint, no sign, not the slightest indication of any route of descent anywhere along the canyon lip.

As good fortune would have it, Pierre's and Aaron's path did take us right to the entrance of Deltatikan, the cliff village constructed over a thousand years ago by the Pueblo people, high on the cliff face, presumable for protection from enemies, be they human or animal. We scaled the low walls between the simple chambered houses, and then spread out and explored every single one of the dwellings, squeezing in by the windows and scaling the house walls in order to clamber up to the roofs. The little adobe houses were folded in beneath the broad and capacious curtain of rock that stretched endlessly upwards and outwards above the concavity that sheltered the village. No earthquakes here, we hoped.... After exploring the twenty or so buildings and wondering what had become of their inhabitants, why they or their descendants had abandoned their fastness, and where had they gone, to disappear forever from the rest of the human race, we sat down together in the cool shade with our backs to the canyon wall, just sitting and thinking, each one quietly enveloped in his or her own dreams, fatigued after the walk in the desert sun, and now bemused by the way we had casually occupied the very heart of another people's history. We looked at each other, some of us growing somewhat uncomfortable at our happy-go-lucky invasion of their homes, their ancestral hearths and their places of worship. Aaron, the poet and scholar of our group, felt this first and with the greatest intensity.

"I think we should leave now, very quietly," he said. "We may have disturbed the spirits of the people who once lived here, and I am sorry for that. I will leave in sadness, carrying with me my respect for them."

Iris was the one who followed him most closely. "Yes, Aaron, you are right. We just blundered in, didn't we, meaning no harm but surely showing no respect. I am going to say a prayer in my heart, now, and again tonight before I go to sleep, for the rest and peace of these people, and for their forgiveness of us for being so clumsy."

So, with something of the quiet solemnity of a religious procession, we took our leave of Deltatikan, retraced our steps with some effort back up the steep cleft down which we had so easily slipped before, and headed back to the truck, our home in the modern USA. We were sad to leave the Pueblo people, but this was their land, not ours, and surely they had not invited us. It was right for us to be on our way.

Leave we did, and without a whole lot of time to spare, for each of us gazed with increasing awe at a great bank of clouds beginning to form, to pile up, over there above the western horizon. If this should prove to be a storm, and it surely looked that way, we had better be ready for it. Desert storms are notorious for their ferocity, and we were meagerly prepared, to put it mildly. It was essential that we should get back to the truck just as soon as ever we could, and decide whether we ought to move the truck to higher ground, if indeed there was any in the area, certainly not to linger by the bank of what was at this moment a dust-dry streambed but which in the space of only ten or fifteen minutes could become such a raging torrent as would tumble along any old farm truck foolish enough to linger on its bank. So we hastened, almost ran, back to the truck, some of us arriving close to exhaustion. Good for Duke, I thought, manhandling two extra backpacks with never a whisper of complaint. I promised myself to have private word of gratitude and appreciation with him later on. Everyone piled into the truck, and I pulled it around and headed back the way we had come, to a rise in the ground, a hillock just off the track not two hundred yards from the blacktop road upon which it looked down, a spot with another grove of bushy scrub pines, good shelter for our campsite and privacy for our latrines.

So we climbed out of the truck once more, and reassessed the situation. The weather forecast on the radio, which had been so optimistic yesterday with no hint of desert storms on the morrow, was now speaking seriously about the chance of something really severe, and warning the public to pay the most careful attention. So I called the group together and broke the news to them, that we might in all likelihood expect a severe storm with little advance warning, at practically any time of night or day. Why were we so dogged by storms, I wondered – first on Holy Cross and now here. We still had the option, or at least I thought we probably still did have it, of hightailing it out of there, rigging the canvas over the back of the truck to ward off the full force of the rain, and heading back to the Institute through the late afternoon and into the hours of gathering darkness, but that option was greeted by howls of protest from my stalwart companions.

"We damn well survived Holy Cross in a mountain storm, and we can survive any goddam desert storm they send along! So forget

it, buddy, we're here for keeps! We're the staying kind of folks!"
This, from, of all people, elegant and suave Caitlin Kennedy, the
young lady, debutante to be, from the Virginia hunt country. What
an unrecorded triumph for the Caronson Institute, thought I, to
broaden the mind of so fair a lass as this, shouting out her convic-
tions to all and sundry, to a sturdy Harlem youth, a young Jewish
boy from Washington, a young visitor from France, and to all the
others.

"Yea Caitlin, yea Caitlin – we're all right there with you!" called
out the others with one voice. So there it was: it was up to me,
either to cancel the trip, play safe, drive back home all those long
miles in the dark, with the steaming scorn of all the boys and girls
behind me while I chickened out, the milksop that they would
think me to be – or to set my mind to contrive how best to face
this troublesome challenge, how to rig up a campsite that might
survive a desert storm striking in the wee small hours, in darkness
illuminated only by constant flashes of lightning, with the heavens
drumming us into insensibility by crashes and volleys of thunder
directly overhead. Alexis, Duke, Iris, and Caitlin, all would sit tight
and brace themselves to survive the immensity of that – but what
about gentle Pierre, his newfound buddy Aaron, young Rosie and
younger Meg, how could I be sure they would be able to keep up
their spirits in such a trial, and more important, what part must
I now play in order to ensure that all came out for the best? We
would have no such stone shelter as had given us refuge so long
ago on Holy Cross Mountain.

Well, first and foremost, thought I, let's be practical. Here
we are, out in the wilderness, with the devil of a storm a-brewing
(but maybe it would yet pass over); night dropping down upon us
even as we hesitate; no supper yet in anyone's stomach; no latrines
planned or dug; no plastic waterproof tent-sheet coverings rigged;
no sleeping bags set out – Jesus holy Christ, what am I all about?
Please let me just wake up in my bed at home and have all this a

bad dream! But I drove that idiocy away fast, and set myself and the team to work. Work we did, unremittingly and to good effect. The thunder growled in the distance, and we cooked ourselves a hearty dinner – bully beef and green beans, cookies and blueberries -- that we had brought with us in the truck, and sat back for an evening of tall stories, reminiscences of Mount Grayling in the remote past and much else beside, even a song or two, until we told ourselves that it was time to turn in. And the thunder continued to growl on, near and far, coming steadily closer. Thinking of which, I had everyone take into their little shelter-tent only the things they positively needed for the night and to stack everything else, particularly any clothing, in the back of the truck. Rain might easily seep in under their sleeping bags.

It must have been about two in the morning when a tremendous explosive crack followed by the deepest of booms shattered the air all around us. We were all wide awake in a second, wondering what had been hit: one of our own company, one of the pine trees, the truck itself, who knows? There was no time for speculation since we heard the squall of rain rushing across the desert to meet us, which it did immediately and with a vengeance, a pounding roar and a fierce hammering upon every surface. All our plastic rain sheets, tied securely though they were to the truck, to tree limbs or to rocky projections, collapsed instantly upon us, and cold water coursed everywhere in darkness pierced by zigzags of lightning and, when we could manage it, by the beams of our flashlights. The canvas cover over the cargo bed at the back of the truck held tight, by some miracle, and we were glad that we had lashed it securely before nightfall. Most of the boys and girls simply abandoned their possessions, sodden and scattered as they were, and gathered at the back of the truck where they helped one another climb in out of the storm. They tumbled over Menannah Lightfoot's spades and shovels that we had used to dig the latrines, but that was of no account. I was not sure that I really was glad that everyone was in the truck, for the truck was just about the tallest object around and could easily attract the lightning, but it would have been difficult in the extreme to force bedraggled and scared youngsters out into the storm once more. Besides, the storm itself abated as fast as it had arisen, and we could hear the rush of the pelting rain as it receded eastwards. It was time to assess the situation and to decide upon a course of action.

"Right!" I called out to the sodden mass of humanity that filled the back of the truck. "Everyone listen to me! No talking now. This is serious business. We've got to find out if everyone is here. Remember the buddy system I started with you back when we were looking for that stone shelter on Holy Cross? You <u>must</u>, absolutely must, see the two people above you and below you in the alphabet – no taking anyone's word for it. Right? Now go to it." That worked like a dream, and everyone was accounted for in a couple of seconds.

"Next, dry clothing," I said. 'Boys, all of you get out of the back of the truck, stand around in front or squeeze into the cab for a few minutes while the girls stay in the back and change into the dry clothes they left here, and then they can take your place in the cab and you can go change. No peeking now! It's going to be a tight squeeze, but we've got to get these things right." And that was accomplished. Even dear Duke behaved himself this time.

Afterwards in the back of the truck they bundled themselves together in friendly abandon, and I stayed right there with them. No one slept very much for the remainder of the night, but decorum and decency were maintained. There was no privacy, only lots of healthy exhaustion.

Daylight! We climbed down and began to sort out the wreckage of our campsite. Clothes and sleeping bags were rescued, soon strung up to dry along with all the plastic sheeting tied to the truck and to the closest low pine trees. It was a sobering moment for all of us when we came across one tree which yesterday had stood a good twenty feet tall. But now it was riven right down the middle into two almost identical halves, one prostrate along the ground and the other swaying uncertainly in the morning breeze. So that was the work of that first bolt of lightning and deafening crack of thunder! It could so very easily have been one or more of us.

"So who was praying for us and protecting us?" asked Aaron. "Do you think it was the God of the Christians or the Jews, or the spirits of the wilderness, the Great Mystery that the Indians tell us about?"

"Le bon Dieu, He is the same everywhere," answered Pierre. "I think the old Pueblo people helped us, because we showed respect to them: we were sorry that we had walked all through their houses without asking, and we left them in peace. In my mind I told them we were sorry deep in our hearts, and I think they heard me." At that Iris and Caitlin stepped forward as if on cue and warmly saluted the boys with a quick kiss. The boys, being younger than the girls and not as tall as them, felt a little abashed.

"My turn for the next hug! Step right up, ladies, step right up!" called out Duke, and the magic moment collapsed. "Who's for breakfast? And what do we have after the rain?"

There was bacon to be fried, and toast, pancakes and coffee or tea, so we all scattered to look for fuel for a campfire. But of course there was no dry wood to be found anywhere after the storm, though we did bring in armfuls of pine branches as sodden as our bedding, and several small handfuls of dry twigs and little branches from under the truck. But how to get a strong fire going, even with all the matches we had with us?

I balled up some dry sheets of paper that I found beneath the dashboard in the truck, receipts for farm supplies I could just decipher, a good many years old, and made them the centerpiece of a small teepee of dry twigs with small needled branches overarching the construct. With the driest possible split branches and twigs beside me, I struck a match, offered up a quick prayer to Mazda,

Wayland, Hephaestus, Tubal Cain and all the other gods of fire, and applied light to tinder. Yes, it flared, it flared beautifully, a little stream of smoke and a tongue of flame reaching some ten inches or more into the crisp morning air. I gently laid split twigs upon the tepee, split side inwards, points erect, and watched with hope at first and then with growing anxiety, disappointment and finally despair, as the smoke at first thickened and whitened, but then the flame dropped down, dwindled and gave up the ghost in a fading wisp of grey-black smoke. Hell, that was all the kindling we had! And now what? Eight anxious faces cast sour glances at me, and I could almost hear, echoing and re-echoing among the far-off hills, the rumbles of nine empty stomachs.

Anyone have a cigarette lighter? No, of course not. Anyone have fuel for a lighter? Damfool question. So what next? No hot breakfast, and at least an hour's drive to the nearest Navajo trading post, which might, or equally well might not, have anything for us to eat. Jeez Louise, as they say – Bloody Hell, as I say. And then I remembered, and at once kind of wished I hadn't. Why, there was that five-gallon can of gasoline in the back of Menannah Lightfoot's farm truck, placed there by Providence (or by the Devil, I wondered) for our exclusive use in times of emergency. And if this wasn't an emergency, pray, what was?

So I went back to the truck, took down the can, and brought it forward. I had had some experience with gasoline and knew very well indeed how totally inflammable and deadly dangerous it was. – 'Hazmats', what an excellent word. -- With care, and with assistance from Alexis, Pierre and Aaron, Iris and Caitlin, I reconstructed the little teepee, this time built of damp and downright wet little branches, and set beside it, a little distance away, a pile of slightly larger branches and fronds, and then again some decent-sized broken tree limbs beyond them all. I was ready. With the greatest care I poured about a sixteenth of an inch of gasoline into an empty soda can, and poured it over the teepee. Telling everyone to stand well back, I struck a match and dropped it onto the pile. A blaze of flame leaped upward several inches, and then fell reluctantly back and extinguished itself. All right, a sixteenth of an inch was clearly not enough for this endeavor, and the branches were clearly too waterlogged. So we dismantled the teepee, poured a little more gasoline into a shallow dish, and soaked the needled branches in the liquid.

After letting them soak for a minute or two, we rebuilt the teepee and wearily all of us set to start the whole process over, when we were utterly taken aback by a whoop of triumph and a barrage of shouts some yards behind us. It was Duke, yes it was! Good grief, what damfool thing had he done now? He had in fact discovered what he took to be a young mountain lion, or at least a bobcat, and he was hollering all over creation in his animal high spirits, having treed the unfortunate creature in one of the ragged twenty-foot pines. We all dropped our tools, and I ordered everyone not to touch anything by the fire on pain of death while we went to find out what was going on. If it really was a mountain lion cub, then the mother would surely be around too, and that would be no joke, no joke at all: she would attack, and certainly she could kill. Duke was beside himself in his excitement, screaming and leaping around, and he had infected a bunch of the others, who frankly ought to have known better. Glancing warily through the branches of the tree in question, I found myself face to face with none other than a frightened and resentful raccoon, cornered at the top of a tree! Poor Duke, how we all began to tease him mercilessly – until we were all cut short by another piercing and much more terrified series of screams from way back behind us.

Whirling around, we saw to our horror a figure racing pell-mell down the slope of the hill, a mass of flames pouring from head to foot high into the air. For one moment we were all frozen motionless in our horror, but then I was the first to master my astonishment and to act. I leaped to my feet and tore after the apparition, my long strides catching up in no time to the short figure all aflame dashing down the hill in front of me. I knocked it – him or her, I knew not – down to the ground and scooped up handfuls of wet sand, my hands together acting as a shovel, until nothing at all could be seen of the now passive and silent, gasping figure but the outline of nose, mouth and eyes. By then everyone else had come up at a run, and I carefully scraped away the wet sand to reveal a pitifully scared little Rosie Durrindale.

Gasping for breath, she told us what terrible thing she had done. Everyone else in the group had won credit for something special or useful on one or other of our trips, but she had done nothing to earn anyone's gratitude or respect, so now when everyone was rushing away to look at the mountain lion, she suddenly saw that her chance had come. She would be the one to light the fire! So she poured out a cupful, yes a cupful, of gasoline into the soda can and dropped in a lighted match, preparatory to pouring the liquid slowly over the damp sticks. Well, as they say, the rest is history -- indeed it was very nearly obituary. She tossed the can away as the flames roared up, splashing the gasoline all over herself. Screaming and staggering to her feet, she tore off down the hill, quite why she didn't know, only to get as far away from the fire as ever she could. And that was when by the grace of God I caught up with her.

I was so angry at her for playing with fire that pity was almost driven out of my system. But the older girls mercifully took over and ascertained that she felt no pain beyond that from the blow I had administered when I felled her in order to quench the flames that looked certain to burn her alive. She sat up, smiled in bewilderment at each of us, and then burst into wrenching tears. She had not a hint of a burn upon her, not a hint at all, and astonishingly her clothes were only slightly singed too, so fast had I pursued her, knocked her flying, and in fact saved her life. First relief overcame her, and then shame at the trouble she had caused and the fact that she had been caught, absolutely caught, in the most direct disobedience to myself, the one person who had for her own good been set in authority over her.

Something bright and flickering caught the corner of my eye, and I turned to look back up the hill to our campsite. Flames! In falling back from the fire Rosie had knocked over the five-gallon can, and most of the gasoline had spilled out onto the ground. I stood up and saw with horror that a small stream was making its way right to our truck. I dashed back up the hill, noticing with relief that the truck had not caught light yet, although the first little flames were already beginning to lick at the rubber tires. There was absolutely no time to be lost. If I waited an instant the truck might well catch fire and then explode, likely enough killing one or more of my charges. I leapt into the cab, started the engine with a roar, and backed the truck at full speed into the grove of pine trees, where it came to a halt against a small trunk twenty yards back from the burning gasoline. The situation was saved, but my relief turned to panic fear in an instant, for I had not looked to see if any hiker had been standing behind the truck, which could well have been the case since people were often coming and going for their possessions. Thank the Lord, no one was there at that moment, all too excited in pursuit first of Duke's 'mountain lion,' and then of poor blazing Rosie. But this was the second time I had positively endangered the lives of my hikers, and I trembled to think there might be a third somewhere ahead of me. Three strikes and you're out.

Meanwhile Rosie had slowly calmed down, sitting, still with sand all over her, on the hillside, and gradually she told me what had happened, how she had come within an ace of killing herself and sending her family and all who knew and loved her into deepest grief. She had used a fuel lighter before, for charcoal on her parents' and her grandparents' grills at home, and she knew, knew intimately, just how to use a fuel lighter on a barbecue grill. But, silly little girl that she was and that she now labeled herself to be, she had had no idea that charcoal lighter fuel and gasoline were clear different things. So she had determined to show the world that there was indeed something that she could do – light a darn good fire, by golly! And light a fire she did, igniting the best part of a soda can of gasoline and thereby coming within an ace of im- molating herself.

With my caustic tongue I lit into her quite hard, I really did, and I am not ashamed of that, no, not in the least. Rosie truly had to be brought to the realization of what her death would have meant, to her near and dear ones, her grief-ridden mother, father and older sisters back at home, to all her extended family, her school friends, to that boy next door whom she looked up to, to all of us in the hik- ing group and everyone at the Institute, students and adults alike, and, yes, to me. I told her that I would have been held criminally liable for negligence in leaving such tools of death within reach of any thoughtless little boy or girl who wanted to pick them up and play with them. My career at the Institute would be over in deep- est disgrace and I would be in serious trouble with the law, but far worse, I would have to carry with me for all my born days the guilt and the responsibility for the death of a fine young girl entrusted to my charge. I did not tell her or anyone about my stupidity in reversing the truck at full speed without looking behind me – no need for that -- but I was trembling all over by this time.

No one had much appetite for exploring the desert any farther, so we simply packed up and drove away. It was a somber and almost silent drive all the way, Rosie sobbing from time to time, imagin- ing of what her friends, and most of all her parents, would think of her. There would be relief at her safety, yes, but there would surely be, on her parents' part anyway, a measure of anger at her for her foolishness and at me for criminal neglect of my duties. Why don't we just not tell anyone, and then there'll be no trouble, Rosie asked Caitlin and Iris, I learned later. No, they replied, the story is bound to get out one way or another, and think of the trouble Edward would get into if he tried to conceal a thing like this. Oh Lord, sobbed Rosie, I'm getting everyone into trouble! Caitlin and Iris just hugged her and held her firm.

I thought it would be best for me to meet with Jonathan Dunkerley-Jones first, and then Rosie would meet with him, either alone or with me present as she wished. She had done nothing flagrantly malicious, and so should be free to make all the decisions she could. She agreed to my plan, and asked me to be with her when her turn came. Both those meetings went off as well as they possibly could. After that Rosie called her parents, and Jonathan and I followed her on the telephone. I was particularly gratified and relieved that Rosie's family, and her father in particular, had not seen fit to throw a load of guilt squarely in my face. In short, when they heard the whole story, they exonerated me at once when they heard I had rushed off to shield the children from an angry mother mountain lion, and fastened every ounce of blame upon their own darling daughter. Finally Jonathan called a staff meeting and told the group what had happened. It was his decision also that we should inform all the students in the Institute: they needed to hear an accurate account before all kinds of rumors and twisted versions began to spread, as surely they would. So once again I had to repeat the story, in words that I almost knew by heart by this time, and I was received in silence. The students were awed by the closeness of disaster, the suddenness at which it can strike when everything seems to be going so well. Lastly I had one more call to make, to Samuel and Rachel Caronson, whose only comment was that it would have broken their hearts completely if the Institute they had founded in memory of their dear son had been stained by the death of yet another young person even in its very first season. Frankly, everyone exonerated me, everyone that is except myself. They would never have felt that way, oh no, not at all, if I had crashed the truck on the way back from Mount Elbert – but no one ever learned about that close-run thing.

Finally, it was over. With an unbelievable sight of relief, I told myself that it was over, it was over, it was over. Rosie could go on living her life as she chose, and I could go on living my life as I chose. This frightening episode and its subsequent period of intense anxiety were over and done with. Rosie and I had a good long talk together, and in a tearful hug, we purged ourselves of all the wretched memories. We were close friends when we parted, and after that we had our own way of winking at each other.

Well, with the return of all the other expeditions, white-water kayakers, horseback riders and rock-climbers, this was a time of celebration and of a long goodbye. This was indeed the final evening of the Caronson Institute, at least as far as its first season was concerned, and Samuel and Rachel Caronson returned before sunset, just in time to take part in the closing festivities. The students had packed up their belongings and were ready to depart on the morrow, and I was too, shortly to be followed by Jonathan Dunkerley-Jones, Bud Tamarack, Rodney Tregannet and all the rest of the staff. Autumn would soon descend upon the Institute and it would sleep until it should awaken to new glories and an ever-broader life in the next springtime, with Samuel and Rachel glad in their hearts at the prospect of another and even more successful season. How poor Simon would have adored all this!

So when all the bags were packed we made ourselves ready for the buses that would take us early in the morning to the local airport and thence back to Denver and home. In a couple of days

I would be headed back to Boston, where I had taken up a teaching position in the English department of the Crittenden School while at the same time attempting to complete my Ph.D. thesis. I might meet the staff members of the Institute again, particularly if I visited Uncle Rod in the summer once more, but it was a strange sensation for me on this final evening to be on the point of saying farewell, not goodbye for a season but truly farewell for a lifetime, to my valiant hikers, one and all members of a team bound together by our unique experiences – the snow-filled corry on Mount Grayling, the stone shelter on Holy Cross, the blaze of sunrise on Mount Elbert, the deep but uncomfortable peace of Deltatikan, even the blaze of poor Rosie... We sat on the grass together as a group and brought forward all those memories, spending time on them one by one as they passed before us, and we told our stories to the staff and all the other young people at the last great fire-lit evening of Caronson Institute 1975. Spread out on the grass around the tall campfire by the pond, people spoke, people sang, people recited, and there was in the air a sense of particular sad happiness.

It was the white-water kayakers who shattered the solemnity of the occasion. "Here, coach Bully Blasky, you've got us good and wet a dozen times and more! Now we're going to dunk you, oh yes, sir, we are!" and they surged forward, laughing uproariously, and seized the vainly protesting Coach Blasky by his wrists and ankles, carried him shoulder-high across to the camp pond, heaved once, heaved twice and yet again, and tossed him fairly and squarely right into the water. He emerged spluttering and laughing, pretending to be furious but in truth gratified at the affection his team had so raucously displayed.

"Now, Mister Hiker King, it's your turn -- Yes Sirree!" shouted out Duke Sutton in his broad baritone voice. And, hesitantly at first, but then with gathering enthusiasm and amid gales of laughter, all my dear friends descended upon me in a cascade, seized my arms and legs, and bore me shoulder-high to the brink of the pond.

"Put out your own fires next time!" called Rosie, blushing furiously at her daring.

"What price desert thunderstorms back in Boston?" asked Alexis, struggling with my ankles.

"Ah, le bon Dieu, may He have mercy on you in the lake!" That was Pierre's farewell to me.

"Come back and see us all – if you can swim," called out Caitlin and Iris together, in gales of laughter.

And then they all swung me as high as ever they could. "One! ... Two! ... Three!"

Whoosh!!

CHAPTER 10
USSR --- 1985

"Look! There it is, it really is! Cool! --- Russia, and I've waited so long! --- So that's it? All pine forests, it seems to me --- Oh God, I'm beginning to feel a bit scared already --- Fascinating, fascinating, this is going to be so great! --- Only one or two roads, no towns, and we're right above the airport already? --- It's just blank, forests and that's all; I didn't expect that, but now I do see a few fields and a railway..." These were among the comments of the twenty American teenagers that my friend and colleague Ellen McCrae and I had, perhaps rashly, undertaken to escort around the USSR for a full month in the spring of 1985. We understood that our plane was descending from its cruising height towards our landing field outside Moscow. But everything about a trip to Russia is unexpected, and our landing, our very first experience, set the tone. I could recognize by now that this was certainly not the approach to Sheremetyevo, Moscow's international airport! The captain of our Aeroflot jetliner announced to us all that there had been an accident to another Aeroflot plane trying to land at Sheremetyevo with jammed landing gear, and all neighboring airports were filled or too small to take our transatlantic jetliner, so we had been diverted to Helsinki.

"Oh no, Helsinki, hell! Oh no, Helsinki, hell! Oh no, Helsinki, hell!" chanted some of the more extroverted and thoughtless (not to say vulgar) of our students, led by Alex Leibowitz and Adam O'Neill, until Ellen McCrae and I shushed them up, ordering them to be more considerate of the discomfort and embarrassment of the crew. "Oh no, the Ugly American already, and we're not even in Russia yet," I groaned.

We made our way through customs uneventfully, the students tired and disappointed, both irritable and excited. Ellen and I were on the point of calling the American consulate for advice how to spend the six hours before the resumption of our travel to Moscow when we were accosted by a tall and attractive young blonde Finnish air hostess who told us in immaculate clipped English that her employer, Suomi Travel, had informed her of the plight of these young Americans and asked her to offer her service as guide and interpreter for the day: Suomi Travel was an associate of our travel agency back in New York.

"Welcome to Helsinki, my home town," our trim and sparkling young guide announced to the students who had crowded around her. She stood out in her ice-blue uniform glinting with polished brass buttons. "I am so sorry about your delay, but I am proud to show you our beautiful city! Now, what would you like to do? Here are three ideas.

First, I can call up a bus and we can tour the city. You will be able to see our famed football stadium, our important parliament buildings, our residential and business districts. Who wishes for this? No one? I think you must be tired from travel, yes?

Oh well, I can suggest two more ideas. You can stay in city centre, walk all through our department stores, very fashionable, and then take a sauna, traditional Finnish steam bath, very refreshing. Any takers? Oh good, half of you or more. Young ladies, you will enjoy very modern Scandinavian design and fashions.

And a last idea from me: if your teachers permit, you can explore Helsinki city on your own, taking in Lutheran Cathedral, very dignified, and the boat docks and marina, so beautiful and where you can purchase reindeer hides. And will also be time for sauna, yes. Who is this for? Ah yes, each has made his or her choice. Good, good.

So, if your teachers permit, I will escort some of you, particularly young ladies, through the fashion centre shopping district, with one of your teachers. And the rest can stay with other teacher and take good walk, like hike, through city, to Lutheran Cathedral and even Russian church, very big one from late Russian Empire, and the harbor, with other teacher, I say.

Listen to me, please, teachers, is that all right? And all will be back exactly here in six hours for onward to Moscow. Anyone late stays in Helsinki, very sorry, then flies back to New York, because Soviet law says no young person enters Soviet Union alone, needs adult companion. And I must tell you, Moscow Airport so busy now, with damaged plane sit sideways on runway and cannot move, so your group will be travelling by overnight train to Moscow. This is not so bad, I tell you. Four to a compartment, good bunks, top and bottom, girls and boys separate, and hot tea served by railway staffs as approaching Moscow."

Fortunately, all went well. Ellen struck up an immediate friendship with Elle Torgensson, the elegant young lady from Suomi Travel, since they were both connoisseurs of Tove Jansson, Moomin Troll and that whole series of books, such a lucky coincidence. They exchanged home addresses and opened what promised fair to be a lifelong friendship.

The rest of the group, boys mainly, went with me to take a good look at the Lutheran Cathedral – white and elegant, with stout white columns beneath a broad pediment, and a clean airy space inside. The Russian church was, the students all said afterwards, gloomy and unwelcoming, threatening rather than attractive.

Helsingfors had been one of the Russian Empire's great westward-facing ports, so a substantial cathedral had been erected in the Muscovite style late in the nineteenth century, all dark red, heavy and sullen. But the docks were charming, attractive indeed with a bright flutter of small sailing craft and ferries to cross the Gulf of Finland to Tallinn or the Baltic to Stockholm. Most intriguing were the racks and piles of reindeer hides displayed for sale, fresh and sparkling clean, but immensely heavy with all that deep undercoat of fur to ward off the Arctic cold. Graham Convey, a tall and muscular lad from the Midwest, was all set to buy one and carry it with him across the Soviet Union, but I felt I really had to discourage him since it must have weighed thirty pounds and he would have his baggage to carry as well. The reindeer hide would have been a wonderful thing to bring back home, but it was just too much. I felt sad and a little guilty.

The sauna, ah the sauna, it was a great success! Boys and girls wrapped more or less securely in long white towels sweated it out in the steam room, urging one another among squeals to dare ever greater heat and to pour more water onto the hot rocks to create even more clouds of steam, and keeping the sauna staff busy maintaining decorum and a bearable level of noise. Julie Salmonson and Ned Bickers took to tweaking at each other's towels amid gales of laughter: those two were an item already. Ellen and I would have to keep an eye on them, which made us feel very middle-aged although we were in fact both in our early thirties. Well, we all came through it, with Ellen and me managing to gain some respect from the students for our resolve not to be left out as boring old adults. I will say this: we sweated it out with the best of them.

Let me describe now, as we were waiting for the night train to Moscow, who we all were and how the twenty students and two adults had come together. Ellen McCrae teaches Russian history and international history at the Margaret Denton School for Girls in Newton, while I teach Russian language and literature at

Brookline Hill Academy, both just outside Boston. It was a natural for the two schools, both single sex, to coordinate their schedules as far as possible, one outcome of that being that for the final month of the senior year they both maintain individual or group projects, such as our tour of the Soviet Union. I must say that of course not every family could afford the cost of a month in the Soviet Union for their son or daughter, or various other trips that the two schools sponsored, but we had established a special fund-raising program to which every traveler made his or her contribution, either financially or by active promotion and fund-raising through alumni and other groups. It was fortunate that one of us was fluent in Russian: it would have been foolish to confine ourselves to translation and to hope and pray that no emergency would ever arise, particularly no medical emergency.

We had taken dinner in the Helsinki railway station building whose frontage to the city had been designed by Eero Saarinen, to the great interest of our History of Art students. So once we had boarded the Russian train and sorted ourselves out into compartments by gender, there was little to do as the train rolled out into the night but to sit around and talk. The delay in Helsinki had made the students more excited if anything, eager to talk endlessly as they lay or squatted on their bunks or lounged in the narrow corridor, talking endlessly. Eventually Ellen and I moved back and forth, back and forth, along the corridor, requiring the foursomes to separate themselves from each other, boys with boys and girls with girls, to take up their places in their own four-bunk compartments, and to shut – and keep shut – the door. But we could not stop them talking, and more than a few of them got precious little sleep that night.

All hope of peace and quiet was destroyed by an inexplicable incident at the Russo-Finnish frontier, one of those frightening and totally unexpected occurrences that mark many visitors' experience in Russia. Some hundred yards short of the border Finnish guards boarded the train, courteously examined our passports and travel papers, and bade us goodnight and a safe experience in the Soviet Union. "Come back again, and this time see our country!" they called out as they smiled, climbed down and disappeared into the darkness. The train rolled forward ever so slowly, crossed the border (as one or two of us crossed ourselves at the same time for good luck), and stopped dead still. We looked at each other: we were now behind the Iron Curtain! Russian frontier police clambered aboard, marked by dark green headbands on their caps and details on their uniforms. No greetings, no eye contact, just a push into several random compartments, and a finger pointed to some suitcase, to be opened and all its contents spread out before the guards, who, I noticed with distaste, seemed to take an interest in the girls' underwear.

Our passports and travel papers passed muster, and the guards were just about to climb down, to an almost audible sigh of relief from our company, when one of the soldiers turned back, pointed to a girl's suitcase on the top bunk, and had it taken down. He did not wait for it to be opened, but peeled back the bunk mattress and drew out from under it a wicked-looking ten-inch long knife, a scalpel or dagger! We all gasped in horror, and Amanda Tillotson whose bunk it was almost fainted on the spot. The guard began to shout, in Russian of course, and to shake the girl by the shoulder. She fell apart in tears and hysterics, with Ellen trying to calm her and to shield her. I tried to speak sense to the guard, but he just roared at us, announcing that he and his comrades would take the terrorist girl away but none of us could accompany her since we were not under suspicion. I tell you, this was a bad moment! Labor camp in Siberia? International incident? Soviet-American Summit shot down in flames? I was trying hard to keep control of myself, Ellen was doing all she could to protect young Amanda, and everyone else was standing around frozen in horror – and then suddenly the entire scene changed. The guard stepped back into the compartment, swung the knife menacingly around in the air a couple of times, and tossed it back onto Amanda's bunk. Then with a guffaw he dropped out of the train, the doors swung to, and once more we were on our way to Moscow. We never heard another word of the incident and of course never reported it in Moscow – it would be our word against that of a representative of the Soviet armed forces -- but one thing is sure: it certainly made a vivid entry in Amanda's journal. As for the guard, well, I could only suppose that he had concealed the knife up his sleeve until he 'discovered' it, and then had a bit of what he considered good, honest, Russian fun with an American girl. This was our first encounter with the 'humor' of Soviet officialdom.

After some hours the sky lightened, and forests and villages gave way to dreary suburbs. Men and women, looking short and thick, trudged steadily along well-worn paths through the dirt towards the bus or train station in order to make their way to work. It was a sad sight, perhaps more somber than sad. Meanwhile the 'train ladies,' as we called them, served us piping hot tea in tall glasses set in metal cup-holders.

The train pulled into the station in Moscow where stood ready to meet us our guide Natasha, as arranged by Intourist. She, a somewhat severe-looking individual wearing sensible clothes and substantial shoes, would be with us for four weeks so it was important that we all get along well together. We dragged out our suitcases and stacked them on the old wooden wagon that Natasha had commandeered, together with the services of a porter. A shabby tour bus took us to our hotel, a glass tower of perhaps seventeen stories set on a hill on the northern edge of the city. Alex Leibowitz and Nan Crandle complained loudly that we not to be close, within walking distance anyway, of the Kremlin and Red Square, but visitors had no choice: they are simply assigned, and I had to tell Alex and Nan to keep their disappointment to themselves. It would do no good to express it, and it might well alienate Natasha, upon whose goodwill we would have to rely for a month. With reluctance we surrendered our passports at the hotel desk, wondering if we would ever see them again, but once again we had no choice in the matter. The students paired off with the roommates they had chosen. Ellen and I had singles.

The rooms were scattered on different floors and it took forever for the infinitely small, solitary elevator to reach the top floor and descend again, letting passengers in and out at every level. Graham Convey, the tall and athletic boy from Minnesota, and a couple of others felt in need of exercise and ran up the ten or more flights of stairs to their rooms. My room was at the top of the building, which I reached by way of the elevator, but I decided to walk down, as did most of the students who had ridden the elevator up to their rooms. In their impatience and excitement at finally being in Moscow many of the students started to run and jump down the stairs. Suddenly I let out a terrific yell, shouting to them all to stop, to walk down slowly and at all times to hold on to the hand rail. I had felt cool fresh air, very fresh in the shaft of the staircase, quite unlike the hot, steamy air in the rest of the hotel – and in a flash I was sure I knew the reason for that. Well, I was right! At one turn in the tall, glassed-in stairway tower where there should have been a six-foot sheet of plate glass window there was instead nothing, simply nothing. Perhaps the glass sheet had been broken, perhaps it had been stolen – at any rate it was certainly not there, and there was no warning notice, so a boy or girl running down while barely touching the stair rail if at all could very easily have taken a headlong plunge fifty feet or more down to the street below. Well, that sobered us up a good deal! Ellen and I explained how rough and unfinished Moscow, and indeed the whole Soviet Union, were -- 'Remont' or 'Under Repair' being one of the commonest signs we saw, soon learned by all the students. Not long after that we noticed on the wall of a large and newly constructed office building a sign announcing proudly "This Building Constructed Entirely from Materials Saved at Other Sites." Well, aha, we thought, we know a thing or two about that.

And came then the city tour on a soon-to-be-familiar bus that had seen better days a good any years ago. Almost half the students missed the commentary, even in Red Square and at the foot of the Kremlin wall, since they were sprawled fast asleep across their seats, having talked away half or more of the preceding night on the train. Natasha lectured on regardless: it was her duty, and she knew that we would be asked to write a report on her work and her coverage when the whole visit was over. Besides, she was a Muscovite and proud of her city, as indeed was every Muscovite we met.

The heart of Old Muscovy! What a strong grip is taken upon one's heart by the presence of ancient Moscow all around one, the home of the tsars from the fourteenth to the twentieth centuries. Our first stopping point was, naturally, the Kremlin, where we were overwhelmed by the dimmed light, the towering iconostases and the frescoes on the columns, arches, walls and ceilings in the three great cathedrals, surmounted by dome after golden dome. The oldest, the Cathedral of the Dormition, where all tsars were crowned, silenced even the most irreverent of our group of young Americans as we wandered through, breathing the very essence of Old Russia. We were loath to go farther and we lingered as long as we could, but all too soon our impatient guide ushered us on, informing us that we had a schedule to follow and that in our spare time we were free to come back if we chose. So we were escorted across the open square and through St. Michael's Cathedral where all tsars before Peter the Great were buried, and on to the small but truly intoxicating Cathedral of the Annunciation, the site of all tsars' weddings. This last cathedral is not much larger than a family chapel, dark inside, but a jewel beyond belief, steeped in the same deep religious atmosphere as the Cathedral of the Dormition but here concentrated in such a way as almost physically to seize hold of each of us, and to draw us in. "Get me out of here, or I'll start worshipping all those tsars," gibed one of our group, Shimon Goldstein from Brooklyn.

I dared to ask Natasha why the domes of the Cathedral of St. Michael were now gilded and gleaming in the sharp sunshine, when they had always been leaden or silver in mourning for the dead tsars interred below. She replied that I was mistaken, of course they had always been golden just like all the other domes -- we had lost count how many -- on all sides in the Kremlin. My guess was that they had been tarted up for the Olympics, but I did not want to alienate her by saying so. It gave me pleasure, however, later to confront her with a postcard purchased in the hotel lobby, showing the domes in question dull silver in color. "Oh pish," she exclaimed in embarrassment, "they were being cleaned" -- but I knew my history.

Soon enough another incident involving postcards took place, this time infinitely more sinister. Many of the students had bought postcards from the kiosk in the lobby of the hotel, and wanted to send them off to the folks back home. This seemed innocent enough and I gave the matter no thought. Two days later, not long before we were due to leave Moscow, all hell broke loose.

A pair of policemen arrived in the hotel lobby early in the morning and demanded to see John Nicholson and the adults in charge of the student group. Johnny, Ellen McCrae and I met with the officials, who were scowling in a hostile and threatening way.

"John Nicholson, that is you, is that correct? You are under arrest for insult to the Soviet people and defacing the image of the Founder of Our Country, the Hero of Our Peoples. You will come with us, now, to police station. One adult, you will come too as witness."

"But I haven't done anything? What's all this about?" blurted out Johnny, growing pale and sweating at the same time.

"Come quietly to Police Station, or will be handcuffs. All will be explained."

So Johnny, together with me as the Russian speaker in our group, rode in the back of a police van to the police station where he was formally arraigned and charged. And at last we learned what it was all about. What an idiot he had been, what an unbelievable, absolute bloody idiot! He had wanted to send a postcard to his kid brother back home, and he had chosen a picture of a benevolent and avuncular Lenin. But then he had been fool enough to draw dark glasses on the face, scars on the cheeks with lines of stitches still showing, and lice crawling down from his scalp. And, oh what a wretched, goddam fool he was, he had not only signed his name but mentioned in the message in his card the name of the hotel where we were staying – and sent the card off openly, not even sealed in an envelope! Good grief, some people really ask for trouble, it's incredible.

Johnny would be held in the jail overnight, and charged in a People's Court the next day. All I could do was tell Johnny I would at once notify the American Embassy in Moscow and his parents if I could reach them. I was pretty sure that all that the Embassy could do would be to keep a watch on Johnny, see what happened to him, and report this to the State Department in Washington, while at the same time requesting the Soviet government to show leniency toward an ignorant and unthinking young boy. And there I had to leave poor, benighted Johnny, alone in his cell, and him not knowing a word of how to communicate with his captors.

The Embassy was as helpful as it could be: a well-spoken young man came with me to visit Johnny in prison and gave him what comfort he could, telling him that in his opinion this was all being staged to make an example of him and that the Soviet government would have no intention at all of creating an international incident out of schoolboy stupidity and rudeness. Johnny did appear to be at least somewhat comforted by this.

I sat around in the hotel all that day in order to be immediately available should any need arise. Ellen took the group on another tour and visit somewhere in Moscow, but to be honest I cannot remember where they went, and I don't suppose they can either: everyone was so worried. Our guide Natasha, however, had her job to do, and nothing would stop her in pursuit of that: there was always those final reports to make at the end of our tour of the country, her report and ours.

Well, the next morning after a night without much sleep, I presented myself in jacket and tie at People's Court No. 15, where the trial was to be held at ten o'clock, Madam Judge-Advocate Kyrilla Leonidovna Serativo presiding. The same young official from the Embassy accompanied me, trying to reassure me that whatever happened the Embassy would do its level best to keep messages flowing through, back and forth, between the boy and his parents, perhaps once a month if the poor lad was incarcerated – but he did not think that was really at all likely. The Embassy could not interfere with the Soviet judicial system, having itself no right of appeal since it was not recognized by the court as a party in the case, and so on and so on. I grew bleak, despair folding in upon me. But surely the punishment for an act of infantile foolishness would not be so very severe, would it? That would all depend on Judge-Advocate Serativo, and I knew nothing at all about her. *Gulag Archipelago*, Solzhenitsyn's three-volume account of the countless horrors of the penal system, rose before my eyes, deprived of sleep as I was.

"All stand for the People's Judge and Advocate!" a voice called out, and the trial got under way. Well, after the preliminaries and all the bureaucratic verbosity common, it seems, to judicial proceedings the world over, the evidence was presented. No defence at all was offered but only the humblest of apologies. The sentence was pronounced:

"Two months at hard labor in a corrective labor camp" – long dramatic pause – "or leave the Soviet Union within twenty-four hours!"

It was over! Johnny collapsed in tears and was handed over to my keeping, with a demand that I purchase a ticket to New York immediately, or surrender John Nicholson to the authorities for transfer to a penal colony.

"I think I'd rather go home, if you don't mind," Johnny managed with a weak half-smile, "and I'm terribly sorry I've been such a nuisance."

The Embassy helped to secure the financing, and I escorted Adam to Sheremetyevo Airport, from whence he flew home to the bosom of his family

The lesson was learned: it was much worse than 'Don't Mess With Texas.'

Ellen and I called a meeting of the students, and I told them something they absolutely, positively had to remember, that they had to assume all the time, rightly or wrongly, that someone in authority was listening in to every single word spoken in their rooms or anywhere else at all, save out in the open air. As I said those words, I was sure someone was listening to me at that very instant. And if any other of you students let me down, I promised, I would be standing there in court positively insisting on months and months of convict labor for them!

When we had calmed down from all that, which took time, believe me, the next excursion in line for us was to process, after a long, long wait in the chill air in a line that stretched way round from the front of the Kremlin to the tree-lined park at the side that had once marked the course of the now buried Neglinnaya River, through Lenin's tomb to pay our respects to what seemed to us to be only an unpleasant, plump wax doll lying fully clothed in bed beneath pink spotlights. That struck all of us as more comic than distasteful, but this time, thank God, our young people had the good sense to look serious all the time, to keep their thoughts strictly to themselves and not to express them in any form whatever, anywhere where Soviet officials might be within hearing range. We all obeyed the guards' instructions to us not to talk in the tomb or to put our hands in our pockets.

It was not even the immensely deep Moscow subway with its endless, steep and speedy escalators and its lavish marble and chandeliered stations, that made the deepest impression upon us, although that was truly awe-inspiring in its own right. It was instead the outing we all took, on a cold night, to observe the changing of the guard at Lenin's tomb at the stroke of midnight. With such a beautiful tumbling cascade of bells as none of us had ever heard before, a fast and free-flowing torrent of tintinnabulation, the great clock on the Kremlin tower struck the hour of midnight, and at that instant three guards began their slow, rhythmic march out from the Clock Tower gateway and along the Kremlin wall to Lenin's tomb, passing only a few feet from us as we stood transfixed at the swinging ballet steps of the soldiers carrying their rifles vertically, supported only by one hand on the butt, and swinging their legs forward far above the horizontal at each perfectly timed step.

'Ministry of Funny Walks," whispered Julie to Ned, and then quickly shut up completely, anxious that he might have been overheard by the KGB.

The little gate on the tomb was opened by the escorting officer, and the guards, with practiced step, moved fast and oh so smoothly in a meticulously practiced routine to take up the place of those they were relieving. These in turn swirled away with the same high-swinging goose-step back through the archway beneath the Clock Tower. We all stood in silence and looked at each other in awe. Never elsewhere have I felt anything quite like the emotion that swelled up in me – and I could see that indeed all of us from the youngest to the oldest felt the same way. Not in any capital I had visited, not in London, Edinburgh, Dublin, Washington, Paris, Brussels, Luxembourg, Berlin, Bern, Stockholm, Helsinki, Vienna, Budapest, Prague, Ljubljana, Zagreb, or anywhere else had I encountered anything remotely like this: I had become lodged in the very heart of someone else's patriotism, deep in the very essence of another culture and one distinctly unfriendly to me and my country – remember this was in the year 1985, in the depths of the Cold War. It was frightening, yet in its way as intoxicating as the daytime visit to the cathedrals from the bygone Land of the Tsars. We were mesmerized, and it was therefore hard for us to tear ourselves away, long after the chimes from the bells had ceased to cascade and the changing of the guard had become no more than a memory.

Natasha managed to offer us a day trip to the small town twenty-five miles away known in Communist times as Zagorsk after a fallen Soviet hero. That settlement is the home of the magnificent Trinity-St. Sergius Monastery, one of the most sacred pilgrimage sites of the Russian Orthodox Church. Dating from the 14th century, it takes the form of a random collection of buildings behind a fortress wall, mostly churches, the greatest in the centre being capped by a gleaming golden onion dome. I was reminded of the Novodevichy Convent in Moscow where the great central church is surmounted by a dome of glaring blue, gaily decorated with wide-spreading golden stars, intricate as snowflakes. Such a monastic assemblage of dazzling domes was likened by a Russian pilgrim long ago both to the prayers of the faithful ascending as incense to the Heavenly Father and on also to Pentecostal flames descending as the Holy Spirit bestowed blessings upon the faithful gathered below.

We filed into the darkened church and took our places, silently standing along the back of the building. A priest or deacon was chanting Divine Liturgy, and in his resonant voice, a true Russian bass that put me in mind of Chaliapin, he solemnly intoned the service, never flagging or hesitating but moving steadily and confidently on, on, and on. After half an hour or so some of our students had had enough, felt they had taken in the atmosphere and that it was time to move on. So Ellen and I let them go, with quick whispered promises that they would absolutely not leave the grounds of the monastery. Meanwhile the bass voice had yielded place to a clear tenor, still in the Orthodox chant, but not comprehensible even to me with my familiarity with the Russian language since the service was sung in Old Slavonic, the ecclesiastical tongue that was ordered to be spread through Kievan Rus by St. Vladimir the Great upon his conversion to Christianity in 987 AD. I glanced across at Ellen and could tell that she was as deeply transfixed as I; we both knew that such chanting had continued absolutely without any interruption at all since the day that St. Sergius had founded the monastery in 1345 right down to this very moment, twenty-four hours a day, three hundred and sixty-five days a year, ceaseless, unbroken, such a chain of divine worship and vocal liturgy as exists nowhere else upon the entire face of God's earth. Even Stalin, evil incarnate though he was, had permitted the worship to continue. And as my readers glance over these words that I have written, the chant of Divine Liturgy goes on, goes on, goes on...

Soon enough it was time for us to leave Moscow, and we settled into the two or three hour customary wait at the airport for the plane that would take us to Tbilisi in Georgia, our next destination. I was idly watching the airport television with its predictable report of bountiful harvests past, present and future on the collective farms, when without notice the screen turned black. After a full five minutes the screen lightened again, but only to an entirely different story. I rushed over to attract Ellen's attention since the new story was all about wildfowl on the Baltic coast of the Soviet Union, in Estonia, Latvia and Lithuania, and I was well aware of Ellen's dear love of birds.

243

Natasha plucked my sleeve and whispered to me that something had happened, some important news story that was about to be set before the Soviet people. "I believe it is a death in the leadership," she murmured. "You know that the members of the Politburo are not young, but important, wise and experienced leaders of the Soviet people. Possibly it is Konstantin Chernenko, the General Secretary, himself – I do not know."

Chernenko had in fact been dying by inches since long before he had been elected General Secretary by his geriatric colleagues on the Politburo. They knew that their positions of power were secure in his hands but might well fall into serious jeopardy if a younger man should take up the reins of power. Chernenko had recently been filmed voting in his special hospital room, and talking with his doctors at the same time. But his emphysema made it impossible for him to complete a sentence, so the record of his speech had been cut and spliced, clumsily. We all joked about the water glass that suddenly appeared on his table, and as suddenly disappeared, but we took good care only to mention this outside in the open air, never within the four walls of any room, hallway, restaurant, or hotel bedroom. Konstantin Chernenko had succeeded Yuri Andropov only a few months ago, and it looked as though he would not last long either, 'Konstantly-about-to-Popov,' as the London paper *Private Eye* satirically named them both.

After talking with officials at an information booth, Natasha confirmed to us that Chernenko had indeed departed this life, and for some reason she, this upright and foursquare Soviet tourist guide and escort, shed some quiet tears into her handkerchief. There had been little respect or affection for the departed leader, but Natasha may have been weeping for her own mortality as in a sense we all do, or perhaps she was anxious about the future of her country with one more member of the old guard slipping quietly from the scene. But now that he was gone, who would take his place? The students, led by the irrepressible Adam O'Neill and Betty Kinglake, began at once to laugh as they placed bets, the favorites being the octogenarian Viktor Grishin, Party boss of Moscow, and the much younger Mikhail Gorbachev, almost a babe in his fifties, who had been standing in on all public occasions for the senile and doddering General Secretary Chernenko.

One other youthful contender had recently dropped out of the running, Grigory Romanov (not related to the tsar's family). He had been party boss of Leningrad but had blotted his copybook seriously just a short time before, when his daughter was to be married and he had determined to make her wedding reception the great social event of the year. For the gala he had requisitioned from the Winter Palace a host of antique silver place-settings, exquisite 18th century china plates, and a great set of wine glasses that had belonged to Catherine the Great. The bride was toasted as was customary: in silence all the glasses of champagne were raised. But disaster struck! Someone let his glass fall to the floor, and the crash was heard across the hall. Ah yes, that fine old Russian custom -- no one shall drink out of *my* glass after this toast! And two hundred and fifty wine glasses from the eighteenth century were hurled down to the floor, every one of them smashed to smithereens. Grigory Romanov could never be forgiven, not that the philistine Politburo cared so much for the irreplaceable glasses as that one of their team had brought scorn, laughter and disgrace upon himself and by extension upon all of them as well, jeering openly abroad as well as secretly at home.

In the airport Natasha suddenly drew herself up on her feet before the group. "Let me tell you a few things, American students! It is very uncultured in Russia, *ne kulturni*, to make jokings and silliness when some one person has died. My goodness, making bets about who succeeds to our country's revered leader, not even yet in his grave, peace be upon him! Never have I heard of such a thing! You may do that in America, I hear many such rude things about your people, they are crude, it is maybe true, I think it is, but here in Soviet Union we are civilized peoples. And what is more, you could spoil your whole tour in my dear country by vulgarness. I am warning you -- I will not take responsibility. When you depart from my country I must make long and detailed report on group's conduct. Do not compel me to talk of rudenesses. Otherwise your eminent teachers may find that in future there is no place for any more student groups from your schools. Then, great sadness, yes?

But to put that behind us! You are good boys and girls in your hearts, only not clever today, *ne kulturni*, not thinking very well. So, and let me tell you one other thing. We are very lucky to be leaving Moscow this day. Every room in every hotel in city will be taken by Party and Government officials and important persons from all over Soviet Union. Foreign student groups arriving today will never see Moscow, but they will learn a great deal about factories in Ukraine, and big wheat fields. We have been very lucky, no?

So now, all is understood, yes? Please to behave, I say, please to behave yourselves! And we go on to Tbilisi! Soviet Republic of Georgia is delightful place, romantic, beautiful, historic, very ancient. I love it, almost my favorite!"

So we flew on by Aeroflot to Tbilisi, where the first thing we did upon arrival was to search for news of who would succeed the unfortunate Chernenko, but there was nothing available on the subject that day. First thing next morning, however, many of us stormed out of the hotel to scour the streets for copies of *Pravda* and *Izvestiya*, finding them on a newsstand not far along the main street of the city. And there Gorbachev was, his portrait filling virtually the entire front page of both papers. A caption below hailed him as the Soviet Union's next leader, a true hero of the people. Incidentally, the prominent birthmark on his scalp had been carefully air-brushed into oblivion where it was to remain for quite some time, until the world press printed frequent and untouched photographs of him, whereupon the Soviet press found itself compelled to follow suit in order not to look foolish. There was just a short note at the foot of the front page of both newspapers, informing the Soviet public that General Secretary Konstantin Chernenko had passed away and that an obituary was to be found deep inside the newspaper – end of notice.

One interesting incident: in one of our intervals of free time, between the inevitable city tour and a visit to a chocolate factory, I took it upon myself with Greg Anderson, Betty Stanton and a couple of other more serious and mature students, to explore the principal Orthodox church, indeed cathedral, knowing that Georgian Orthodoxy was not entirely identical to Russian and wondering whether I could discern the differences. What I did spot took me quite by surprise, for there in a corner next to a stout column in the dark medieval cathedral stood Natasha herself among the smoky icons, rapt and attentive to Divine Liturgy, her lips moving gently through the words. We all watched her cautiously from a distance, becoming convinced that she was there for spiritual nurture, not from idle curiosity. After perhaps ten minutes she moved slowly away, looking cautiously around her as she did so. Then with a start she saw us. None of us showed any recognition, and she slipped away. Similarly none of us said a word to her about that encounter at any time thereafter. We felt that the security of her job might well be at risk if American visitors reported that they had witnessed their own official guide from Intourist attending to her devotions in a Christian church.

The highlight of our stay in Georgia was a visit – dare I say a pilgrimage? – to the town of Gori, birthplace of Josef Stalin. On its way there our tour bus, distinctly even shabbier and more antique than the one assigned to us in Moscow, wheezed its way out of the lowlands and up, up between the high open hills, foothills of the Caucasus, making a stop at the top of a pass. We all piled out into air that was delightfully cool, the atmosphere dry, the sun bright, the short-cropped grass a deep and inviting green. The students at once began to run and play games as juvenile as tag, forgetting that they were fully fledged teenagers, and rejoicing, celebrating in fact, at having time to romp in freedom after the dust and diesel fumes of Soviet cities and the stuffiness of a Soviet tour bus. The focus of our attention, to which the students after a time paid somewhat reluctant heed, the reason in fact for our bus stopping at all, was the ruins of one of Georgia's oldest monastic churches atop the summit of a low, steep hill nearby. The ruins caught the immediate and deep attention of Ellen and myself, and of the History of Art students, but I regret to say that its appeal was lost on most of the youngsters. A steep conical dome surmounted the limestone central tower of the church, and the exterior walls of the building were thickly covered on all sides with sculptures of Biblical scenes and of episodes in the lives of saints. Some were instantly recognizable: Abraham and Isaac, the Transfiguration, St. Michael the Archangel and the dragon, the Dormition of the Virgin, but many others were beyond us and there was no one to ask. It was, however, a moving experience to stand there, gaze up, and immerse oneself in the religious culture of one of the very oldest Christian communities in the world. Only Ethiopia and Armenia, I understood, declared Christianity to be the official religion of the state before Georgia, all of them many, many years before the conversion of Constantine and centuries before there was any pope in Rome. The church itself, we were informed, dated from the ninth century, and had only been abandoned in 1919 during the disastrous Civil War. Clyde Browning, Elsie Patterson and a few other of the more mature or spiritual students joined Ellen McCrae and me in taking good note of all this.

And so, on to Gori. A broad central avenue sweeps through the town past the municipal office buildings, from one of which hung suspended a sheet displaying a fifteen-foot portrait of Chernenko. Where had that sprung from, I wondered? Had the town fathers planned the demonstration, in anticipation of Chernenko's death? Across one corner of the portrait stretched a great black band topped by a bright red rosette. At least someone somewhere was mourning the departed leader, we thought, or at least wished to appear to be doing so. Opposite that, near the centre of the street, stood a tall and garish structure, rectangular in shape, open on all sides, and bountifully decorated with garish loops and folds of colored curtain, great widespread flowers and branches of trees, all rendered in plaster. The whole was simply a covering, a screen from the ravages of the weather, for the simple ramshackle peasant's hut standing alone beneath all this sumptuous extravaganza. This, this was Stalin's childhood home, preserved, or perhaps recreated out of nameless scraps, for posterity. And by it stood a tall statue of The Man with a Mustache, likely enough the only one now left standing in the entire Soviet Union, where his image had once turned its baneful eye upon the citizenry of almost every community from the Baltic to the Pacific, from the Arctic Ocean to the Himalayas. Pictures of Stalin and small plaster busts could be found for sale in the tourist shop nearby, again almost the only ones for sale anywhere in the country in 1985. In our greed, we fair gobbled them up! Natasha was not amused; doubtless her family, like everyone else's, had suffered brutally in those dark decades.

And then it was time for us to bid farewell to Georgia and to whirl off to Yalta, a special destination indeed. The flight from Tbilisi to Simferopol, capital of Crimea, is not one often taken by foreign visitors, and we had heard all the old saws about the shortcomings and alarums of Aeroflot. Yes, the seats were distinctly uncomfortable, being tubular steel frames with canvas slung between and the whole screwed down to the bare metal floor, like old porch furniture back home. And yes, the meal offered to us was not exactly the most appetizing, consisting as it did of large grey pieces of cold chicken distributed from a large and equally grey metal bin by the gloved hand of a large grey-faced matron whose stout form made it a challenge for her to move down the central aisle. She could not turn: she had no sideways. After this delectable repast she counted the knives and forks, and upon the plane's landing would allow no one climb down from the aircraft until every last piece of the silverware had been accounted for, including one stray fork that had slid down into the canvas crease of someone's seat -- why anyone would want to purloin such an item beats me, but it had to be somewhere on the plane, and there it was, leaving its own particular stain on the seat that the next passenger would occupy. Ascent in the plane had been sharp and cornering so steep that I wondered if my metal chair might not be wrenched loose from its screw holes in the floor and send me tumbling into the aisle. Descent was equally sharp and sudden, and the plane bounced merrily up and down into the air several times along the runway before it finally drew to a halt at the entrance to the airport building.

We were escorted into a stuffy and antiquated tour bus (surprise, surprise) in Simferopol Airport, and driven for what seemed like hours across the fields and sloping hills of Crimea, much of the landscape still grey-brown and somewhat desolate-looking though lightened here and there with the green of new crops. Even the acres of vines showed comparatively little leaf, which surprised us in what we had expected to be full springtime. We had hoped more from the alleged subtropical paradise described so enthusiastically by tsarist and communist writers, from courtiers of Catherine the Great in her memorable visit, down through Chekhov to the present. Our bus rolled along the dusty road, slowly and gently uphill all the way, mile after mile – and then suddenly and without warning we reached the top of the long slope. Before us lay our first view of the Black Sea, and between us and the sea we faced a steep descent of several hundred feet. Cliffs and crags rose up on all sides, and the road wound precariously among them, dipping down between truly impressive soaring peaks, icy and snowbound even in May against a rock-hard steely blue sky.

The town of Yalta, when finally reached, proved to be a gentle and welcoming place – as indeed anywhere would have been to us, after the stark dreariness of Simferopol and the many miles of plain seeded fields and sprouting vineyards all the way south from the centre of Crimea to the coast. Our hotel was a workers' paradise, housing when full at least a couple of hundred dutiful sons and daughters of factory and farm workers for their free vacation, but half empty in springtime.

More than anything else we were all struck by the scenery of the undercliff. Here the mountains soared above us, shielding the coast from wintry northern gales, and far below the escarpment there lies just above the foot of the cliffs a strip of land a hundred yards or so across at the widest, yet miles and miles long above the sea. Here indeed was subtropical Russia, the land of a gentle Mediterranean climate, most welcome to us all. The Black Sea itself, however, did not in the least invite any single one of us for a dip, not even Graham Convey, the most stalwart and determined of our youths, for the sea was grey, there were no waves, there was no sand but stones and gritty gravel, and there were no tides at all. Disappointing, yes – but if superb beaches had been our top priority we should never have left the good ole U.S. of A. Exploratory walks among the little fishing boats along the curving harbor front and through the renowned tropical gardens pleased us, especially Ellen McRae, and Betty Lanton, Jane Blakesmith and some of the other girls, but nothing matched our tour of Livadia Palace, the summer home of the tsars and the site of the 1945 Yalta Conference. The gardens were lush, and we took appropriate note of the sleeping stone lion that Churchill had coveted and unsuccessfully begged Stalin to present to him: poor Winston was distinctly miffed that day. We entered the long hall, at the far end of which, roped off and inaccessible, stood a circular table and red, padded wooden chairs exactly as they had been placed for the Big Three and their advisers in February 1945.

Our local guide, being a bit of a wag, invited our students to step aside to take a look at the place on the polished wooden floor where Franklin Roosevelt's footsteps could still be seen. The students hesitated, looked quizzical and turned skeptically toward one another, and Ellen and I exchanged really doubtful glances, but on the persistent urging of the guide they all pressed forward and followed him to where he pointed to a spot behind a sofa and a circle of armchairs set close to one corner of the room.

"Got you!" he exclaimed joyfully. "Got you! Oh you poor, foolish, ignorant American students, you didn't even know that your President Roosevelt could not walk! How sad to grow up in your powerful country and to know nothing, nothing at all. What a tragedy! Your two teachers here have failed you, failed you sadly, yes they have, absolutely! Why don't you come to study in the great Soviet Union? Here you would learn something! We would surely see to that. Yes, we would. No ignorance permitted here!" And he burst out laughing.

Shrugs, groans and sullen looks were the response of our young people, as the guide laughed them out of countenance. I was proud of our students, and Ellen was too, that they had not risen to the bait and entered into an argument with a Soviet government employee – they had learned that that was not a good idea at all.

Our bus took us along the undercliff, traveling steadily westward away out of the town. Oh good, we thought, maybe we will have a chance to see Sevastopol! Many of us, especially Ellen with her background in international history, had studied the Crimean War of the 1850's in some detail and longed to visit the battlefields of the Alma, Balaclava and Inkerman, especially to inspect for ourselves the site of the charge of the Light Brigade with its manic combination of terrible error, failure, courage beyond belief, dash and splendor – but alas, that was not to be. Sevastopol was, and remains, one of Russia's most significant naval bases, and no foreigner, not even a teenager, might be permitted to catch a glimpse of it, even from a distance. After all there have been 'innocent' young spies with cameras, and even as recently as in the 1980's foreign visitors were not permitted to photograph any bridge at all anywhere in the entire USSR for fear of giving to the West an idea of where to attack – this even at the time of our visit in 1985, twenty-five years after the U-2 incident that had shot down the 1960 summit meeting before it ever took place. Long before the 1980's both sides in the Cold War possessed satellite photos with minute details of every inch of their opponent's landscape. With my extensive background in Russian literature, I longed to see Old Sevastopol, the scene of the siege that Tolstoy described so dramatically in his *Sevastopol Tales*, the book that made his name and was 'must' reading in Petersburg society long before he wrote *Anna Karenina* or *War and Peace*. But the bus swung irrevocably around and headed back to Yalta, and the next day we were taken inexorably back to Simferopol, where we waited three hours (seemed like six) in the dreariest of all Soviet airports (which is saying quite something) for the plane that eventually took us to Leningrad, our final destination.

Ah, Leningrad – St. Petersburg -- the Jewel of the North founded by Peter the Great as a showplace of Russia and her future as a European power to be reckoned with, stands out larger than life with its immense distances, its vistas across the broad Neva, its long avenues and above all with its many, many magnificent palaces. Visiting here is one long gasp. Like Moscow, its older brother, this city swallows up the visitor in a sustained burst of Russian pride and patriotism. This was clear in Communist times, but strikes the visitor even more forcibly if he arrives long after we did, in the twenty-first century when acres of gold leaf have been newly lavished on the palaces and the statuary, and when the inevitable squalor that clouds every Russian city has been tucked into back streets and areas when tourists do not often find themselves venturing.

We walked miles – one always seems to walk farther in a city than in the country -- the length of the Nevsky Prospekt, peeling off to take in the Cathedral of Our Lady of Kazan which, to the great amusement of our young Americans, especially Shimon Goldstein and Nan Crandle, had been converted into a museum of anti-religion, with exhibits specializing in religious persecution, in pillage and in martyrdom. We also all paced around Gostinyi Dvor, the principal market building dating from the early nineteenth century, which in 1985 still housed the equivalent of five and dime stores, Woolworths and so on, with a good variety of low-cost items for sale, but which I had seen back in 1976 when great shallow bins along the alleys were filled with such mundane items as can-openers. At that time the only sounds in the whole area were the rustle of feet on the dusty wooden floors and the light clatter as prospective buyers picked up, inspected, and tossed back the can-openers they rejected. The only acceptable ones were those stamped with a manufacturing date at the middle of the month: those made at the end would have been smashed together any old how, in order to complete the quota, and those assembled at the beginning of the month would have been made by workers exhausted over from the terrific rush of finishing last month's quota and hung over from subsequent celebration. In the early twenty-first century this lovely early 19th century complex of shops has been taken over by Givenchy, Prada, Gucci and the fashion houses of New York and Paris, and has become a notorious resort of pickpockets.

We ducked into Dom Knygy, the largest bookstore in town, mainly in order to buy political posters. These were wonderfully cheap, at the most seventy-five cents for full color, and those in one or two colors for about a quarter and up. The students snapped them up as souvenirs, the boys above all eager for this kind of authentic souvenir, choosing the ones they wanted by number on the display, first lining up at the display to choose them and write down the numbers of the particular posters they wished to buy, then again at the sales booth to pay for them, and then finally taking the receipt back to the sales clerk's line to collect the posters themselves: three long, slow lines. The posters had been intended for eager Soviet students to decorate the inside left-hand corner of their classroom that a generation or two before would have housed an icon and a candle. Nowadays the posters were also bought by factory workers who wished to gain credit with their superiors with a display of fervor for Lenin and the Marxist state. I must say I could not restrain myself here, and in Moscow and anywhere else where I could find them I bought up, on this trip and on several other visits to the Soviet Union, as many posters as ever I could carry in one great roll. This was for classroom display back at Brookline Hill. As we left the Soviet Union at the end of this particular trip the customs officials insisted that I open the entire roll, just in case I had hidden in it letters from Soviet citizens to anyone outside. This was a bore, unrolling and packing up again as neatly as I could, but I felt I had my revenge when I looked back at the customs shed after I had reassembled my roll, and noticed that the entire floor for many yards in every direction was bestrewn with fluffy scraps of below-grade Soviet wrapping paper, already wafting hither and thither all across the hall. By the way, I enlarged this collection over many years, eventually in my retirement selling my three hundred or more posters to Princeton University twenty years after the Soviet Union had collapsed for a profit that I estimated as close to five hundred percent -- a capitalist's handsome profit from the Soviet state.

Any travel account will describe to the reader the famous sites and sights of Leningrad, now once more St. Petersburg, so, as in my account of our time in Moscow, I will confine myself to narrating just a few experiences particular to our group.

First then, here's an incident that took place in the old tsarist Astoria Hotel, one of the most distinguished in the city. I remembered that the hotel dining hall was well worth a glance since its pilasters were all sheathed in polished copper reminiscent of the capitals of the pilasters in the Catholic cathedral in Vilnius, – and I remembered distinctly that there was a small exhibit hanging from a column in the lobby that would intrigue anyone who saw it. So I took some of our people in, principally History of Art students, and crossed over to the remembered column. It was bare! I described to the disappointed students that there used to hang there a framed copy of the menu headed by a large swastika for the victory dinner that Hitler had planned to hold in the hotel before the entire destruction of the city. Peter the Great had made a mistake, Hitler averred: the world did not a require a city upon this site. It would be a matter of no concern if all its three million citizens should perish with the city. While we were milling around and the students growing restless, the hotel manager, who happened to be passing through the lobby at that moment, came over to see if he could be of service to these foreign visitors. I explained that we were most eager to see the extraordinary menu.

"No, sir, you are entirely mistaken," he insisted, as firmly and politely as he could. "There is no such document. There never has been such. I have worked in hotel many years. I know hotel. If such item you describe did exist, I would know. Very sorry, sir, you are completely in mistake, completely. I cannot help you. Good day, and enjoy your visit."

And that was that, yet another example of a familiar lesson: in the Soviet Union truth is what authority decrees to be true, not something independently verifiable. That is entirely consistent with Marxist-Leninist doctrine, I assured the disappointed students. This was a useful educational lesson for them, both in Communist political philosophy and in the realities of the Soviet system.

Outside once more, we admired the equestrian statue of Nicholas I which had survived the Revolution not because he was a liberal father to his people -- oh no, far from it, a brute if ever there was one -- but because this massive bronze statue of horse and rider stands up on only the horse's two hind feet, a very dramatic example of sculptors' skill. At first it faced a royal palace and had its back to St. Isaac's Cathedral, but the clergy protested and swung it around, refusing to countenance the rear end of a horse directed at the house of God. But in the night royal servants stole forth and swung it back again, and pivoted thus it has remained. Incidentally, on the plinth Nicholas I is portrayed in bas-relief planning the first railway in the Russia Empire. It ran -- of course it did -- from St. Petersburg to Tsarskoe Selo, the 'village' of the tsars' summer palaces some twenty miles from the capital.

Wherever one might be in Leningrad the Great Patriotic War is always at the back of one's mind. Ellen and I simply had to take our students to Piskarovskoye Cemetery, the place of interment of no fewer than one million citizens of Leningrad who had lost their lives in the most terrible siege in the history of the mankind. It is impossible to visit this cemetery and remain unmoved. Long grassy mounds stretch away on either side from the central gravel path leading up to a symbolic memorial statue. It is not the statue or the appearance of long plain grassy mounds of communal graves that overwhelm the visitor: it is the knowledge that an entire million of our fellow human beings lie here dead, frozen and starving, by the will of Adolf Hitler as carried out by the ever-obedient German Army under the watchful eyes of the SS. Present in the minds of each of was the knowledge that under every single one of these long grassy mounds, dozens of them, lie the broken remains of ten thousand citizens of Leningrad. The deep trench was dug, the bodies filled it to the top, and the earth was piled up over. All had to be completed in just a few weeks as the siege lifted, or typhus and plague would break out all over the ruined city. Our students moved slowly along, whispering in groups, some crossing themselves, some fingering the stars of David or the crucifix that hung from their necks, many holding tight to one another, some even close to sobbing as though they had known the dear dead. Piskarovskoye is not a savage site like Auschwitz: it leaves much more to the imagination than a visit to an extermination camp ever can, and it is all immensely sobering. This cast a pall over our entire group: clearly it had been very important for all of us to come here, mourners and pilgrims that we were. We thought too of the paradoxes of Russia, the cruelty, the spirituality, the sentimental kindness.

Our hearts and minds stayed with the siege after our visit to the cemetery as we walked along the first blocks of the Nevsky Prospekt up from the Admiralty, whose elegant spire writes upon the sky a signature of the city. There is a small, well-worn sign on the wall of a building there, inscribed in letters now eroded and very hard to decipher "Warning! Do not walk on this side of the street. Shells are more likely to fall here." A metal rack below always carries a long, slender bunch of fresh flowers. The sign refers of course to the totally unprovoked German attack. Nearby there is a photograph of an emaciated and desperately starving Leningrader holding in his hand a lump of 'bread,' in reality half sawdust or hay, his food ration for the day. Grim in its way is also the account of how tanks assembled in the Kirov Works were driven straight from the production line into battle. Those works, once the largest factory complex in the world, were the site of the start of the workers' march on Bloody Sunday in 1907, now commemorated by massive and very striking wrought iron gates and fencing stretching for many yards across the front of the works, having been requisitioned from the property of some aristocrat in the fashionable quarter of St. Petersburg.

Ellen and I wanted to devote some time to the scientists, zoologists or natural historians in our group, so we took them, especially Nan Crandle, Clyde Browning and Amanda Tillotson, to the Natural History Museum. This is an even sadder place than others dedicated to the display of stuffed carcass after stuffed carcass, for here, we discovered, many of the cases are completely neglected with the glass even parting from the metal or wooden frames, so that moths and such have made their way in and are slowly and irrevocably devouring whole sections of the back of a leopard here, the leg of an antelope there. Most reprehensible of all, however, is the neglect of the two glass cases displaying the remains of mammoths, the only two such in the entire world! The poor beasts looked so tired, dusty, grimy and grey, exhausted and really done in. One was of a young adult female who had slipped into a crevasse and broken her hip, preventing her from clambering out. She died *in situ*, and some of her frozen flesh was eaten by the 19th century team who discovered her. The other, now little more than a tattered reddish rug with a folded trunk and small tusks at one end, resembled a large golden retriever that had been run down by a car and the body left outside a couple of winters ago. This mammoth had been in life a mere baby that had somehow lost its mother and been buried by a landslide after it had collapsed from hunger and exhaustion. All agreed, the display was as disturbing as it was fascinating, for these are veritably the only mammoths to be seen in the world, anywhere at all.

What should I write about Palace Square, the Winter Palace, the Hermitage, St. Isaac's Cathedral, the Peter-Paul Fortress, and all the other sights of this extraordinary, captivating city? There is just too much, and one could see in the faces of our students who had so nobly borne up through our difficult entry to the Soviet Union, our unforgettable visit to Moscow, our sojourn in Tbilisi and our springlike days in Yalta that they had just about had enough of Russia -- had enough of the food too, the endless heavy and not quite fresh bread, the croquettes of nameless meat stew that pursued us from one city to another, the yogourt that was half grey water and half solid and cheesy, the metallic taste of 'fruit juice,' and the labor of having to do all one's laundry oneself in one's hotel room, brushing one's teeth in Pepsi so as to avoid the tap water and fear of giardia, and, and, oh so much more... It was time to go home, and we knew it: the glory of travel had palled, the enchantment of Mother Russia, the fearsome embrace of the Russian Bear, the remote mysteries of Orthodox chanting and icon-kissing, all had begun to coalesce in the minds of these young people. So, in keeping with that spirit, I will write no more here about all the other sites we visited in Leningrad – ah, Petersburg, Petersburg, you call me back all the time! – and conclude with the entirely characteristic difficulty, the near-disaster we confronted even in extricating ourselves at Leningrad Airport from the hug of the Russian bear.

Well, leaving the Soviet Union is a serious business, every bit as fraught as entry into the workers' paradise. We took our final journey in a familiar, stuffy, so-so clean Soviet tour bus, and bade farewell to Natasha, presenting her with a delicate necklace and matching earrings of liquid silver and turquoise created by Hopi craftsmen in Arizona, a tribute that I had brought with me for our guide whoever she might be and that we all felt Natasha deserved for helping us all along the line from that first morning so long ago when we descended sleepily from the Helsinki train at the Moscow railway station. Natasha was not permitted to enter the airport building but embraced each of us in turn and wept more than a little at our departure. For a whole month we had become her family, her children.

Inside, Passport Control came first: there is a certain air of finality as one enters the little passageway opposite the official's booth and the metal doors shut with a clang both behind one and before. Then the guard in his green-tabbed uniform takes his good time to search through one's passport, several long minutes for each of us, examining each and every entry, even resorting to a magnifying glass where necessary. Finally the passport is slid back across the counter and the exit gate opens. The official never looks up, having no interest in whatever individual passes before him, provided only that the passport satisfies his inspection. And then one is on one's way.

But the traveler has to have a boarding pass as well, of course. These were not individually printed paper tickets such as one might expect, but old, worn and soiled halves of baggage tags from long ago! But we were told they were important, and we had to hang on to them, almost for dear life.

Our suitcases were spread out for inspection, open and facing the inspector, with packets of nylon stockings, *Playboy* magazine and even bluejeans displayed on top, for any official to spirit away with him as he pleased, for which tip he would (probably) expedite our departure from the airport building onto the bus that would ferry us across the tarmac to our plane, ever so far away out there.

Then the bus itself was inspected, not for our sakes nor for any political pollution that we might be bringing with us, but for escaping Soviet citizens. First it was thoroughly searched inside, seat backs, baggage racks, floor spaces, everywhere. And then soldiers swept to and fro under the bus mirrors the size of trashcan lids fixed to the ends of long poles, while another guard scanned the whole underside with a powerful flashlight. No wretched absconding Soviet citizen was found -- there were none. So we boarded the bus and were driven far out onto the tarmac in order to board our plane, an Aeroflot jetliner that would take us back to JFK airport in New York.

The very last formality was to hand back the scruffy little boarding tags that had been handed to each of us half an hour ago. Easily done, we thought, here it is, in my pocket all the time. And we began to file up the steep steps into the plane.

"Halt, every person! Stop right there! About face, and all descend from airplane, everyone please to do this, exactly now!"

This was not an order that anyone could disobey. Out on the tarmac, miles from anything save our patiently waiting plane, the bus having driven away and the portable steps up to the plane also having been hitched on behind the bus after our descent from the plane, we stood around in groups and wondered what last snafu had delayed our departure. We were so close to going – it could not possibly be anything important, or so we thought… But oh dear, one of our company had simply been unable to lay her hands on her miserable little boarding tag, search all her pockets as she might. It just had to be poor Amanda Tillotson again, the frightened young girl whose bunk bed in the train all those long weeks ago had harbored an assassin's knife. Why, oh why did it have to be her? As the only adult woman in the group Ellen pushed her way past the students, gave me a glance that told me this was best left to her, and confronted the American girl and the Russian official.

"Well, what on earth is the problem?" Ellen asked in some irritation. "You know she is one of us, an American student. You have seen her passport and have stamped it. Look, there it is, in her hand for you to inspect again if you want to."

"Please, is serious problem. No one permitted to enter airplane on Soviet airfield if has not official boarding pass. Is Soviet law. I cannot make exception. This young person must find boarding pass. We can wait. She must turn out all her baggage, her suitcase and her hand baggage, all her pockets and every place else where she could carry ticket."

And that was exactly what poor Amanda Tillotson, once more on the absolute verge of tears, had to do, as fast and as thoroughly as she could. "Nothing," she said to the Soviet official after a quick glance through everything, looking piteously up from her knees. "I am sorry, very sorry, there's nothing there! I can't find it anywhere." And she looked at Ellen and me in despair.

"Very well," said the official. "All of you will wait here. My colleague and I escort young lady back to reception building to enter airport police headquarters for female colleagues to strip-search this student. Strip-search is very efficient. No one ever hides anything anywhere on person, even in stomach or inside personal body cavities, without our experienced female police agents finding it. Very efficient, some painful I regret, but often not very much of bleeding. This foolish young person will soon regret she has tried to conceal official paper from Soviet security forces. We will find paper, and she will remember experience."

Amanda was by now in complete meltdown, floods of uncontrollable tears. "I insist," Ellen stated to the border guard, "I insist that I accompany this young person. She is a minor and in my care. What is more, a full report of your actions will be made to the American Embassy in Moscow, to the Consulate in Leningrad, to the Soviet Foreign Office, to Aeroflot, and to every single other place and office that I can think of!"

"Very sorry," he answered with a commanding sneer on his face. "Is Soviet law. Can make no exception, not even for gracious young student. Boarding pass must be found or she does not depart. Rest of you must go tonight, yes of course. All your papers stamped by Soviet government officials say you depart tonight, so please you must go. That is Soviet law, no question. You depart, for New York. But she stays alone, by herself, until this is all explained and appropriate reports have been made and accepted by superior officers. This may take a week, or more than week. She will stay in airport in strict police custody because she has concealed important Soviet document and refuses to hand it over to state organs. Please to understand that always Security Police is very concerned with attempts to violate Soviet border regulations, because of illegal incursions of Western agents. I repeat and assure you: American student will be lodged in own cell and carefully guarded in Soviet police detention area, good security, no concerns."

Ellen bent down with Amanda, who had completely lost control of herself by this time, and helped her open up her hand baggage, a backpack in which she had her travel documents, a magazine and a book to read on the plane, a folding plastic raincoat and her toothbrush and comb. We also opened up her suitcase and spread out in the wind on the open tarmac all her clothes, her souvenirs, and, to her embarrassment, her personal toilet items. By now the poor girl was hysterical, envisaging a Gulag camp in Siberia and never seeing her family and home again.

"Take a hold of yourself, my dear," Ellen said. "Stand up straight right next to me, and we will see what can be done I promise you we will get this sorted out – and I will never let you go back to the airport buildings without me coming with you."

But in her heart of hearts Ellen was as terrified on Amanda's behalf as was Amanda herself. This whole situation was totally outside our experience. The only additional thought I had was why on earth these bloody Russians cared a fig for a scrap of a torn baggage label that had served as a boarding pass. I just couldn't understand that, not at all.

Suddenly a shrill cry rose from one of Amanda's close friends, who were all hugging each other in tears by this time. "There it is! Isn't that it, sticking out of the top of her boot? I bet that's her boarding pass!" And yes, there it was, the corner of a shabby, greasy little card poking out of Amanda's ankle boot. Saved, thank God Almighty, saved!

"Yes, very good, young miss," said the frontier guard with what I took to be a disappointed smile. "All is now in order. Proceed, and please not be so careless in all the rest of life, particularly not when facing organs of the Union of Soviet Socialist Republics. Do you hear?"

"Yes sir," was all that Amanda could manage through her sobs.

And we flew away, we flew away. Dear Ellen McCrae was first to catch on what must have been the dread significance of that wretched little scrap of paper. A departing traveler taking it away with him, could later have arranged by some means for it to be delivered back to the Soviet Union, into the hands of some citizen who could use it to engineer his own escape or to have it reproduced many times for his friends.

I truly believe the sighs of our relief added to the force of jet propulsion of our airliner – and no group has ever cheered more lustily than ours upon landing at JFK many hours later. But, as Ellen and I learned later from reading our students' journals, they had not truly hated the Soviet Union, not at all – except poor little Amanda Tillotson who vowed never, ever, ever, to set foot in Russia again all her life long, a vow I am sure she will keep as long as she lives. As for all the others, they had emerged from the Soviet experience as so many of us do, with a host of paradoxical emotions, constant unease coupled with a deep respect for how direfully these people have suffered and continue to suffer, and an awkward love-hate for that tempestuous, all-embracing, deeply religious, brutally hurtful and in every way completely unforgettable Angel, Devil, Spirit and Wraith that answers to the name of -- 'Russia.'

ABOUT THE AUTHOR

 George Wrangham was born, raised, and educated in England. He graduated from Eton College and King's College, Cambridge, with a BA with honors and an MA, both in history.

A retired teacher of history and English, Wrangham served as the head of the history department at the Shipley School in Bryn Mawr, Pennsylvania, and now teaches night school.

Wrangham has published articles on history teaching in multiple international journals as a member of the International Society for History Didactics. He is well-read in European, American, and Russian history, and in English literature.

An avid birder for over seventy years, Wrangham is married with four adult children and six grandchildren. He lives near Philadelphia.

Made in the USA
Middletown, DE
22 July 2015